GENERAL HISTORIES

Prelude to the Total Force: The Air National Guard 1943–1969

Charles Joseph Gross

Air Force Systems Command

OFFICE OF AIR FORCE HISTORY
UNITED STATES AIR FORCE
WASHINGTON, D.C., 1985

Library of Congress Cataloging in Publication Data

Gross, Charles Joseph.
    Prelude to the Total Force: The Air National Guard, 1943–1969.

    At head of title: General histories.
    Bibliography: p. 225.
    Includes index.
    1. United States—Air National Guard—History.
I. United States. Air Force. Office of Air Force History. II. Title. III.
Title: General histories.
UG853.G76   1984   358.4'137'0973   84–7432

ISBN # 0-912799-15-3

For sale by the Superintendent of Documents, U.S. Government Printing Office,
Washington, D.C. 20402

United States Air Force
Historical Advisory Committee
(As of October 1, 1984)

Mr. DeWitt S. Copp
The Voice of America

Dr. Haskell M. Monroe, Jr.
University of Texas at El Paso

Dr. Philip A. Crowl
Annapolis, Maryland

Gen. Bryce Poe, II,
USAF, Retired
Alexandria, Virginia

Dr. Warren W. Hassler, Jr.
Pennsylvania State University

Lt. Gen. Thomas C. Richards,
USAF
Commander, Air University

Brig. Gen. Harris B. Hull,
USAF, Retired
National Aeronautics and Space
Administration

Lt. Gen. Winfield W. Scott, Jr.,
USAF
Superintendent, USAF Academy

Dr. Alfred F. Hurley (Chairman)
Brig. Gen., USAF, Retired
North Texas State University

Mr. Eugene R. Sullivan
The General Counsel, USAF

iii

The Author

CHARLES J. GROSS wrote this history during 1978–1979 as part of his doctoral program in military history at The Ohio State University. He holds bachelor's degrees in political science (1964) and education (1970) from The Ohio State University and an M.S. degree in American history from Utah State University (1973). The PhD was granted in 1979. From July 1964 to September 1969, Dr. Gross served as an intelligence officer with the United States Air Force. His assignments included a twelve-month tour of duty at Tan Son Nhut AB, South Vietnam, as officer-in-charge of the Target Analysis Section, 12th Reconnaissance Intelligence Technical Squadron. The author began his air reserve career in 1972 and spent nearly three years with the Ohio Air National Guard's 179th Tactical Fighter Group. From 1976 to 1984, he was assigned to the Air Force Intelligence Service Reserve. Currently, he is a reserve major assigned to the Office of Air Force History, Headquarters USAF. Dr. Gross joined the USAF historical program in May 1979 at Headquarters Air Force Logistics Command. He is now a civilian historian with Headquarters Air Force Systems Command.

Foreword

Among the oldest and most enduring of America's military traditions is the reliance for defense on citizen-soldiers. From the settlement of the colonies in the 17th century, Americans relied not on long-service professional troops but on citizens to defend against invaders and to mount expeditions against Indian or European foes. Until the late 19th century, the colonial and state militias—the free, able-bodied males enrolled in units in their local communities—provided the soldiers to man our wartime armies and in peacetime, the military forces to maintain domestic order. Even after a national military establishment was created and state militias in the 19th century began to degenerate into paper organizations, the theory and the substance of citizen-soldiering remained the foundation of national defense. With our wide ocean barriers east and west, and neighbors north and south who posed no substantial military threat, the army and the navy served as shields behind which the nation would have time to mobilize its citizens. Then these regular forces, as cadre, would absorb the manpower of the country and lead it into battle—and victory.

Late in the 19th century, several factors began to threaten the policy of mobilization, and with it, reliance on the citizen-soldier. One was the sheer size of modern armies and the complexity of conducting war, which required a force that was adequately trained for combat before hostilities began. Another was the need for sound advanced planning and an officer corps that could both lead men in battle and manage logistics, transportation, and mobilization planning. In effect, modern war and the staff system required to conduct it called for an educated, professional officer corps and a large, trained corps of non-commissioned officers. If the nation relied on citizen-soldiers, these individuals would have to fit into a national military structure upon mobilization. Thus, the modern National Guard was born.

A second factor altering the federal-state militia relationship was technology. With the complexity of the steel and steam navies of the late 19th century, untrained, part-time sailoring, never a viable part of our naval tradition once the age of sail began to wane, became virtually impossible. Navies needed to be manned and ready for the early, crucial battles that might determine command of the sea. Air forces presented similar requirements: proficiency in operations necessitated constant peacetime practice; and from the aviators' viewpoint, fleets of the most advanced aircraft had to be prepared to overwhelm the enemy at the beginning of a conflict. Budgetary limitations on the numbers of aircraft in peacetime, and the intensely complex logistical, maintenance, research and development, and training establishments necessary to support the air arm made a part-time, amateur force seem wholly inapplicable to air power.

Nevertheless, from the beginning of military aviation, the National Guard was interested and involved. In 1909, less than a year after the Army purchased its first airplane, the First Aero Company, Signal Corps, New York National Guard, came into existence in New York City. By the time of its pre-World War II mobilization in 1940, the National Guard from throughout the nation could provide twenty-nine observation squadrons manned by nearly 5,000 officers and men. In early 1946, with the creation of the first Air Guard unit, and then with the formation of the Air Force as a separate, independent military service the next year, the Air National Guard emerged as a separate reserve component and began its modern development into a viable, powerful member of the aerospace team.

In this study of the origins and evolution of the Air National Guard, Dr. Charles J. Gross, himself a former guardsman and a professional historian, currently at the Air Force Systems Command History Office, chronicles this tranformation. In the 1940s, the active duty Air Force was not particularly sympathetic or supportive of an Air National Guard. Focused on creating an Air Force as a separate service, carving out its role in the air-atomic age, and changing from piston to jet engines in an austere budgetary environment, the regulars saw no real purpose for part-time, state air forces. If anything, an Air Guard threatened the funding of an adequate regular force. Given the Guard's record of poor readiness and its successful resistance to direction from Washington, the Air Force leadership would have been just as happy to see the Guard eliminated.

In 1950, the difficult and in many respects unsuccessful mobilization of the Air National Guard for the Korean War, forced the Air Force into reforms, and the Guard itself to accept greater peacetime control by the active force. Through the 1950s, by means of expansion, more modern aircraft, and more closely coordinated planning and policy-making, the Guard began to increase both in effectiveness and in the respect it engendered from the Air Force leadership. Late in the decade, increased bugetary pressure on the Air Force, combined with the Eisenhower administration's emphasis on reserves and the Congress' support for the Guard, led to a more favorable view of the Guard by the Air Force. Also, Air Guard leaders themselves realized that they had to institute various reforms and better integrate the Guard with the regular force. Most importantly, the Guard in the 1950s won for itself, in continental air defense, in tactical aviation, and in airlift, meaningful missions that it could perform effectively on a continuing basis in peacetime. In mobilizations during the Berlin crisis in 1961–1962, in the Pueblo crisis and the Southeast Asian War in 1968, the Guard proved its competence and excellence.

The expanding role of the Guard and its close cooperation with the Air Force are Dr. Gross' themes, explaining the rise of the Guard to the prominence it plays in today's air operations. He pulls no punches in recounting the conflict between Guard and regular Air Force, or in explaining how each side maneuvered to safeguard its interests. However, the author also shows how common concerns and mutual dedication to the national defense overcame parochialism and led from cooperation to integration. The result was displayed for all the Air Force to see in the professionalism of Guard units in the 1960s mobilizations. Guard and regular Air Force had become vital to each other; in return for modern aircraft, a substantial peacetime mission, and upon mobilization integration into the wartime force, the Guard accepted de facto control by the regular Air Force. As Dr. Gross concludes, the concept of "state militia" was altered far beyond the changes wrought earlier in federal-state military relations. The Air Guard was ready for the "Total Force" policy of the 1970s. The dilemma of maintaining a reserve fully capable of fighting the air war was solved. By the 1980s, the Air National Guard, at the same time inheritors of a military tradition extending back before 1776, and users of the most advanced technologies of war, could prove that citizen-soldiers need not be second to any airman in the world.

RICHARD H. KOHN
Chief, Office of Air Force History

Acknowledgments

This work was originally prepared as a doctoral dissertation at The Ohio State University. From the time I began the research through the presentation of the dissertation, and finally the publication of this volume, many individuals and organizations gave the project their unflagging support.

To the officers and enlisted personnel of my former Air Guard unit, Ohio's 179th Tactical Fighter Group, I owe much of the inspiration for this book. Their enthusiasm and professional skills dispelled the tired images of "weekend warriors" and "sunshine patriots" that have often marred the reputations of military reserve programs in this country. Professor Allan R. Millett, my advisor at The Ohio State University, was the first to suggest that the Air Guard might be an excellent topic for serious historical research. He ably guided me through the research and writing of the original manuscript.

The Office of Air Force History partially financed the research with an Air Force dissertation year fellowship. Dr. George Watson and Mr. David Schoem of the Reference Branch made many valuable records available from Air Force holdings and opened the doors for me to do research in several valuable documentary collections. Other USAF historians helped arrange interviews with Air Force and Air National Guard officials who had played key roles in the development of the Guard.

The staffs of the Manuscript Division, Library of Congress, the Modern Military Branch, National Archives, the John F. Kennedy Library, the Dwight D. Eisenhower Library, and the Lyndon Baines Johnson Library gave me invaluable research assistance as did those of the USAF Historical Research Center, Maxwell Air Force Base, Alabama. The Executive Vice President of the National Guard Association of the United States, Maj. Gen. Francis S. Greenlief, NGUS (Ret.) and his staff were most helpful, as were personnel of the National Guard Bureau. Lt. Col. James L. Delaney and Lt. Col. Delores Bumpers, Air National Guard historians, provided valuable documents and helpful editorial comment as did Mr. Gerald T. Cantwell of the Office of History, Air Force Reserve. I interviewed many individuals in connection with this research. Although the comments of each and every one of them were helpful, I am especially indebted to: General Greenlief, Gen. Leon W. Johnson, USAF (Ret.), Maj. Gen. John J. Pesch, ANGUS (Ret.), and Gen. Curtis E. LeMay, USAF (Ret.). Maj. Gen. Winston P. Wilson, ANGUS (Ret.), who did more than any other person to build the Air Guard into a fine military organization, generously provided his expertise on the subject.

Dr. Richard H. Kohn, Chief, Office of Air Force History, and Col. John Schlight, Deputy Chief, committed the resources of their organization to publishing the dissertation as an official USAF history. Mr. Herman Wolk, Chief, General Histories Branch, enthusiastically assisted the author in refining the original work. I am further indebted to Mr. Lawrence J. Paszek, Senior Editor, for designing the book and guiding the manuscript through the publication process, Ms. Mary F. Loughlin for contributing her editorial expertise, Ms. Anne E. Shermer for selecting the photography and completing the layout, and Ms. Ann W. Caudle for proofreading the entire volume.

Most of the photographs were selected from the Air Force and Army collections held by the Defense Audiovisual Agency. However, the Air Force Association, National Guard Bureau, and Air National Guard units from New York, Minnesota, Ohio, and Indiana generously provided photographs from their historical files. These contributions have enriched the book immeasurably.

I dedicate this volume to my wife Barbara. Without her love, moral support, and prolonged efforts on the typewriter, I would never have completed this undertaking.

Contents

Photographs

Introduction

The shadow of the Minuteman statue falls across the village green in Lexington, Massachusetts. The statue symbolizes America's oldest military legacy, the citizen-soldier. In colonial times, minutemen were members of small elite companies within the organized militia. They agreed to turn out for immediate service in defense of their communities while the more cumbersome ordinary militia units were being assembled. Today their historic role is perpetuated by the Air National Guard, an elite volunteer force of citizen airmen maintained in a high state of operational readiness as a reserve component of the United States Air Force (USAF).

Although it can trace its heritage to the colonial minutemen, the Air Guard is a relatively young and comparatively unknown military organization. It did not become a separate reserve component until 1946. However, the National Guard's aviation program was well established long before then. The program originated even before the Wright brothers were able to convince the U.S. Army that the airplane had military possibilities. On May 30, 1908, the First Aero Company, Signal Corps, New York National Guard, was formed at the Park Avenue Armory on 34th Street in New York City. It consisted of approximately twenty-five aviation enthusiasts who had volunteered to learn ballooning. Two years later, the unit financed and built its first aircraft at a cost of $500. The investment depreciated in 1910 when the do-it-yourself aircraft crashed on takeoff during maneuvers. In 1911, the First Aero Company made its first successful entry into heavier-than-air flight when the Curtiss Aeroplane Company loaned it an airplane and a pilot. The pilot, Beckwith Havens, later joined the unit as a private and is recognized as the National Guard's first military aviator. When he flew the unit's airplane at joint Army-National Guard maneuvers in 1912, the regular Army contributed only two flying machines to that affair.[1]

Through World War I the development of National Guard aviation remained limited. An aeronautical detachment was established in the California National Guard's Seventh Coast Artillery Company in February 1911. The Missouri National Guard organized a Signal Corps air section the following month. New York's National Guard organized its Second Aero Company at Buffalo in 1916. These small units were largely the product of the initiatives of local aviation enthusiasts. State or federal financial support for these programs was minimal. Aircraft and balloons were purchased almost entirely through private contributions. In 1915, for example, the Aero Club of America equipped New York's First Aero Company with five airplanes costing $29,500. And, in 1916, when New York's two National Guard aviation companies were mobilized (the first such organizations ever called into federal service) several members brought their own personal aircraft with them.[2]

In April 1917, the War Department decided that National Guard aviation units would not be mobilized during World War I. These units were disbanded and most of their personnel volunteered individually for active duty. One guardsman, Raynal C. Bolling, an attorney for U.S. Steel and Commander of the First Aero Company, accepted a commission as an Army aviator once his National Guard unit was disbanded. He headed a mission to Europe in June 1917 to gather technical information on Allied aircraft industries. This mission provided technical guidance for America's aircraft program during the war. Col. Bolling was killed on March 26, 1918 by German infantry fire while on an automobile reconnaissance of the Somme battlefield.[3]

During the 1920–1921 reorganization of the National Guard, aviation units achieved a permanent place. In 1920, the War Department, at the urging of Guard aviation enthusiasts and a few regular Army air officers including Brig. Gen. William (Billy) Mitchell, announced plans to include "aero units" in postwar National Guard infantry divisions.[4] Between 1921 and 1930, all nineteen National Guard divisions organized air observation squadrons. Whether or not such squadrons should have actually been organized or merely carried on paper had been the subject of much General Staff debate in 1919 and 1920. Eventually the availability of some 8,500 surplus World War I military aircraft had tipped the scales in favor of the former option. By 1930, the War Department was looking to the National Guard for more than divisional observation squadrons. Faced with smaller budgets and pressured by Army fliers for increased emphasis on aviation, it allowed the Guard to organize ten additional observation squadrons. These air units were not attached to divisional units. Most of them appeared on National Guard troop lists as "Corps Aviation Troops."[5]

The National Guard was ordered into federal service beginning in September 1940. Its aviation units furnished twenty-nine observation squadrons manned by some eight hundred officers and four thousand enlisted men. Although some units retained their numerical designations, all were ordered to duty as nondivisional formations. Eventually, most of their personnel were scattered across the rapidly expanding Army Air Corps as individuals rather than members of organized National Guard units. Their skills and enthusiasm were a valuable addition to the Air Corps whose total active duty strength had risen only to 51,185 by the end of 1940.[6]

The Air National Guard first emerged as a separate reserve component of the armed forces after World War II. Significant wartime contributions of individual National Guard aviation personnel notwithstanding, the Air Guard was primarily a product of the politics of postwar defense planning. This study, covering the 1943–69 period, examines the origins of the Air Guard during World War II and traces its gradual evolution from a postwar flying club into an outstanding firstline reserve component of the U.S. Air Force.

The Air Guard has played an increasingly important role in the total Air Force structure since World War II. Portions of the Air Guard were mobilized for service during the Korean and Vietnam Wars. Air Guard units also reinforced America's active duty military strength during the 1961–62 Berlin Crisis. Its fighter-interceptor squadrons have participated in the Air Force's air defense runway alert program since 1953. Increasingly, since then, Air Guardsmen have been integrated into daily Air Force operations in a broad variety of missions ranging from military airlift to the installation of ground-based communications equipment.

By the late 1970s, the Air Guard accounted for a substantial portion of the Air Force's post-Vietnam flying unit strength. During fiscal year 1977, it contributed forty percent of Tactical Air Command's fighter squadrons, fifty percent of its reconnaissance squadrons, and over sixty percent of its tactical air support units. Approximately one-third of the Military Airlift Command's airlift units were Guard outfits. Although their aircraft were not the most advanced types, these units substantially augmented the active Air Force. Through realistic training, Air Force management policies that demanded virtually the same standards of operational performance as their active duty counterparts, and the skilled services of a large cadre of full-time technicians, Air Guard units were maintained in advanced states of readiness. Despite these impressive figures, by 1982 the Air Guard was still a relatively small force of just over one hundred thousand personnel. Its annual budget of nearly $2.2 billion represented under four percent* of the total Air Force budget.[7]

Judged by its performance during the last two decades, especially the outstanding contributions of Air Guard fighter units sent to South Vietnam in 1968, the Air Guard has been one of the most successful military reserve programs operated by the armed forces. Nevertheless, relatively little scholarly attention has been devoted to it. Professional military men also have largely ignored the topic in their broad analyses of America's long-term national security requirements. More glamorous topics like nuclear strategy, weapons research and procurement, and the military's role in national security affairs have dominated their attention since 1945. Air reserve programs have not received much serious attention. The few studies available have generally concentrated on the problems of the Army's reserve components, especially the National Guard. Moreover, scholars analyzing

---

*This figure does not include considerable support provided by the Air Force outside the Air Guard's budget. For example, all weapons systems and support equipment were funded by the Air Force, which also paid for the costs of instructors and facilities needed to train air guardsmen. On the other hand, the Air Guard's budget defrayed its own personnel, military construction, operations, and maintenance costs.

Brig. Gen. William (Billy) Mitchell advocated forming aero units within National Guard infantry divisions.

A searchlight and floodlight operated by the 1st Aero Company, New York ANG, at Mineola Field, Long Island.

Capt. Raynal Cawthorne Bolling (center) leads the first mass flight of military aircraft in the United States, Nov. 18–19, 1916. Captain Bolling was the first commander of New York's First Aero Company. (A National Guard Heritage Painting by Woodi Ishmael)

Courtesy National Guard Bureau

(Above) Private First Class Beckwith Havens, the National Guard's first military aviator, on an aerial photo mission in Texas. Havens flew his Curtiss plane in joint National Guard-Army maneuvers in Connecticut in 1912.

(Right) Lapel device worn by members of New York's 1st Aero Company.

(Below) Biplane owned by Philip Wilcox—the 1st Aero Company's first aircraft.

Courtesy New York ANG

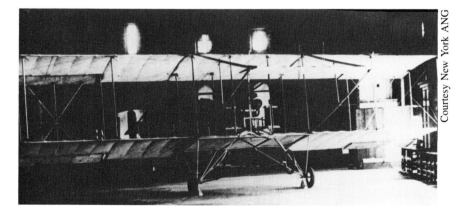

Courtesy New York ANG

5

the National Guard have tended to emphasize its role as an organized political pressure group rather than its military functions. The Air Guard has been virtually ignored except for passing references to it as an exception to the general pattern of reserve program difficulties. These omissions have created a significant void in our understanding of reserve programs and those factors which could contribute to their success as military organizations. This study of the origins and evolution of the Air Guard attempts to fill that void.[8]

This is not a study of the Air Guard as a political pressure group. Nor is it an examination of the Air Guard's state role in disaster relief and preserving legally constituted authority. Both of those subjects are extremely important but have not been addressed here. Instead, this work focuses on the Air Guard's central military role as a reserve component of the U.S. Air Force, and emphasizes the evolution of relations and policies between the Air Guard and Headquarters, United States Air Force.

This emphasis was shaped by three primary considerations. First, a review of the literature of American military history revealed that scholars had neglected the military role of reserve programs, especially air components of the American armed forces. Second, I was extremely impressed with the enthusiasm and professional competence of the Air Guard during my own service as an intelligence officer with the Ohio Air National Guard's 179th Tactical Fighter Group from 1973 to 1976. Third, it was apparent that the Air Force's reserve components have come to play an increasingly important role in that service's ability to carry out its global military missions. For these reasons, I concentrated on the Air Guard as a national military organization focusing on policy issues at the headquarters level and the Air Guard's institutional evolution.

Chapter I

Forged in Politics, 1943–1946

The modern Air National Guard was established after World War II. Its first unit, Denver's 120th Fighter Squadron, was activated in April 1946. Unlike its prewar cousin, a collection of twenty-nine National Guard divisional aviation observation squadrons with some 4,800 personnel, the Air Guard was an expression of the drive for an independent Air Force. War Department plans developed during World War II, called for a postwar Air Guard which would be a highly-trained combat reserve force capable of rapidly augmenting an independent Air Force. It would consist of 58,000 men organized into 514 units. The heart of the program would be eighty-four tactical flying units including seventy-two fighter and twelve light bomber squadrons. On paper, the Air Guard seemed a formidable military organization. It appeared to marry the independent air power assumptions of the Army Air Forces, presumably vindicated during World War II, and the historic citizen soldier traditions represented by the National Guard.[1]

The appearance, however, was deceiving. The postwar Air Guard program was neither a happy marriage nor a rational expression of the alleged air power lessons of the war. Until the Korean War, the Air Guard more closely resembled a government sponsored flying club than a formidable first line reserve component of the Air Force. The Air Guard program was a product of the politics of World War II planning for the postwar American military establishment. It reflected the determination of Gen. George C. Marshall, Army Chief of Staff, to gain the support of the National Guard Association of the United States for a postwar system of universal military training. In return, however, the National Guard wanted assurance that it would continue to occupy its position as the Army's first line reserve force.

General Marshall dominated the War Department during World War II. His ideas heavily influenced wartime planning for the postwar Army. Marshall firmly believed that the political, economic, and technological uncertainties of the twentieth century required the United States to maintain a redoubtable military establishment. If America wanted to avert or minimize the effects of a third world war, she could no longer afford to virtually disarm in peacetime. Marshall, in common with other professional military officers, believed that the fundamental answer to the uncertainties of the age was increased peacetime military prepared-ness. In this Marshall faced a dilemma. He realized that national security policy was not created in a political vacuum. His reading of American history had taught him that his fellow citizens would rapidly dismantle the nation's military machine and would not tolerate a large standing Army once the Axis powers had been defeated.[2]

The answer to Marshall's dilemma had been suggested by his old friend and mentor, Brig. Gen. John McAuley Palmer. Palmer had been recalled from retire-ment to active duty by Marshall in November 1941. Marshall, according to Palmer, had asked him to help ". . . develop a postwar military system that would be consistent with our traditions, and one which might therefore expect favorable consideration by the American people and Congress."[3] Palmer was a long time advocate of the "citizen Army" concept. He was convinced that American citizens could become excellent part-time soldiers if given proper professional training and isolated from the state politics surrounding the National Guard. The vehicle to achieve this would be a system of universal military training conducted by the regular Army for all able-bodied males. This large pool of trainees would be organized into a strictly federal reserve force. Palmer had publicly advocated this approach in his capacity as Gen. John J. Pershing's personal representative to Congress when it considered postwar military policy after World War I.[4]

General Marshall was sympathetic to Palmer's ideas. His experience with the American Expeditionary Force in France during World War I had shown him the merits of a citizen army trained in peacetime by professional soldiers to shoulder the bulk of America's wartime combat burdens. By the summer of 1943, Marshall had accepted Palmer's proposal as the basis for the War Department's postwar plans. Universal Military Training would substitute a massive citizen reserve force for a large peacetime professional Army and would minimize the financial burdens of national defense. Organization and training of the reserve force would be strictly a federal affair. The National Guard, with its divided state-federal loyalties would be dissolved as a federal reserve force.[5]

On July 22, 1943, a Special Planning Division was established to coordinate detailed War Department planning for demobilization and the postwar Army. Palmer served the planning division in an advisory capacity. In the summer of 1943, the Army Air Forces (AAF) also established its own postwar planning offices—the Post War Division, under Brig. Gen. Laurence S. Kuter, the Assistant Chief of Air Staff, Plans, and the Special Projects Office, under Col. F. Trubee Davison. Wartime service rivalries and the desire to achieve an independent postwar Air Force had helped push the AAF into this activity. The separate War Department and AAF postwar planning staffs, with no formal joint planning mechanism, worked largely in isolation from each other. They also lacked ade-quate guidance from either the Joint Chiefs of Staff or civilian officials within the executive branch of government. Predictably, these two staffs, along with their equally isolated Navy counterparts, developed quite different versions of America's postwar national security requirements.[6]

The Army Air Forces, although part of the Army, had evolved in the direction of an autonomous military service by the time it commenced its own postwar planning in 1943. The political motivations and military assumptions behind the AAF's postwar plans were quite different from those which animated Marshall, Palmer, and the Special Planning Division's staff. Fundamentally, AAF planning had one overriding goal: to build the best possible case for an independent postwar Air Force. The doctrine of strategic bombardment was the heart of the AAF's case for independence from the Army. The wartime AAF headquarters was dominated by advocates of strategic bombing. They firmly believed that future wars would be brief and highly destructive affairs quickly decided by the superior application of air power against an opponent's homeland.[7]

The AAF's "Initial Plan for the Post War Air Force" was completed in February 1944.[8] It described a huge (approximately one million) peacetime active duty Air Force structured to carry the burden of postwar security with little Army or Navy support. The cutting edge of this force would be 105 combat air groups.

Brig. Gen. John McAuley Palmer, long-time mentor of General Marshall, advocated universal military training and a federal reserve force.

As Assistant Chief of Air Staff, Plans, Brig. Gen. Laurence S. Kuter stressed the need for maintaining active duty forces, rather than relying on the Reserves or National Guard for air strength.

9

There was no room in this plan for universal military training, an organized federal reserve force, or the state-controlled National Guard. However, the War Department directed that subsequent plans include these forces and reduce the active duty force. Army Air Forces leaders and planners did not abandon their quest for an active duty Air Force built around the strategic bombardment mission. They remained cool toward universal military training and constantly stressed that forces-in-being, not reserves, were the key to modern defense. They were confident that the public and Congress would eventually accept their vision of America's postwar national security requirements. Adoption of the massive retaliation doctrine by the Eisenhower administration in the early 1950s vindicated their optimism if not their strategic insights.[9]

The initial postwar plans of both the Special Planning Division and the AAF neglected the National Guard. Guard officers had become alarmed by the treatment they had received at the hands of the War Department early in the war. Army public relations coverage of the mobilization, reorganization, and training performance of National Guard divisions had been extremely poor. Numerous stories had appeared in the public press concerning the problems experienced by National Guard units after they had been called into federal service in 1940. Basically, guardsmen believed that they had been made scapegoats for the inadequacies of prewar Army plans, organization, facilities, and equipment. Personnel controversies further clouded the scene. Pressure had been placed on Guard units for men to fill the Army's rapidly expanding officer candidate schools. At the same time the War Department's pre-Pearl Harbor decision to create a relatively youthful officer corps limited eligibility for active duty in each rank to certain prescribed age brackets. Through this age policy, the Army sought to create a more energetic and aggressive field leadership. However laudable its intent, this policy disqualified numerous Guard officers from active duty assignments and led guardsmen to believe that its real purpose was to eliminate the leadership of the Guard in order to create vacancies for the young officers of the regular Army.[10]

Compounding the anxieties of the National Guard, its formal participation in the War Department's planning process appeared to have disappeared by mid–1943. Section 5 of the National Defense Act of 1920 required the War Department to consider the views of National Guard and Reserve officers when formulating plans and policies pertinent to their components of the Army. The prescribed mechanisms for this advice were War Department committees on National Guard and Reserve policy. On May 2, 1942, the Secretary of War had suspended their operation for the war's duration. Another development that had troubled guardsmen was the removal of the National Guard Bureau from the War Department's Special Staff in April 1941. The bureau was then placed in an obscure and powerless position under the Commanding General, Army Service Forces. There, it was relegated to a largely record keeping function. Consequently, the bureau was no longer able to defend the interests of the Guard within the innermost councils of the War Department. The suspicions of guardsmen were increased by rumors that the War Deparment's secret plans for the postwar Army excluded the National Guard altogether. The absence of Guard participation in the planning process, General Palmer's public advocacy of an entirely federal military reserve system, and, what leading Guard officers felt was the shabby treatment of the National Guard during the war fueled the fear that the Army was determined to destroy the Guard.[11]

Guard officers, through their powerful lobby, the National Guard Association of the United States (NGAUS), became politically active. Maj. Gen. Ellard A. Walsh of Minnesota was President of the National Guard Association and its companion organization, the Adjutant Generals' Association. He was given "a blank check on the small funds available and general mandates to proceed in behalf of the Guard."[12] Walsh established a Washington headquarters for the association with a permanent office where he prepared to defend the Guard's interests against the regular Army. The postwar military planning process, already complicated by interservice rivalry and parochialism, was about to be introduced to the pressures of American domestic politics.[13]

The Guard, represented by its chief political organ, NGAUS, had a reputation as one of the most effective pressure groups in American politics. It enjoyed four crucial advantages as an organized lobby. First, and most significant, the Guard was a public institution sanctioned by the Constitution's militia clause. Its defense mission gave the Guard a patriotic claim on public resources unmatched by interest groups outside the government. Second, the Guard was a nationwide institution with units deeply rooted in communities in nearly every congressional district. These community ties were especially appealing to congressmen. Third, the Guard profited from its close connections with state governments and political party organizations. Each state Guard organization was administered by an adjutant general, usually a political appointee of the governor. Historically, governors had used the Guard as a source of patronage, but the practice had been drastically curtailed after World War I. More importantly, many Guard officers were active in partisan politics, and their political activism enhanced their relationship with governors and congressmen. Finally, the National Guard Association of the United States was a tightly disciplined organization with clear and readily-communicated basic goals.* Membership was restricted to officers and included the Guard's

---

*Since its creation in 1879, NGAUS had promoted three basic goals. First, it sought to guarantee the Guard's role as the first line combat reserve component of the active duty Army. Second, it worked for increased federal financial and technical assistance that would make the Guard's combat reserve role credible. Third, it battled to retain the Guard's dual state-federal status so that it could preserve its organizational autonomy. In most respects, NGAUS was extraordinarily successful in achieving those objectives. However, it was forced to exchange much of the Guard's autonomy for additional federal supervision and money. The federal government exercised extensive authority over the Guard as a result of this exchange. It prescribed the number and kind of Guard units, as well as their manning authorizations and locations. Further, it established standards of health and professional competence for Guard personnel, provided advisers and materiel, supervised Guard training, dictated codes of military justice, and could order the Guard to active duty at the direction of the President or Congress.

entire commissioned cadre. They were subject to a well-developed system for recruiting members, selecting leaders, and enforcing internal discipline. Membership dues were collected through the military chain of command. Many of these officers were devoted to the Guard. They made it either a full-time career or an activity central to their lives. Thus, the Guard's constitutional status, patriotic image, internal discipline, political activism, and enthusiasm all combined to magnify its influence.[14]

Drawing upon its distinctive advantages as an organized political pressure group, the National Guard Association employed several techniques to promote its basic goals and protect its interests with Congress, the primary focus of its attention. Essentially, the Association relied upon communications between congressmen and individual guardsmen in their districts. Sometimes it used grassroots letter and telegram campaigns to alert congressmen to the Guard's position on issues. The organization could also stimulate messages from home-state friends of key congressmen when attempting to influence their votes. More typically it relied upon selective pressure applied to a few congressmen who had direct authority over Guard matters by virtue of their committee assignments. This same efficiency was also demonstrated by the Association at congressional hearings. Guard spokesmen were frequently selected not only for their expertise, but also because they came from the same states as key members of these committees. Congressmen generally encouraged this technique regardless of its transparent intent. Association officials personally lobbied congressmen on issues considered important to the Guard. Carefully cultivated friendships often facilitated the Guard's appeals to Congress.[15]

Another important source of the Guard's influence was its ability to provide Congress with useful and reliable information on reserve affairs. The National Guard Association drew upon the expertise of its own staff as well as the National Guard Bureau and the adjutants general to keep Congress informed about matters affecting the Guard. Since the Association was not subject to control by the executive branch, it could provide independent information which Congress could use to challenge existing reserve forces policies. Such independence and expertise in reserve matters was highly valued by Congress.[16]

The National Guard Bureau was the other major object and instrument of the Guard's influence. Because of its historical role as administrator and chief adviser on Guard affairs within the War Department, as well as the fact that its chief was a Guard officer, the bureau was strongly committed to defending the Guard's interests within the federal government. It was also well placed to provide early warning of official proposals that might impinge on the Guard's status. Consequently, the bureau was a natural, albeit dependent, ally of the Association. It was obligated to the latter for its success in administering the Guard. When it wanted more money or authority from Congress, the bureau relied upon the Association for political support. Within the War Department, much of its au-

Gen. George Marshall with Maj. Gen. Ellard A. Walsh, President of the influential National Guard Association.

Courtesy Minnesota ANG

thority depended upon this partnership. The bureau's requests and policy positions were backed by the Association's political influence, and since it ultimately depended upon the Association's power, the bureau was obligated to defer to its wishes.[17]

General Walsh was determined to use these political resources to insure the Guard's survival as the nation's first line combat reserve force after World War II. On January 2, 1944, he held a preliminary meeting with General Palmer to discuss the Special Planning Division's postwar military plans. Next, a conference was arranged between the division's staff and the representatives of the National Guard Association concerning the Guard's place in the postwar military establishment. Four sessions were held during February 1944 in the offices of the National Guard Bureau.[18] National Guard representatives made their position clear to Maj. Gen. William F. Tompkins, head of the Special Planning Division, and his staff. They argued that "the National Guard would be a first line reserve [of the Army of the United States] . . ." and that "we would view with suspicion and distrust any action of the Special Plans Division so long as the National Guard had no representation thereon."[19] They also made it clear that provisions of Section 5 of the National Defense Act of 1920 required National Guard participation in the formulation of all War Department policies and regulations affecting the organization, distribution, and training of the Guard and must be complied with. In sum, they would accept nothing less than a guarantee that the National Guard would participate in the postwar planning process, maintain its position as the Army's first line civilian reserve component, and retain its dual state-federal status.[20]

Palmer, reversing his previous position, sided with the guardsmen. He convinced Tompkins and Marshall that the National Guard's prewar status must be retained in the postwar Army. However, the reasons advanced for this recommendation were primarily political rather than military. It had become evident to both Palmer and Tompkins that any effort to eliminate the Guard's status by merger into a purely federal reserve would result in a political battle in the Congress. They feared that such a fight would weaken and perhaps fatally delay Congressional enactment of a system of postwar universal military training prior to the war's end. The price of National Guard support for universal military training was assurance that the Guard would remain a major element in the postwar Army. General Marshall, who believed that an adequate system for postwar universal military training had to be enacted before wartime enthusiasm for military service waned, accepted these essentially political arguments.[21]

At a special joint meeting of the National Guard and Adjutant Generals' associations held in Baltimore, in early May 1944, General Walsh publicly attacked the Army. His annual report opened with the declaration that the meeting would determine whether or not the National Guard would continue to occupy its primary position in the nation's peacetime military reserve system. Walsh followed with an exhaustive, one-sided history of American military policy from the perspective of the militia and the National Guard. He portrayed their relationship with the regular Army in the blackest of terms. Walsh denounced the "Regular Army Samurai" as a greedy, caste-conscious, self-serving elite bent upon destruction of the National Guard in order to aggrandize their own careers. The National Guard Association, he declared, must be prepared to represent its views on postwar military policy before Congress.[22]

At the same time, Walsh mounted more direct pressure on the War Department by publicly threatening to stall postwar military legislation in Congress. In a bitter letter to the House Select Committee on Postwar Military Policy, he blasted the Army's treatment of the National Guard. He charged that "the National Guard never has and is not now receiving the wholehearted support from the regular Army that it should, or which is contemplated in law."[23]

Rejecting the argument that legislation molding the postwar military establishment should be enacted quickly to avoid any postwar backlash, Walsh argued that such a procedure would guarantee the loss of public support. The National Guard Association was willing to support universal military training if trainees were given the option of joining the National Guard afterwards, but final determination of these matters should be deferred until after the war. At that point,

America's citizen-soldiers would have returned home and their opinions could be heard.[24]

The National Guard Association's political pressure eventually paid off. On the recommendation of General Tompkins, the Secretary of War approved formation of a General Staff committee on the postwar National Guard composed of Army and Guard officers. The committee, which served from August 1944 to September 1945, with all members assigned to Tompkins' Special Planning Division, studied policies affecting the postwar National Guard. On May 17, 1945, the National Guard Bureau was removed from the Army Service Forces and reestablished within the War Department. The bureau had been conducting a study on the Guard's postwar position. Responsiblity for the study rested with its Requirements Division, whose chief became the bureau's liaison with the Special Planning Division and the General Staff Committee on National Guard Policy. The bureau was not satisfied to insure the mere survival of the National Guard at its prewar troop level of approximately 242,000 men. It had polled Guard commanders on active duty with the Army and pushed for a substantial increase in the postwar manpower allotment.[25]

Within the War Department, planning for the future of the National Guard was part of a continuing struggle between aviators and ground force officers over the size and composition of the postwar Army. On May 31, 1944, General Tompkins solicited recommendations on the postwar Army from various General Staff divisions and major commands including the Army Air Forces. The only real guidance that accompanied this request was an arbitrary troop level ceiling of 1.5 million men for the Army developed in 1943. Even before Tompkins' request, the AAF and the Army ground forces had staked rival claims to postwar strengths that threatened this troop ceiling. The AAF's 105 group plan had called for a million-man Air Force while the Army ground forces were asking for 780,000 men including 400,000 trainees provided by a universal military training system. A compromise plan was developed in August 1944 calling for a total Army strength of 1,093,050 professionals and 630,217 trainees annually. This plan would have designated the AAF as the primary M–Day [Mobilization Day] force with 75 air groups and a strength of 430,000 professionals. Seventy-five groups did not satisfy the aviators. They still insisted on 105 groups.[26]

On November 11, 1944, General Marshall shattered the postwar planners' design for an Army of 1.1 million men. Marshall demanded a reexamination of postwar military strengths by the Special Planning Division. He wanted a small professional force backed by universal military training. A new plan was formulated. Total Army strength was projected at 1,015,000 men. The Army Ground Forces was to consist of only 100,000 regulars and 320,000 trainees. The projected total size of the Army Air Forces was even smaller. It was to be limited to 120,000 regulars and 200,000 trainees. Under this new plan, the AAF, which had been insisting that 105 air groups were needed to insure national security, got only 16 groups. Gen. Henry H. Arnold, Commanding General, AAF, strongly disagreed with this plan. He argued that domestic politics and budgetary considerations should not be elevated above national defense needs.[27]

The Army Air Forces had first begun seriously considering the prospect of postwar National Guard air units in the late summer of 1944. The resulting Air Staff "Study of the Air Component of the Post-War National Guard," approved on October 21, 1944, assumed that state-controlled armed forces with federal status would continue to exist and envisioned that these state forces would include an autonomous air component corresponding to the projected postwar independent Air Force. It reflected the AAF's reluctance to assign important missions to the Guard by recommending that approximately ninety percent of the projected air component should consist of antiaircraft artillery troops. The balance would be allotted to flying and possibly aircraft control and warning units.[28] Thus, at the outset, AAF planning established a negative pattern of expectations. This pattern relegated National Guard air units to distinctly secondary roles and provided them with inadequate resources. Such thinking plagued the program through much of its history.[29]

Despite the reservations of the Air Staff, the National Guard, including its air component, had assured its postwar existence as a first line military reserve force. General Tompkins, testifying before the House Select Committee on Postwar Military Policy on June 15, 1945, affirmed this. He noted that the War Department "contemplates retention of our two reserve components of the Army . . . the National Guard and the Organized Reserves . . ." with the former "our first line of reserve in an emergency."[30] The Guard, he continued, should continue to perform its dual function as an instrument of internal security for the individual states in peace and an instrument of national security in war. To that end Tompkins presented the basic War Department recommendation:

> to strengthen and improve the National Guard so as to make it capable of immmediate expansion to war strength fully able to furnish units trained and equipped, for service anywhere in the world. In time of war, when called into national service, the National Guard should be able to defend the critical areas of the United States from land, sea, or air attacks and assist in covering the mobilization and concentration of other reserve forces.[31]

The National Guard, which had feared extinction as a wartime reserve force in 1943, had forced the War Department to accept it in the postwar Army. It had been given a clearly stated mission that implied an expanded troop strength; and it would be able to recruit from the universal military training system proposed by the War Department to reach that expanded level. Politically, the National Guard had paid its debts before Tompkins testified. General Walsh, speaking for the Guard before the committee on June 5, had supported universal military training.

The struggle within the War Department over the size and composition of the postwar Army continued through 1945. General Marshall insisted on a small, balanced professional force backed by a huge reserve system. The Air Staff, firmly wedded to the forces-in-being concept, argued that only a large, active duty Air Force could adequately fill America's postwar national security requirements. This issue was resolved on August 27, 1945, when the War Department directed that the Army Air Forces' postwar structure would consist of four hundred thousand men and seventy groups. These levels were to be reached by July 1946 and to remain frozen until February 1947. The plan was approved by Gen. Dwight D. Eisenhower, Army Chief of Staff, in December 1945 and by the Joint Chiefs of Staff in January 1946.[32]

Many in the AAF and on the War Department General Staff opposed the Marshall and Palmer vision of the regular Army as essentially a small training and organizational cadre for hordes shunted through a universal military training system. To complicate matters further, the Navy loomed as an even more formidable challenger for what appeared likely to be extremely limited postwar military budgets. In this conflict of interests, planners continued to struggle with questions relevant to postwar policies for the National Guard.[33]

General Marshall, faced with growing opposition to his postwar plans within the War Department, evidently sought to strengthen the hand of the reserve component planners. On July 28, 1945, the Special Planning Division's Committee on National Guard Policy was augmented by four additional officers drawn from both the Guard and the regular Army. The most politically prominent of the new members was Maj. Gen. Milton J. Reckord of Maryland—a former president of the National Guard Association and the current chairman of its legislative committee. Marshall recalled Reckord to Washington, D.C. from his active duty assignment in Europe to chair both the expanded National Guard policy committee and an overall "Joint Staff Committee on Postwar Planning for the National Guard and Reserve."[34] Reckord, for his part, favored universal military training and expected to see a small postwar regular Army backed by a substantial National Guard with the remaining requirements for a balanced Army filled by an organized reserve.[35]

The joint staff committee made some changes in the recommendations previously approved by Secretary of War Henry L. Stimson and General Marshall. The most important of these provided that "when the requirements for a balanced force in the Army of the United States necessitate the allocation to a state of troops or equipment, the housing of which would impose an inequitable burden on the state. . . . the federal government will contribute its equitable share of the expenses of constructing and maintaining the required facilities."[36] They also prepared, in conjunction with War Department civilian officials, a troop basis plan for the Army's organized reserve units. Their proposal anticipated "a National Guard of . . .perhaps 500,000."[37]

The joint committee's policy proposals were approved by the Secretary of War on October 13, 1945. Officially titled "War Department Policies Relating to

(Left) Secretary of War Henry L. Stimson decided to accept the Joint Staff Committee's proposal for a dual component reserve system.

(Below) Maj. Gen. Milton A. Reckord receives a Second Cluster to the Distinguished Service Medal from General of the Army Dwight D. Eisenhower. Having earned the honor in the European Theater during World War II, General Reckord returned home to serve as Adjutant General for the State of Maryland and chairman of the War Department Committee on National Guard and Reserve Policy.

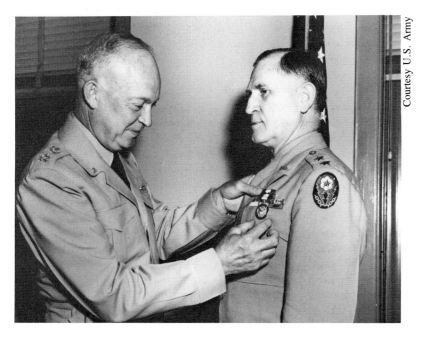

the Post War National Guard and Organized Reserve Corps, 13 October 1945," these proposals clearly committed the War Department to the creation of dual component reserve systems for both the Army and the Army Air Forces. The National Guard, composed of organized units, retained its prewar position as the Army's first line combat reserve force. Individuals needed to bring organized units up to fully authorized strength and to replace combat losses, as well as those units which neither the active Army nor the National Guard could provide, would be supplied by the U.S. Army Reserve. The War Department's proposals also added a new reserve organization to augment the postwar AAF—the Air National Guard. The Air Guard, like the National Guard, was intended to be the primary source of organized combat ready units. It was envisaged as an M–Day organization capable of rapid expansion to wartime manning levels and full operational readiness. Individuals and air units that neither the Army Air Forces nor the Air Guard could supply would be provided by a strictly federal AAF reserve program paralleling the Army's. And, despite the lack of a clear state-related mission, the Air Guard would share with the National Guard a dual state-federal status.[38]

These plans, commonly known as Approved Policies 1945, established the official basis for Army Air Forces planning of its postwar reserve programs. The AAF implemented them through separate plans for the Air National Guard and the Air Force Reserve. The original AAF reserve components plan implementing Approved Policies 1945 was prepared by the Assistant Chief of the Air Staff for Operations and presented to the Air Staff on October 9, 1945. At that time, certain revisions were directed. An ad hoc committee within the Air Staff then drew up a revised plan, dated November 1, 1945, that implied an air defense orientation for the Air Guard. It called for twelve wing headquarters commanding twenty-four fighter groups, twelve aircraft control and warning organizations, fourteen anti-aircraft artillery brigades, and three light bomb groups.[39]

Although some Air Staff officers realized the wisdom of any plan that would increase public support for the AAF, the general attitude about the Air Guard's ability to fulfill an M–Day role remained skeptical. The skeptics were especially critical of the Guard's ability to operate and to maintain highly technical equipment.[40]

Regardless of these negative assessments, the Commanding General, Army Air Forces, approved the revised plan on November 26, 1945. He forwarded it to the Army Chief of Staff the same day with the recommendation that it be approved for initial implementation and further planning. The plan was returned without action on December 4, 1945 pending decisions on the organization, strength, and composition of the postwar Army. The AAF was instructed to keep the plan current. Finally, on January 30, 1946, the Army Chief of Staff directed the "piecemeal" activation of National Guard air units under the revised AAF plan.[41]

On February 9, 1946, the Guard Bureau officially announced the Air Guard plan to the states and territories. Formal unit allotments were made to those states which had already approved their proposed units. Based upon the response of the states and further study of the plan, minor changes were made. Augmentations were recommended by the National Guard Bureau. The final Air Guard Plan, calling for 514 units, was agreed to in the spring by Gen. Carl Spaatz, Commanding General, Army Air Forces, and Maj. Gen. Butler Miltonberger, National Guard Bureau Chief. Spaatz forwarded it to the Army Chief of Staff who approved it on April 25, 1946.[42]

The final plan targeted June 30, 1947 as the completion date for postwar organization of the Air Guard. It retained the twelve wing headquarters envisaged in the preceding plan. Tactical flying units would consist of seventy-two fighter squadrons and twelve light bomber squadrons. The federal government agreed to furnish aircraft, supplies, instructors, and pay. The states were to furnish men, bases, and storage facilities. Projected strength was set at about 58,000 men with the states allocated quotas based on their male population between eighteen and thirty-five. Each state would receive at least one tactical flying unit. Air bases were to be located near large population centers to make recruiting easier.[43]

The revised AAF plan assumed that the Air Guard would be an air defense force, primarily equipped with fighters. Fighters were deemed especially suitable for the Guard because of their size, relatively low maintenance costs, and versatility. Air defense would be relatively easy to sell to the states as an extension of the traditional militia role. Light bomber aircraft were found suitable for similar reasons of size, flexibility, and economy. Transports and heavy bombers were not considered appropriate for the Air Guard. Perhaps more significantly, Army Air Forces planners were faced with the problem of disposing of large numbers of surplus, yet still useful, fighter aircraft no longer needed by the rapidly shrinking postwar establishment. The Air Guard's initial allocation of missions and aircraft was probably heavily influenced by these factors. Since the first permanent program of National Guard aviation in 1920, its tactical organization and missions appear to have been more heavily influenced by the availability of surplus military aircraft than any other single factor.[44]

The Air Guard plan, which emerged in 1945–46, was an outgrowth of the politics of planning for the postwar military establishment. It was foisted upon an unenthusiastic AAF because of General Marshall's desire to minimize postwar defense spending and to create popular support for a viable peacetime military system based on universal military training. Marshall wanted this system in effect before America's historical distaste for compulsory peacetime military service and expensive standing armies could reassert itself. To avoid a time-consuming and politically damaging fight with the National Guard Association, he had reluctantly agreed to preserve the Guard's established position as the Army's first line reserve force.

Army Air Forces' headquarters took a different view of America's postwar requirements. Lacking meaningful experience with its own organized reserve flying units and determined to build the best possible case for an independent Air Force, the AAF's postwar planners stressed the necessity for a large Air Force-in-being built around the strategic bombardment mission. Their reading of the military lessons of World War II convinced them that an active duty Air Force, held in instant readiness for combat, would be the only decisive military organization in future wars. They were convinced that those conflicts would be short, destructive affairs decided by the superior application of strategic air power. Within this context of AAF organizational self interest, little attention was devoted to the necessity for reserve forces, especially state-controlled organizations like the Air National Guard. Air Staff officers were extremely skeptical of the ability of any amateur force of citizen-airmen to master adequately the sophisticated technology of modern aerial warfare. Nevertheless, General Marshall, determined to win National Guard Association support for his postwar plans and to stretch austere postwar military budgets as far as possible, directed the Army Air Forces to create the Air Guard as part of a dual component air reserve system. The Army Air Forces bowed to Marshall's pressure to minimize the political problems the AAF faced in achieving its long-cherished goal of independence from the Army. Many of the difficulties that plagued the Air Force-Air Guard relationship until the Korean War can be traced to the strained circumstances surrounding the Air Guard's creation in 1945–46.

Chapter II

Struggle for Control, 1946–1950

On June 30, 1946, Denver's 120th Fighter Squadron became the first postwar National Guard aviation unit to receive formal federal recognition. On May 26, 1949, the last of the Air Guard's projected 514 units was organized. On paper, the Air Guard had become a formidable military organization. Its officer corps had largely escaped the taint of state political patronage which had harmed the image of the prewar National Guard. Air Force officers considered its pilots, virtually all World War II combat veterans, to be well-qualified for their assignments. Celebrated combat pilots like Joe Foss,* serving as a fighter squadron commander, provided an especially glamorous aura.

Air Guard tactical units consisted of seventy-two fighter and twelve light bomber squadrons. Its nontactical units included thirty-six aircraft control and warning units, three tow target squadrons, three air service group detachments, and three weather stations. These primary organizations were supplemented by numerous Air Guard support units. By February 1950, the Air Guard's aircraft inventory consisted of 2,401 planes, including 211 jet fighters. Its fighter aircraft strength represented nearly seventy percent of the Air Force's total fighter strength in the continental United States. By June 30, 1950, its personnel strength was 44,728, including approximately 3,600 pilots. This force, built in four years, was a considerable accomplishment. To national guardsmen, it vindicated their faith that the American militia tradition could be successfully adapted to the demanding requirements of modern aerial warfare.[1]

The Air Guard, however, was far from ready to play its intended role as the Air Force's primary mobilization day reserve force in 1950. Propeller driven fighters, which dominated its aircraft inventory, were quickly driven from the skies

---

*Lt Col Joseph J. Foss of the South Dakota Air National Guard had won fame as a Marine Corps pilot during World War II.

by MiG–15 jets during the Korean War. Some air guardsmen privately considered their tactical units to be nothing better than glorified flying clubs formed into forty-eight small state air forces. Regular Air Force officers could see no compelling military justification for these state-controlled organizations whose missions were entirely national. Moreover, they could point to the fact that, although Washington paid ninety-seven percent of the Air Guard's bills, it could not tell it how or when to train. Most of these Air Force officers were convinced that the Air Guard's anomalous state-federal status precluded its immediate use in a national emergency. Operational readiness tests conducted by the Air Force during 1949 tended to confirm these pessimistic assessments. The inspectors concluded that, on the average, it would take Air Guard fighter units 86.6 days after mobilization to become fully prepared to carry out their primary operational mission.[2] This delay in the air defense of the United States appeared to be especially untenable after the Soviet Union tested its first atomic bomb in 1949. Lt. Gen. Ennis C. Whitehead, writing in November 1949, noted that " . . . at best the Air National Guard represents aircraft in flyable storage."[3] Whitehead was Commander of the Continental Air Command (CONAC), the Air Force command responsible for inspecting and supervising the training of the Air National Guard. Many professional Air

Marine combat pilot Maj. Joseph J. Foss at the Sioux Falls Army Air Field, South Dakota, 1944. After World War II, Foss returned to South Dakota and began dual careers in the National Guard and state politics.

Force officers shared his skepticism about the military utility of the Air Guard. U.S. Air Force Headquarters, reflecting the growing doubts and frustration with the Air Guard, in concert with the Continental Air Command, suggested in January 1950 that the Air Guard be written off as its primary combat reserve force. The Air Force wanted to give the Air Guard less demanding missions than air defense. These missions would include troop transport, direct air support of ground troops, and civil defense. The Air Force, in effect, rejected the Air Guard's image of itself as twentieth century aerial minutemen. These missions implied greatly reduced levels of federal support for the organization.[4]

The troubled Air Force-Air Guard partnership reflected the traditional American hostility between the militia and the professional military. An unhappy postwar political necessity, their relations sank to a new low on the eve of the Korean War. At the base of the partnership's difficulties lay continuing Air Force skepticism about the wisdom of having an Air Guard and the unresolved fundamental questions about the ability of the active duty establishment to direct the training of its principal combat reserve force. Hoping to resolve these problems, the Air Force struggled with the National Guard Bureau and the states for four years to gain greater operational control of Air Guard units. This struggle, including an abortive drive to convert the Air Guard to a strictly federal reserve force incorporated in the Air Force Reserve, was ultimately futile and counterproductive. More significantly, it diverted the Air Force and Air Guard from establishing a working relationship that would have enabled them to constructively address the problems which delayed the Air Guard's emergence as a viable combat reserve force. The Truman administration's austere postwar defense budgets also significantly slowed the pace of the Air Guard's initial development, thereby further exacerbating its serious problems with the Air Force. Finally, poor planning and neglect by the Air Force also delayed the Air Guard's development.

The most basic problem troubling Air Force-Air Guard relations during the 1946–50 period was the question of command authority. The Air Force and its predecessor, the Army Air Forces, had insisted from the inception of planning for the postwar military establishment that there was no military justification for a dual component air reserve system. The Air Guard, it argued, would have an entirely federal mission, the air defense of the continental United States. Such an aerial force would lack the state missions of the National Guard such as disaster relief and internal security. The exigencies of American politics had prevailed, however, and the Air Force was forced to develop a working relationship with a reserve component it did not want and could not adequately control.

Air Force authority over the Air Guard was marginal at best. Although it supplied aircraft, equipment, and operating funds to the Air Guard, domestic politics made it virtually impossible to use this support as a lever to force compliance with Air Force policies and procedures. Once federal recognition had been granted to an Air Guard unit, the Air Force's authority was essentially limited to conducting annual inspections and supervising training programs it did not control. Air Force advisers assigned to Guard units could only suggest, not command. Command remained firmly lodged with the various states until Air Guard units were called to active duty. The Air Guard was fiercely protective of its state militia status. Moreover, many state authorities were determined to treat their Air National Guard contingents as if they were nothing more than miniature air forces that had to be operated strictly within their own state boundaries when not in active federal service.

Considerable tension developed between the Air Force and the Air Guard because of this relationship. Initially, this quarrelsome atmosphere focused upon Lt. Gen. George E. Stratemeyer. Stratemeyer was the first commander of the Air Defense Command (ADC), organized on March 21, 1946.* In addition to the air defense of the United States, ADC had been burdened with a variety of miscellaneous and distinctly second-rate missions. These included administration of Reserve Officers' Training Corps (ROTC), Air Scouts, and the Civil Air Patrol. Finally, the command ran the Air Force Reserve and discharged the AAF's inspection and training supervision responsibilities relative to the Air National Guard.[5]

From the beginning, Stratemeyer was apprehensive about the Air Guard's ability to successfully participate in the air defense of the United States. However, he had to rely on the Air Guard to provide the bulk of ADC's fighters. The Army Air Forces' air defense fighter force in the spring of 1946 consisted primarily of two night fighter squadrons. But they, like their Air Guard counterparts, existed only on paper.[6]

Stratemeyer was forced to exercise his limited authority over the Air Guard within a complex and cumbersome system of command growing from the latter's state status. Lines of authority and communication between AAF Headquarters, ADC, the National Guard Bureau, the states, and individual Air Guard units were confusing, time-consuming, and often ineffective. AAF Headquarters had delegated to ADC its responsibilities to inspect and supervise the training of the Air Guard. Stratemeyer, in turn, sought to exercise these responsibilities through the commanders of ADC's four numbered air forces. Regular AAF instructors, assigned to specific Air Guard units, and command level inspection teams, actually implemented these AAF functions. Command jurisdiction, however, remained with the states. Unless authorized by prior voluntary agreements between ADC and the governors concerned, Stratemeyer could not command Air Guard units during sudden national emergencies. These units remained under state command until a congressional declaration of war or emergency allowed them to be mobilized for federal service.

---

*On March 21, 1946, Gen Spaatz directed establishment of the AAF's three major combat commands—Strategic Air Command, Tactical Air Command, and the Air Defense Command.

A separate channel of communication for administrative and logistical matters ran from the Commanding General, Army Air Forces to the Chief of the National Guard Bureau, and then to the states. War Department General Staff Circular No. 5–14, dated June 3, 1946, had given the National Guard Bureau (NGB) responsibility for all Air Guard functions except the supervision of training. As late as June 1949, no Air Force directive could be made applicable to the Air Guard without the specific concurrence of the bureau. Within the states, administrative control was exercised through the adjutants general, representing their respective governors, to the various Air Guard unit commanders. These unit commanders could not, while their units remained in state status, exercise command jurisdiction over any of their sub-units located in other states. This complicated arrangement was inconsistent with accepted professional principles of military organization which sought to combine authority and responsibility in a single easily-understood chain of command.[7]

Stratemeyer recognized the shortcomings of his authority and organizational relationships with the Air Guard. He early antagonized the National Guard Bureau by trying to strengthen his control of Air Guard units. In March 1946, Stratemeyer had been charged with the responsibility for maintaining the Air Guard and the Air Force Reserve "in a highly-trained condition of readiness."[8] The importance of this mission statement was underscored by the fact that the Air Guard's seventy-two fighter squadrons, when organized, would constitute virtually the entire air defense interceptor force available to the Air Defense Command. Likewise, the Guard's projected aircraft control and warning units would provide the bulk of America's air defense radar capability. Stratemeyer wrote Maj. Gen. Butler Miltonberger, Chief of the National Guard Bureau, emphasizing that "the mission of the air national security [of the United States] . . . has been assigned in large measure to the Air National Guard."[9] Since the Air Defense Command "was originated to place under one commander the primary responsibility for the efficiency and effectiveness of the Air National Guard . . . I feel I must be responsible for organizing and administering the Air National Guard in its federally recognized status."[10] Stratemeyer also proposed that National Guard Bureau functions relevant to the Air Guard such as the actual allocation of federally-owned aircraft and equipment be transferred to ADC.[11]

This request received a chilly reception at the Guard Bureau. On May 10, 1946, General Spaatz, Commanding General of the Army Air Forces, informed Stratemeyer that federal statutes limited ADC's control of the Air Guard while it remained in its state status. Apparently Miltonberger had lectured Spaatz on the meaning of those statutes. After what Guard spokesmen later described as a "knock-down drag-out fight" in the spring of 1946, Spaatz had agreed that the AAF, including ADC, would go through the National Guard Bureau on Air Guard matters.[12] Spaatz noted that ADC's authority was essentially restricted to prescribing organization and training standards, furnishing equipment, and conducting inspections. In all other respects, the Air Guard was under the complete control of the state authorities. Stratemeyer, henceforth, would work closely with the Guard Bureau and the state adjutants general. However, he would make no agreements binding the Army Air Forces. Spaatz would do that.[13]

Another touchy issue was the selection of Air Guard bases. This was usually done by state adjutants general in conjunction with state and local politicians. States that had operated aviation units of National Guard infantry divisions prior to World War II attempted to have Air Guard units established in the same local areas. However, in situations where entirely new units were being created, the choice was largely political, although consideration was given to the availability of personnel to man the units. The Air Force could only advise the states on the location of Air Guard airfields. The states jealously guarded their prerogatives in this area.[14]

State officials encountered many problems in acquiring suitable facilities for their proposed Air Guard units. Because of dramatic wartime advances in military aviation technology, most prewar facilities were inadequate for the new types of aircraft Air Guard units were to receive. During the war, National Guard aviation facilities had been used by the Army Air Forces. The airfields had been greatly expanded, runways lengthened, fueling facilities improved, additional operational and maintenance buildings constructed, vast parking aprons and numerous dispersed hardstands provided, and extensive taxiways established connecting these facilities. When the war ended, most of these facilities became surplus to the needs of the federal government and were turned over to the War Assets Administration for disposal. This was done without any consideration of the possible requirements of the Air Guard or Air Force Reserve. If detailed facilities requirements for the Air Guard had been established prior to the war's end, the Air Guard would have had its pick of whatever it needed.[15]

Unfortunately, the War Department did not have a detailed plan for the Air Guard until some time after V–J Day. Once airfields had been turned over to the War Assets Administration, the military having indicated no need for them, local communities were given the opportunity to acquire them. Communities quickly took advantage of this opportunity to gain control of valuable aviation facilities which, in many cases, had been municipal airports prior to the war. They then signed leases on the facilities with commercial aviation or other interests. Frequently, these leases excluded or greatly restricted future Air Guard use of the airfields.[16]

In some instances the Army Air Forces came under attack from congressmen and local officials for pressing the states to speed the acquisition of local airfields to house their Air Guard units.[17] Stratemeyer had written Spaatz outlining problems in securing airfields for the AAF's reserve components. The ADC Commander lamented the

> . . . lack of a policy with reference to which activity, ANG [Air National Guard] or Air Reserve, has priority in acquiring of airfields and facilities thereon. In numerous

(Above) Maj. Gen. Butler B. Miltonberger, Chief, National Guard Bureau, (center) and Col. W. A. R. Robertson, Chief of the bureau's Aviation Group, (left) examine the cockpit of a P–80 jet fighter flown by Lt. Col. Herschel Green. The P–80 was one of the fighters the Air National Guard acquired in its postwar modernization program.

(Left) Lt. Gen. George E. Stratemeyer, first commander of Air Defense Command, tried to bring the Guard in line with Air Force training standards.

instances, facilities are being held for Air Reserve activities which . . .will be requested in the very near future by the various states for their ANG programs. . . . Hq AAF is presently declaring excess to the War Assets Administration all facilities other than those required by the interim and postwar Air Force and Air Reserve activities. . . . In this way, many facilities which this headquarters [ADC] feels will be requested [by the states] for use in the ANG program at some later date are lost. . . . This command is placed in the position of competing through the War Assets Administration with civilian agencies for the use of airfields and facilities which are essential to the mission of this Command . . . the air security of the United States. [18]

Some states, according to Stratemeyer, were slow in requesting airfields for their planned Air Guard units. They were reluctant to commit themselves to a program that might involve a considerable expenditure of their own funds for maintenance of these facilities. He criticized the War Department for failing to inform the governors of an AAF recommendation that seventy-five percent of the operational expenses of these ANG airfields be borne by the federal government. Stratemeyer also asked, in effect, that the Air Defense Command be given final responsibility for the selection of Air Guard bases. [19] Stratemeyer's conclusion reflected a deep-seated anti-militia bias and his own frustrations in dealing with the Air Guard. He found it hard to consider air guardsmen as part of America's first line of defense no matter how well organized and trained. For him, the Air Guard was of necessity an augmentation force to supplement the regulars. It could never be part of the first team. [20]

Spaatz, in his reply, noted that Stratemeyer was to restrict himself to advising on the selection of Air Guard bases. The politically sensitive states would retain absolute authority over the selection of bases regardless of ADC's requirements. State reluctance to acquire airfields was overcome when the War Department agreed to the Army Air Forces' proposal to defray three quarters of the annual operating expenses. Administratively, this economic arrangement was accomplished through service contracts between the states and the federal government. Individual contracts, obligating both parties to the three-fourths (federal), one-fourth (state) formula for airfield operating expenses, were drawn up for each airfield. [21]

On June 5, 1946, the Army Air Forces changed ADC's mission statement with respect to the Air Guard. Henceforward, ADC would simply discharge the responsibilities of the AAF regarding the organization, training, and maintenance of the Air Guard, subject to policies established by AAF. No mention was made of maintaining the Air Guard in a "highly-trained state of readiness" as had been the case in the original mission statement two months earlier. [22] In short, Stratemeyer's responsibility for the Air Guard, his primary source of air defense units, now covered only training and inspection. Resentment on the part of the Guard Bureau and the states had evidently caused this change in ADC's original sweeping assignment with respect to the Air Guard. Stratemeyer's first attempt to gain greater control of the Air Guard had been totally ineffective. It had only heightened long-standing National Guard suspicions of the regular military establishment.

Stratemeyer grew increasingly disillusioned with the Air Guard's slow development. On September 25, he wrote Spaatz once more concerning the Air Guard's problems. The ADC Commander was prepared to recommend abandoning the Air Guard's air defense role altogether. He wrote:

> Our present national security and particularly our security five to ten years hence, depends to a large extent on states accepting their responsibility for creating ANG units which can immediately be called into federal service for effective use on the outbreak or threat of hostilities. If, as happens to be the case at present, they are not disposed to accept this responsibility, I believe the War Department should recommend another system for providing national defense in the air.[23]

Air Guard political independence and the problems it posed were illustrated again later that same year. A bitter conflict between the Air Guard and Air Reserve for scarce funds, equipment, aircraft, and airfield sites had generated substantial ill-will for the publicity conscious Army Air Forces. Guardsmen had been es-

Courtesy Minnesota ANG

Air National Guard hangars at Holman Field, Minnesota, 1949. An active base, Holman received the F–51, T–6, B–26, and C–47.

pecially vociferous in their criticism of the AAF. Responding to this pressure, in December 1946, the War Department issued a "Clarification of War Department Policies Pertaining to the National Guard and Organized Reserve Corps." The statement emphasized that:

- War Department mobilization plans depended upon the enactment of a system of universal military training.
- All M–Day forces must be capable of promptly performing military missions.
- The only M–Day forces which the Organized Reserve Corps would provide would be those which the Regular Army and National Guard [including Air Guard] could not supply.
- Priority in facilities, funds, and equipment would be given M–Day units.[24]

The Guard had clearly won its claim to priority over any strictly federal reserve force in the postwar struggle for missions and resources. Once again it had used its superior organization and political influence to advance its own interests.

Despite its official priority over the Air Force Reserve, the early progress of the Air Guard program was slower than the Air Defense Command expected. Recruiting lacked the expected stimulus of universal military training, and was far behind schedule early in 1947. At the end of February, only 1,746 officers and 3,562 enlisted men were on board. Only thirty flying squadrons had been federally recognized. To receive federal recognition, a unit needed to have twenty-five percent of its authorized officers and ten percent of its authorized enlisted men present for duty.[25]

Stratemeyer believed that ADC's inadequate command authority over the Air Guard was the principal cause of this unsatisfactory progress. However, another vital factor, which he ignored, was the absence of adequate and predictable levels of federal funding. Air Guard funds were severely curtailed in fiscal year 1947. Congress had appropriated $110 million for the entire National Guard for that period. Faced with a budget shortfall for the active duty Army, Congress allowed the War Department to divert $53 million of the National Guard's appropriation to it. After a fight in Congress, the Guard managed to have $4.4 million restored to its budget. Total Guard obligations for FY 1947 amounted to approximately $62 million. The National Guard Bureau had anticipated spending some $33 million on the Air Guard alone that year under the original $110 million appropriation. General Reckord of the National Guard Association told Congress that the original War Department plan for the postwar National Guard, including its air component, had called for expenditures of $200 million in 1947 and $300 million in 1948. He claimed that the severe cuts in the FY 1947 budget had "hamstrung" efforts to develop a strong National Guard in accordance with the War Department's original plans.[26]

Army Air Forces Headquarters reacted to the FY 1947 National Guard budget cuts by temporarily suspending the organization of additional Air Guard squadrons. The original plan called for 514 units including eighty-four tactical squadrons. This was cut almost in half. On March 14, 1947, the AAF's Commanding General announced an "interim-ceiling" of 272 Air Guard units.[27] The fiscal year 1948 National Guard appropriation permitted this to be raised to 308 units, still far short of the final goal. The AAF believed that the 308 unit program would leave the Air Guard an unbalanced force. Its tactical flying squadrons would be inadequately supported by service, engineer, and communications units. However, the Chief of the National Guard Bureau was determined to emphasize the development of tactical units. Support and technical units could await the restoration of adequate budgets. He felt that this policy would save potential airfields and equipment for Air Guard use. Furthermore, it would aid recruiting.[28]

Although the Air Guard's personnel strength had risen to 10,105 and 257 units had been federally recognized by June 30, 1947, the program still was unready to contribute operationally ready flying organizations to the Air Defense Command.[29] The cumulative impact of severe funding cuts, recruiting problems, inadequate command arrangements, and a host of other difficulties was best reflected in the AAF's June 1947 plan for the Air Guard. It stated that " . . . the role of the Air National Guard in air defense was not firmly enough established [by June 1947] to enter into specific [AAF and ADC] air defense plans."[30]

The overriding concern of AAF headquarters in 1947 was the long sought goal of complete independence from the Army. This objective became a reality in September when the Army Air Forces became the United States Air Force under the terms of the National Security Act of 1947. The newly created Air Force, inheriting the AAFs' problems, was hardly an effective fighting force. Postwar demobilization had reduced personnel strength from 2.25 million on V–J Day to 303,000 in May 1947. Combat effective air groups had plummeted from 218 on V–J Day to two in December 1946. By June 1947, the number of combat-ready groups had only grown to eleven. The Air Staff's long-term goal of building an active duty establishment of seventy combat air groups remained frustrated by the small postwar defense budgets of the Truman administration and its policy of dividing these budgets evenly among the armed services.[31]

Faced with inadequate budgets and a critical shortage of combat-ready active duty air units, the Air Force declined to devote any substantial portion of its slender resources to building a viable reserve program. Not surprisingly, the Air Guard's development lagged behind the War Department's original postwar estimates, and Air Force Headquarters, reacting to that slower development, provided the Air Defense Command with another revised mission statement on December 17, 1947. In recognition of the " . . . patently unready state of the Air National Guard . . . it directed ADC to plan for the use of the Guard whenever its units were operationally ready to perform their air defense mission."[32] The Air Force, however, still intended that the Air Guard would eventually provide the bulk of its interceptor force. Even if Congress authorized the active duty force of seventy combat air groups, only twelve regular fighter-interceptor squadrons would be allotted to ADC. With a fifty-five group Air Force, only nine regular flying squadrons would be given an air defense mission. At the close of 1947, ADC's interceptor force consisted of only seven regular Air Force squadrons. This slim force had no operationally ready Air Guard fighter units to augment it.[33]

By the end of 1948, the Air Guard still lacked a fighter force that the Air Force could draw on immediately in a national emergency. A number of problems continued to impede the organization of its individual units. Although enormous numbers of pilots had flown combat missions during the war, some Air Guard units found it difficult to recruit adequate numbers of trained pilots. It had been exceptionally difficult, especially in some rural communities, to find qualified officers who could devote the time and effort necessary to organize and command flying squadrons. In several instances, state authorities had asked the Air Force to loan them regular officers on a temporary basis to actually command Air Guard units during their initial organizational phases. Rank limitations in Air Guard units were part of the problem. Many higher ranking Air Force reservists were unwilling to vacate their grades to accept lower ranking Air Guard positions, while Navy and Marine reserve fliers wishing to join the Guard experienced unnecessary delays. Further, no adequate program had been developed to train young pilots to replace the Guard's aging fliers. The Chief of the National Guard Bureau forecast a shortage of six hundred pilots in the grade of lieutenant by 1950 unless the situation was rectified. Qualified non-flying support officers also were difficult to obtain. The recruiting problems were partially solved by the Selective Service Act of 1948 which virtually brought the Air Guard up to its phased program strength; however, this also filled its ranks with many untrained youths seeking to avoid the draft. Further military service remained unattractive for most enlisted veterans of World War II.[34]

Another crucial shortcoming involved the inadequate size of the authorized caretaker detachments for Air Guard units. These personnel, later known as technicians, were full-time state employees responsible for maintaining equipment, aircraft, and administrative records. They were required to be National Guard members of their units. Later recognized as a key factor in the Air Guard program because of the extraordinary continuity and expertise they provided, their limited numbers created a critical problem in 1948. Air Force Headquarters recognized that "unless additional full-time personnel [i.e., caretakers] are provided the Air National Guard program is in danger of collapsing."[35]

Further, command relationships, which still had not been resolved in a manner consistent with professional military principles by the end of 1948, damaged existing training programs. Air Guard commanders were neither compelled nor disposed to accept Air Force direction. Air Force instructors could only advise them on training and operational matters. And unless informal agreements had been reached between the political authorities, Air Guard unit commanders could not exercise effective control of subunits located in other states. In effect, each state continued to operate its own little air force.[36]

Early in 1948, General Stratemeyer made a second major attempt to establish a better relationship between the Air Force and the Air National Guard's tactical units. At a unit commanders' conference held during February at Brooks AFB near San Antonio, Texas, Stratemeyer advanced a proposal to strengthen his operational control of Air Guard units. His plan envisioned a purely military chain of command. The commanders of the Air Defense Command's numbered air forces would deal directly with their subordinate Air Guard wing commanders. The wing commanders, in turn, would be able to deal with the air group commanders below them regardless of whether or not they were located in the same state. Neither governors nor adjutants general would intervene in this proposed operational chain of command.[37]

Stratemeyer had foreshadowed this proposal three months earlier when he had urged his Air Force commanders to make voluntary agreements where possible, with state governors placing Air Guard units under the Air Defense Command in peacetime. He had cautioned that ADC's short term plan did not contemplate the use of any Air Guard units "primarily due to their universal lack of unit proficiency at the present time." However, once they had reached a "usable state of proficiency," he wanted his Air Force commanders to prepare to employ them immediately upon their federalization.[38] This required prior agreement with the state governors on a voluntary basis. Several of these agreements were apparently in effect when Stratemeyer called his San Antonio unit commanders conference.[39]

Guardsmen present at San Antonio included the Chief of the National Guard Bureau, Maj. Gen. Kenneth F. Cramer and the President of the Adjutants' General Association, Maj. Gen. Raymond H. Fleming, as well as many state adjutants general and air unit commanders. They were receptive to Stratemeyer's proposal, viewing it as a means to increase military effectiveness. For some adjutants general it represented only a formalization of existing agreements between their states and the Air Force to expedite the latter's assumption of command during annual training and national emergencies. By July, the proposal's final version had been sent to all states and the District of Columbia. Thirty-five of forty-nine adjutants general accepted it.[40]

Unfortunately for Stratemeyer, two of the most politically influential guardsmen were not present at San Antonio. General Walsh, President of the National Guard Association, and General Reckord, Chairman of the association's Standing Committee on Legislation, were extremely influential in shaping opinion within the Guard establishment. Both were old-line officers and fierce partisans of the Army Guard. They interpreted Stratemeyer's proposal as a threat to the National Guard's distinctive character as a state militia force.[41] Walsh was especially vehement in condemning Stratemeyer's plan as just one more example of a long series of attempts to replace the Guard with an entirely federal reserve force. Speaking to the 1948 annual conference of the National Guard Association at St. Louis, Missouri, Walsh denounced Stratemeyer's initiative:

> The step taken . . . in my opinion . . . is destructive and illegal, for there is no authority vested in the Chief of Staff of the Air Force or Chief of the National Guard Bureau to determine policy. This can only be done as provided by . . . the National Defense Act. This, and other laws, were enacted by Congress for the protection of the National Guard. The continued attempts of the Department of Defense and the Regular Army to destroy the National Guard as it exists today, is eloquent testimony as to the needs of . . . protective measures.[42]

Walsh's major target was the Secretary of Defense's Committee on Civilian Components, popularly known as the Gray Board. The board, chaired by Assistant Secretary of the Army Gordon B. Gray, had been appointed to study military reserve programs. It called for an end to the dual component reserve systems of the Army and Air Force established in 1945. The board's "Report to the Secretary of Defense by the Committee on Civilian Components" noted that using the National Guard "with its present powerful armament is not generally suitable in the execution of state missions in case of riots or other civil uprisings."[43] The report concluded that "national security requires all services have one federal reserve force."[44] These federal reserve forces, unlike the National Guard, would be established under the army clauses of the Constitution rather than its militia clauses.[45]

Air Force Headquarters supported the Gray Board's basic conclusions. It had never been happy with the dual component air reserve system. The Air Defense Command's subsequent inability to assert command authority over Air Guard units reinforced its initial skepticism. Col. Bruce K. Holloway, an Air Staff officer who later became Commander of the Strategic Air Command, reflected this skepticism in a memo to General Stratemeyer. He asserted that as long as "command jurisdiction remains with the states it precludes appreciable worth in an emergency unless federal control can be gained three to six months prior to an expected attack."[46] General Spaatz had outlined the Air Staff's basic position on the reserve unification issue in a January 1948 memo to Secretary of the Air Force W. Stuart Symington. He noted that several studies by the Air Staff "indicate that the best interests of the Air Force and of national security would be best served by consolidation under federal control, of the existing Air National Guard and Air Force Reserve."[47] Sensitive to the political controversy bound to be generated by such proposals, Spaatz suggested that the Air Force should defer its public position on the issue until after the Gray Board had made its report. He informed Symington that, due to the controversy, the Air Staff had developed plans for either unification of its reserve components or retention of the status quo.[48]

There was some dissatisfaction within the Air Guard's ranks concerning its status as a dual state-federal force. Lt. Col. Thomas G. Lanphier, Jr., Commander

(Above) Maj. Gen. Ellard A. Walsh, NGAUS President, presents the delegates at the association's annual banquet, September 1948. At this conference, General Walsh denounced General Stratemeyer's plan for a chain-of-command linking Guard and active duty units.

(Right) Appointed Chief of the National Guard Bureau in 1950, Maj. Gen. Raymond H. Fleming had previously served as President of the Adjutants General Association.

of Idaho's 190th Fighter Squadron, and a member of the Air Staff Committee on Air National Guard Policy, had compiled a distinguished combat record during World War II as a fighter pilot in the South Pacific. In April 1943 he had intercepted and shot down the Japanese aircraft carrying Admiral Isoroku Yamamoto. In 1948 Lanphier was elected President of the Air Force Association, a civilian lobby organization devoted primarily to the interests of the active duty Air Force.[49]

Writing for the January 1949 issue of *Air Force,* the Air Force Association's magazine, Lanphier made his case for the Air Guard's federalization and consolidation with the Air Force Reserve. He argued that his Idaho Air Guard squadron

Courtesy Air Force Association

Col. Thomas G. Lanphier, Jr. As President of the Air Force Association, he called for federalization of the Air National Guard and its merger with the Reserve program.

was nothing more than a small, independent air force. Although the federal government paid 97 percent of its expenses and supplied it with combat aircraft, it "does not presume to tell us specifically how, when or where to fly, and has no authoritative way of checking or insuring the quality of our training."[50] Lacking specific instruction and inspection from the Air Force, the Air Guard was no better than the individual civilian who acted as its senior officer. Consequently, the states operated forty-eight varied training programs. The problems generated by this lack of standardization were compounded by the duplication inherent in maintaining two reserve programs—both competing for the taxpayer's dollar. Lanphier dismissed the argument that the Air Guard had a state mission with the caustic comment that "an air arm is about as useful to the governor of the sovereign state of Idaho as a bombsight to a freight train."[51]

Lanphier concluded that, as presently constituted, the Air Guard was nothing more than a flying club for those few pilots fortunate enough to be able to join its tactical squadrons. As long as their training was not standardized and strictly supervised by the Air Force, this situation would prevail. He urged that in the name of both operational readiness and economy the Air Guard be federalized and merged with the Air Force Reserve.[52]

James V. Forrestal, the first Secretary of Defense, also strongly supported the creation of a single, federal reserve system for the Air Force. His initial annual report to the President put the issue in clear perspective:

> National preparedness is a national rather than a state responsibility. Retention by the states of control over military forces with a solely national mission violates the sound principle of delegation of authority with responsibility.[53]

37

Forrestal strongly recommended that President Truman initiate measures to consolidate the Air Guard with the Air Force Reserve under federal direction. He wrote:

> The most careful review of the Gray Board Report and our experience with the implementation of Executive Order No. 10,007 have led to the conclusion that an effective civilian air component requires the unification of the Air National Guard and the Air Reserve in a single wholly federal, Air Force reserve. This conclusion . . . has the unanimous concurrence and full support of the Secretaries of the Army, Navy, and Air Force and of the JCS [Joint Chiefs of Staff].[54]

The Secretary of Defense reemphasized the purely national mission of the Air Guard in a memo to the President. The Air Guard was intended to be an M–day air defense force. It was inconceivable that its tactical flying units would ever be used to preserve domestic law and order. Forrestal then went on to the heart of the Air Guard's problems:

> Under present circumstances those federal agencies responsible for national prepared-ness exercise only a negative type of supervision over the Air National Guard. . . . The situation is further complicated by the impracticability of attempting to organize, operate and train effective combat forces when the components are under the control of forty-eight different 'commanders-in-chief.' The present nature of Air Force activity is such that artificial geographical restrictions seriously handicap the preparation of the Air National Guard for its national mission.[55]

In closing, Forrestal said: "Strongly recommend your approval for immediate initiation of measures to effect the consolidation under federal direction of these civilian air components." He noted that both he and Secretary Symington wanted to meet with Truman at an early opportunity to discuss the matter.[56]

President Truman had grown increasingly impatient with the slow progress of the Army and Air Force reserve programs. Although faced with the growing intransigence of the Soviet Union, and the continuing failure of Congress to enact universal military training, the President had been reluctant to ask for a major expansion of the active duty military establishment. Rather, he had been forced to settle for reintroduction of the draft in June 1948 and an increased emphasis on the reserves to strengthen America's military power. His Executive Order 10,007, dated October 15, 1948, had grown out of his determination to improve the military readiness of the reserves. The President had specifically focused his order on the sagging reserve programs of the Army and Air Force. He pointedly contrasted their civilian components with the reserve programs of the Navy and Marine Corps. They were asked to follow the Navy's example by appointing high ranking officers to head their reserve programs. The President directed that all "General Staff" divisions give increased attention to reserve programs and that young, vigorous regular officer instructors be assigned to train reservists. Further-more, adequate training facilities were to be provided.[57]

The Air Force had started to strengthen the administration of its reserve forces early in 1948. However, Executive Order 10,007 and rapidly deteriorating relations with the Soviet Union forced it to adopt a fundamental organizational change. The centerpiece of this change was the Continental Air Command established on December 1, 1948. CONAC absorbed both the Tactical Air Command (TAC) and the Air Defense Command. It also obtained nine fighter squadrons from the Strategic Air Command (SAC). General Stratemeyer, ADC's Commander, became CONAC's first commander. The paramount influence in CONAC was ADC. It's old headquarters and most of its staff were simply redesignated headquarters CONAC. Old ADC regulations were retitled CONAC regulations. All four of ADC's numbered air forces as well as two of the Tactical Air Command's came under CONAC's jurisdiction. The Tactical Air Command and ADC were reduced to minor operational command headquarters within the new CONAC organization.[58]

The basic operational concepts behind the creation of CONAC were the release of additional Air Force resources for reserve programs and the development of a flexible pool of tactical fighters within the continental United States. This meant that all of the Air Force's fighter resources in the United States, including the Air Guard, were supposed to be trained in both tactical offensive and air defense operations. In reality, it meant that air defense had been firmly established as the second highest priority within the Air Force behind the Strategic Air Command's nuclear offensive mission. Consequently, all of CONAC's fighter units began to emphasize air intercept training. Within the context of this increased concern over the nation's air defenses, Air Guard units still constituted the majority of the Air Force's stateside fighter strength. They accounted for sixty-three percent of its potential fighter squadron strength.[59]

Unfortunately, neither the creation of CONAC nor the increased emphasis on air defense addressed the core problems that inhibited the development of the Air Guard prior to the Korean War. The federal funds available to the Air Guard increased from $45 million in FY 1948 to $78 million in fiscal year 1949, but this was far short of the $161 million requested by the Guard Bureau. Adequate funding simply was not available. Moreover, CONAC was no more able than its predecessor to establish firm operational control of the Air Guard. This point was illustrated at the second annual Air Guard unit commanders conference at Orlando, Florida, in April 1949. The conference was sponsored by Stratemeyer's successor as CONAC Commander, General Ennis C. Whitehead. Although the assembled officers were conciliatory toward the Air Force, Whitehead got only a reaffirmation of CONAC's weak training supervision of their units. Command jurisdiction of nonmobilized Air Guard units was rejected. Opinion within CONAC continued to cite the lack of adequate Air Force operational control of Air Guard units as the major factor in the Guard's inadequate operational capabilities. A complete federal takeover of the program was the implied corrective to the situation.[60]

Although President Truman wanted to invigorate the reserve programs of the Air Force, he was reluctant to risk his political prestige in the drive to federalize the Air Guard and merge it with the Air Force Reserve. He recognized the "political dynamite" inherent in any such proposal.[61] Consequently, the burden of obtaining the necessary legislative action fell entirely upon the Department of Defense and the Air Force. On December 15, 1948, the Secretary of Defense directed the Air Force to prepare legislative proposals for consolidation of the Air National Guard with the Air Force Reserve. Lt. Gen. Elwood R. Quesada was directed by Gen. Hoyt S. Vandenberg, Air Force Chief of Staff, to chair an ad hoc Air Force committee that would study factors relating to the intent and effect of this proposed legislation.[62]

Quesada, in 1946 the first commander of the Tactical Air Command, was the Special Assistant to the Chief of Staff for Reserve Forces. His position on the Air Staff was a relatively new one. It had been created late in 1948 in response to President Truman's order to upgrade reserve programs. Quesada's job was to formulate plans and programs for both Air Force civilian components; he had to rely upon other Air Staff agencies to implement them. Quesada also served as the liaison between the Chief of Staff, the Air Staff, and Air Force major commands on reserve matters. His appointment was tacit recognition of the inadequate Air Staff attention to reserve matters since the end of World War II. Prior to the creation of this new post, all reserve matters, including the Air Guard, had been the responsibility of a small Civilian Components Group buried deep within the Directorate of Operations. The group's four officers and five civilians had been headed by Brig. Gen. John P. McConnell, who subsequently became Air Force Chief of Staff. Although the Air Staff was organized on a functional basis with each of its directorates responsible for all regular and reserve forces planning within their own particular specialties, most of the directorates had given inadequate attention to reserve matters. Consequently, the burden of reserve forces' planning had fallen primarily upon General McConnell's small and politically impotent Civilian Components Group. Quesada's appointment represented a dramatic upgrading of the reserve forces planning function on the Air Staff. Underscoring this change was the substantial increase in the strength of the staff directly responsible for coordinating reserve forces planning—under Quesada it grew from nine to forty-four persons.[63]

General Quesada's top priority was to rebuild the floundering Air Force Reserve. In an interview in *Air Force Magazine,* he declared "the past program has been pretty poorly conceived and poorly executed."[64] He noted that the original postwar plan sought to train as many reservists as possible—an unattainable goal. Air Force funds, equipment, and facilities could adequately train only 65,000 air reservists, approximately fifteen percent of the total program. Under a new plan, these inadequacies would be addressed; for example, the trainers and cargo aircraft that all Reserve organized flying units then operated, regardless of their assign-

As a special assistant to the Chief of Staff, Lt. Gen. Elwood R. Quesada brought Reserve and ANG matters to the attention of the Air Staff.

ments under existing mobilization plans, would be replaced with tactical aircraft. Quesada, however, emphasized that because it was still considered an M–Day force, the Air Guard would continue to enjoy priority over the Air Force Reserve. Air Staff planners did not anticipate having Reserve units fully operationally ready until an unspecified period following M–Day.[65]

General Quesada neglected to mention that one of the major problems retarding the Air Force Reserve's development had been the priority given to the Air Guard after World War II. The Air Guard, despite its problems, had found it much easier to attract veteran combat pilots than the Reserve. Air Guard units were flying relatively high performance P–47 and P–51 fighter aircraft. Air reservists, meanwhile, had to settle for AT–6 trainers and C–46 and C–47 transports, if they had any aircraft at all. Budget requests for the Air Guard were usually greater than those for the far larger Air Force Reserve. For example, the Air Force budget for Fiscal Year 1949 requested $52 million for the planned 1.5 million-man Reserve while $56 million was requested for the 57,000-man Guard. The Air Guard also had priority in the acquisition of airfield sites. In sum, many of the Air Force Reserve's problems were due to its inability to compete with the better organized, politically influential, and officially favored Air National Guard.[66]

While General Quesada was planning the revitalization of the Air Force Reserve, the long-festering struggle for control of the Air Guard reached a critical point. Secretary of the Air Force Symington, with the approval and encouragement of Secretary of Defense Forrestal, was determined "to push for the federalization of the Air National Guard."[67] Quesada's ad hoc committee had been directed to study policies and procedures upon which to base legislative proposals creating a single reserve component for the Air Force.[68] Backed by the Gray Board's report and the support of the Secretary of Defense, the Air Force sought Congressional elimination of the Air Guard's dual state-federal status. The desired legislation would give the active duty establishment the full authority it felt it needed to prepare the Air Guard for its air defense mission. Air Force officials believed that this mission was a strictly federal affair, that it made little sense to have a state-controlled force fulfilling it. They felt that federalization would reduce or eliminate the problems impeding the Guard's scheduled development and potentially slowing the availability of its units in an emergency.

The federalization issue was resolved in February 1949 during House Armed Services Committee hearings on H.R. 1437, a bill to authorize the composition of the Army and the Air Force.[69] Representatives of the National Guard Association attacked Title II of the bill. General Walsh charged that Title II would permit federalization of the Air Guard. Noting the profederalization conclusions of the Gray Board and its endorsement by the Secretary of Defense, Walsh disputed the Air Force contention that H.R. 1437 would preserve the existing status of the Air Guard. He then cited language in the bill which called for sixty-one Air Force Reserve groups but made no specific mention of the Air National Guard. General Reckord developed the same theme. He charged that the Secretary of the Air Force could gradually kill the Air Guard because of Title II's vague language. He urged the Armed Services Committee to rewrite the bill to insure the separate existence of the Air Guard. He then attacked the Air Force's handling of its own wholly federal civilian component, the Air Force Reserve. Reckord charged that the regular Air Force had done almost nothing with the Air Force Reserve for three years despite spending nearly as much money as had been spent on the Air Guard. He called the Air Force Reserve a strictly paper organization. The Air Force, he alleged, had failed in its duty to the Air Force Reserve over which it had complete control. Reckord claimed that the Air Guard was a far more advanced reserve component and implied that it owed its superiority to its relative independence from the Air Force.[70]

Reckord also called for a major increase in the authorized size of both air reserve components. He argued that Congress should mandate that the Air Guard and the Air Force Reserve would each consist of 35 air groups manned by 100,000 personnel. At that time, the Air Guard was limited to 27 groups with an authorized personnel goal of approximately 57,000. The actual strength of the Air Guard at the end of Fiscal Year 1948 was only 29,000.[71]

The National Guard Association's attack on the Air Force brought an immediate response from Secretary Symington. Testifying before the same committee,

Symington emphasized that "when I came into the Air Force three years ago . . . it became obvious that one of the most serious problems the Air Force would have, would be the so-called civilian components: the Air Reserve and the Air National Guard."[72] He stressed that the amount of money available for the civilian components of the Air Force had been very limited and their problems great. Getting to the heart of the issue, Symington asserted that "one of the things the Air Force looked forward to [after World War II] . . . was the responsibility of controlling their own civilian components comparable to the . . . Navy."[73] Nevertheless, in the final days before enactment of the National Security Act that had created a separate Air Force, frequent compromises were made in order to insure passage of the bill. During that period, according to Symington, "National Guard interests wedged into the act the fact that the National Guard Bureau would continue to handle the Air National Guard along with the National Guard."[74] This meant the Air Force's principal first line reserve component would continue to be administered by Army officers, a particularly galling circumstance for a military service which had struggled for years to free itself from the Army. Symington, seeking to rebut Reckord's charge that any federal Air Force reserve component would be allowed to languish by the regulars, noted that the Air Guard had been given priority over the Air Force Reserve as a matter of policy.[75] "We have concentrated on the National Guard [as opposed to the Reserve] . . . We gave the Guard every favored position we could plus modern airplanes as against old trainers we gave the Reserve."[76] Symington then criticized the dual component air reserve system created in World War II. That system, he charged, "has made it impossible to administer [civilian components] efficiently in the past."[77] Symington denied that the Air Force was trying to destroy the Air Guard through the proposed language of H.R. 1437.[78]

Representative Carl Vinson, Chairman of the Armed Services Committee, was frustrated by the bitter impasse which had developed between the Air Force and the National Guard during hearings on H.R. 1437. On February 3, he directed representatives of the committee's staff, the Air Force, and the National Guard to sit down together and draw up an amendment of the bill. The amendment would specify that the Air Force of the United States would consist of three components: the regular U.S. Air Force, the Air National Guard, and the Air Force Reserve. He told them to prepare a mutually agreeable amendment over the weekend and submit it to the committee the following Monday. On February 8, 1948, the proposed amendment was read and unanimously accepted by the committee. It firmly established the Air Guard as a legal component of the Air Force of the United States and increased its authorized personnel ceiling to 100,000.[79]

The National Guard had won everything that it wanted from Congress. The continued existence of the Air Guard had been written into law. Federalization was a dead issue in Congress. The Air Force would have to work with the state-controlled Air National Guard.

On February 18, the Air Force publicly acknowledged its defeat. A press release noted that General Vandenberg had directed General Quesada's committee to broaden its study of reserve affairs by studying methods of improving the Air Guard's readiness and ways to facilitate rapid federal control of Air Guard units in a national emergency. Other matters to be studied included the effectiveness of the Air Force Reserve and ways of improving it. Members of the committee, in addition to Quesada, included Air Staff officers, the Special Assistant to the Secretary of the Air Force, the Chief of the National Guard Bureau and the Chief of its Air Force Division, Air Force Reserve officers called to duty, and representatives from Quesada's office.[80]

The February 1949 issue of the *National Guardsman*, official magazine of the National Guard Association, announced a new training agreement between the Air Force and the Air Guard.[81] In an effort to insure closer Air Force supervision over the training of Air Guard units for their M–Day mission, all states and the District of Columbia had agreed to permit the Air Force to direct training through its normal tactical command channels. The plan was similar to the one offered by General Stratemeyer over a year earlier. The new agreement provided that:

> On all matters pertaining to operations for training purposes in the preparation of Air National Guard units for . . . their federal mission, the Chief of Staff, U.S. Air Force,

Rep. Carl Vinson, (right) Chairman of the House Armed Services Committee, discussed legislation with Air Force Secretary Donald Quarles (left). Rep. Overton Brooks (seated) also attended the hearing, February 1957.

through his designated commanders may exercise training supervision—as differenti-
ated from command jurisdiction—over Air National Guard units by means of normal
military channnels.[82]

It also provided that Air Guard commanders could exercise training supervision
over their subordinate units when those units were training for their federal mission
regardless of whether or not they were located within the same states. The Air
Force, which had been determined to achieve total control of the Air Guard via
federalization, had been compelled to settle for closer training supervision.[83]

Despite these developments, the struggle for control of the Air Guard had not
ended. The central focus of the battle now shifted to the role of the National Guard
Bureau. Originally the Division of Militia Affairs, the bureau had been made part
of the War Department in 1908. The National Defense Act of 1916 had renamed it
the Militia Bureau by which it was known until 1933 when it became the National
Guard Bureau.[84]

The Air Force and bureau saw the latter's functions quite differently. To the
Air Force, the bureau was a channel of communication between the Chief of Staff
and the state military authorities. Its proper function was to carry out the directives
of the Air Force concerning the administration, supply, and equipping of Air Guard
units in preparation for their federal mission.

The bureau interpreted its mission in broader and more activist terms. It did
not wish to confine itself to the passive administrative role envisaged by the Air
Force. Rather, in accordance with its interpretation of the National Defense Acts of
1916 and 1933, it saw itself actively participating in the formulation of all plans
and policies relevant to the administration of the Air National Guard. This
interpretation was reinforced by language inserted into the National Security Act
of 1947 that required the Air Force to go through the bureau on matters relevant to
the Air Guard. The bureau, in effect, actively represented the Air Guard's interests
within the Air Force and the Department of Defense. General Reckord, reflecting
this view, referred to the bureau as "our salvation."[85]

Discord between the bureau and the Air Force stemmed from 1946 when,
according to National Guard spokesmen, the Army Air Forces had not only tried to
seize command and control of the Air Guard but also "went into the National Guard
Bureau and demanded that the Bureau turn our money over to them . . . ."[86]
General Spaatz had been forced to go through the National Guard Bureau on Air
Guard matters after what he called "a knock-down drag-out fight" over control of
the Air Guard's share of the fiscal year 1947 National Guard appropriation.[87] The
bureau had won that scrap and had also rebuffed General Stratemeyer's efforts to
gain greater command jurisdiction over the Air Guard in the spring of 1946. Guard
spokesmen had been determined to preserve the bureau's prerogatives. Testifying
before the Senate Armed Services committee during its 1947 hearings on unification of the armed forces, General Reckord had made a strong and successful
argument to prevent division of the bureau into separate ground and air compo-

nents housed respectively in the Departments of the Army and the Air Force. His argument was directed specifically against Air Force attempts to circumvent the bureau. He had told the senators:

> We [the National Guard] do not care what language you give us [in the unification bill] so long as you give us the Bureau with language that will be sufficient so that everybody concerned will understand they must deal on National Guard matters through the Bureau. . . . All the time, not withstanding the corrective action taken a year ago [i.e., General Spaatz agreeing to go through the Bureau on AAF matters], there is not a week passes but what we run into trouble . . . where the Air Corps ignores the Bureau, ignores the governors of the states, and the adjutant general and issues orders to the air unit in the state. That is what we must overcome.[88]

The National Security Act of 1947 had established the National Guard Bureau as a joint bureau of the Departments of the Army and Air Force.[89] Its chief, usually an Army guardsman on active duty with the rank of major general, reported directly to the civilian secretaries of both departments. Within the bureau, a separate Air Force Division was established in October 1948 to replace the Aviation Group that had previously handled Air Guard-Army Air Forces matters. The Air Force Division chief and his Army counterpart both reported to the Chief of the bureau. The bureau's Chief, Major General Kenneth F. Cramer, was determined to run the Air Guard according to his own standards, not those of the Air Force.[90]

A vital function of the Guard Bureau was to prepare and defend National Guard budget requests before Congress. Air Guard budget requests first had to be coordinated with Air Force headquarters.[91] The bureau and its National Guard allies consistently fought for higher Air Guard budgets than either the Truman administration or the Congress had been willing to authorize prior to the Korean War. For example, for fiscal years 1947 through 1949 the bureau requested approximately $536 million for the Air Guard. Only $154 million was actually made available. This reduction dramatically slowed the Air Guard's pace of development. It made it impossible to complete the organization of all 514 units by July 1, 1947 as originally projected.[92]

In 1947, the War Department, which controlled the Guard's budget, diverted $53 million from the National Guard's total $110 million appropriation to help meet the expenses of the active duty Army. This action, reflecting the frantic postwar competition of all military components for extremely scarce resources, virtually "brought the organization of the Air National Guard to a halt" according to General Cramer.[93] To Cramer, this action underscored the recurrent failure of the federal government to provide adequate financial support to the greatly expanded postwar National Guard program that the War Department had promised in *Approved Policies, 1945*. The detrimental effect of inadequate funding was one of the few issues that the bureau and the Air Force agreed upon.[94]

The Air Force, however, was dissatisfied with its inadequate control of Air Guard funds. This was particularly galling because these funds were still, in 1949, administered by the Department of the Army through the Guard Bureau. The Air Force, which had spent many years struggling to free itself from the grip of the Army's ground-oriented hierarchy, felt that Army policies and budget priorities were not especially sensitive to air requirements. After the transfer of control to the Department of the Air Force with fiscal year 1950, the situation was complicated by the reluctance of the Chief of the National Guard Bureau to predicate Air Guard budget requests upon programming data established by the Air Staff. In a memo to the Chief of the Guard Bureau, written in late 1949, the Special Assistant to the Air Force Chief of Staff for Reserve Forces made this point. He emphasized that procedures for preparing the Air Guard budget were the prerogative of the Air Force Chief of Staff. The Chief of Staff, he claimed, had merely delegated responsibility for preparing this budget request to the Guard Bureau.[95]

The Air Force was also frustrated by the National Guard Bureau's determination to function as an operating agency with an active policymaking role. The bureau, for example, had directed that Air Guard units would only comply with Air Force manuals and regulations that had been first coordinated with the Guard Bureau. Consequently, Air Guard units often disregarded Air Force directives. In some instances, according to an official Air Force history, these units even actively circumvented such directives "by securing authority from the National Guard Bureau to use any system best suited to their desires and fantasies."[96] As late as the end of 1949, no Air Force directive could be made applicable to the Air Guard without the express concurrence of the Guard Bureau's chief. This situation further encouraged the lack of standardization in Air Guard training and procedures.[97]

The tensions between the Guard Bureau and the Air Force culminated in an open confrontation late in 1949. The Chief of the National Guard Bureau, General Cramer, precipitated the crisis when he unilaterally relieved the head of the bureau's Air Force Division, Maj. Gen. George Finch. Cramer's action was partially the result of a personality conflict with Finch. The men hated each other. Both were intensely ambitious. The deeper roots of the dismissal, however, lay in the continuing struggle between the Air Force and the bureau for control of the Air National Guard. Cramer was an Army Guard officer. Finch was an air guardsman.

The Air Force felt that Cramer was poorly informed about the Air Guard and had no right to take exception, on his own authority, to certain policies which the Air Force had established for its state-controlled reserve component.[98] Its officials charged that Cramer had, on many occasions, when directed by the Department of the Air Force to promulgate lawful policies and regulations, "delayed implementation so as to affect adversely the training of the Air National Guard."[99] Examples of Cramer's obstructionism cited by the Air Force included a delay of over eleven months in promulgating a decision to establish an air staff in the headquarters of all state and territorial National Guard organizations; an eight-month delay in implementing an Air Staff decision to prohibit split training assemblies for pay purposes; and a three-month delay in an Air Force decision to increase the combat crew strength of tactical units. The real issue, however, was the failure of the bureau's chief to allow the Air Force Division to administer the Air Guard program. As a consequence, according to General Vandenberg, Air Force Chief of Staff:

> Important policies involving the Air National Guard have been handled by officers inexperienced and uninformed in Air Force policies and procedures. This situation deteriorated to the point where the Chief of the National Guard Bureau issued instructions that no one in the Air Force Division . . . would prepare any correspondence on any subject . . . without his personal approval.[100]

On August 10, 1949, Vandenberg's headquarters directed Cramer to use the bureau's Air Force Division for the purposes for which it had been created. Cramer replied that he could not comply with the directive. On September 26, 1949, Cramer issued a memo relieving Finch from his duties.[101] General Vandenberg noted in a memo to the Secretary of the Air Force that this action "was taken without any prior consultation with any representative of the Department of the Air Force. Also, . . . [it] was taken without any reference to the Army."[102] A personal conference between Vandenberg and Cramer did not alleviate the problems between the bureau and Air Force Headquarters. The bureau was technically complying with Air Force requests and directives, but its compliance did not extend beyond the letter of instructions. General Finch was reinstated, but his division was still, in effect, being bypassed.[103]

The situation led to a joint inquiry by the Inspectors General of the Army and the Air Force at the direction of their respective service secretaries. The Inspectors General recommended that General Finch be relieved from further duty with the National Guard Bureau. Further, they advised that a joint board of officers should be appointed by both Secretaries to recommend changes in the bureau's organizational structure and internal operating procedures. The Chief of the National Guard Bureau, they argued, should be directed to comply fully with provisions of any Air Force directive relating to staff procedures on matters pertaining to the Air Guard. In a separate recommendation, the Air Inspector General called for the relief of General Cramer as head of the bureau. The Inspector General declared that General Cramer:

> was reluctant to do anything which the Air Force requested him to do if it were not in accord with his personal views . . . [Cramer] so hamstrung the Air Force Division of his office with restricted memoranda that they could not possibly have the independence of action that he himself (i.e., Cramer) admitted was maintained by agreements entered into . . . with the Air Force Division when his office was created . . . [the Air Inspector General personally had] grave doubts it will be possible in the future to work any more harmoniously and effectively with . . . General Cramer than in the past because of his inflexible and contentious attitude about detail and his insistence on following the same pattern of conduct with respect to the Air Force that he has with the Army.[104]

After receiving the report of the Inspectors General, the Secretaries implemented some of its recommendations. A joint board of inquiry was appointed to investigate the situation within the Guard Bureau. The board, commonly referred to as the "Miltonberger Board," was headed by the former Chief of the National Guard Bureau, Major General Butler Miltonberger. The Department of the Air Force implemented another recommendation of the Inspectors General. It rewrote several National Guard Bureau regulations pertaining to the organization of the bureau as it affected the Air Guard and submitted them to the Miltonberger Board.[105]

(Left) Army Maj. Gen. Kenneth F. Cramer, National Guard Bureau Chief, aroused the Air Force's ire when he relieved Maj. Gen. George Finch, Chief of the Bureau's Air Force Division.

(Below) USAF Chief of Staff designee Gen. Hoyt S. Vandenberg (right) with the incumbent Chief Gen. Carl Spaatz (left) and Secretary of the Air Force W. Stuart Symington. General Vandenberg inherited the Air Guard-Air Reserve controversy, sharing General Spaatz's concern for the readiness posture of the state-controlled units.

The Miltonberger Board reported its findings and recommendations to the Secretary of the Army on March 31, 1950. It rejected the creation of separate National Guard Bureaus for the Army and Air Force as unnecessary and undesirable. It found that any action, consistent with the law, taken by the Air Force regarding the organization and function of the bureau insofar as the Air Guard was concerned was a matter of primary concern to the Air Force. In matters of joint interest to the Army and Air Force, the bureau's structure and operating procedures must conform to the joint operating policies of both services. The board concluded that the existing organizational structure and current operating procedures of the National Guard Bureau were inconsistent with sound staff principles. On this premise, the board reviewed and rewrote a proposed Department of the Army Regulation, No. 10–230–1, entitled "Organization and Functions of the National Guard Bureau."[106] It also rewrote the proposed Air Force regulations for the Air Guard. The board stated that "if faithfully implemented, the proposed regulations and related allocations of functions should result in sound internal and administrative operating procedures" and would "eliminate the top-heavy overhead of the National Guard Bureau by removing . . . functions and duties which could be more properly and effectively performed by the Army and Air Force Divisions [of the bureau]."[107]

General Cramer's defense of his actions clearly revealed that they were part of his effort to assert the bureau's independent role in the policy process. Addressing the annual meeting of the Adjutants General Association in February 1950, Cramer focused on this issue:

> One of the greatest difficulties which confronts the Bureau is the fact that planning [for the National Guard] whether policy is involved or procedures or programs, that all too often difficulty arises because we [i.e., the bureau] have not been given an opportunity to participate. . . . We believe that the Bureau was created for the purpose of giving advice and assistance to the Army and Air Force in the preparation of all plans and procedures.[108]

The bureau's policy role, in Cramer's view, should be exercised by its chief. However, the Secretaries of the Army and Air Force ignored Cramer's assertion of authority. They concurred with most of the recommendations of their Inspectors General and the Miltonberger Board. In the spring of 1950, administrative action was taken, at their direction, to revamp the internal organization and operating procedures of the National Guard Bureau. Fundamentally, these changes strengthened the authority of the bureau's division chiefs to administer the Army and Air National Guard in accordance with the directives of their respective active duty military services. The power of the bureau chief to interfere with the operations of the Army and Air Force divisions was greatly reduced.[109]

The one remaining issue in May 1950 was the future of Cramer and Finch. Finch had been reinstated as head of the bureau's Air Force Division in 1949 at the insistence of the Air Force Chief of Staff. The Secretary of the Army wanted to remove Finch. The Secretary of the Air Force was opposed to this unless Cramer, who had precipitated the crisis, was removed at the same time.[110] The Korean War finally resolved this impasse. Cramer was called to duty with the 28th Infantry Division. General Fleming was appointed acting head of the bureau. Meanwhile, the Army and Air Force Chiefs of Staff agreed to reassign General Finch.[111]

Despite its limited victory over General Cramer in early 1950, the Air Force remained disenchanted with the slow progress of the Air Guard. CONAC's authority over it was still essentially restricted to training supervision and annual inspections. Although all 514 units envisaged in the original plans for the postwar Air Guard had been formed by mid–1949, their ability to perform operational missions was another matter. CONAC inspectors had conducted operational readiness tests of many Air Guard units during their annual summer encampments in 1949, the first year that large numbers of these units had trained together in their wing organizations. The results of the tests were not encouraging. National Guard officials complained that "the inspections which have been made by officers of the Air Force . . . are finding that a number of our units are unsatisfactory because of the fact that adequate facilities have not been provided." They argued, with justification, that providing funds for the purchase or improvement of these facilities was the responsibility of the federal government, not the individual units. Adequate funding for this purpose had not been forthcoming. Consequently, the Air Force had been forced to readjust some of these unsatisfactory ratings.

Inadequate facilities, however, were only part of a larger problem. Based upon the 1949 inspections, CONAC had estimated that, on the average, it would take Air Guard fighter units nearly three months of intensive postmobilization training to attain full operational readiness. Paradoxically, the Air Guard's future potential as an M–Day air defense force was further endangered by its planned conversion to more modern aircraft. The Air Force intended to equip all Air Guard fighter units with jets. It assumed that only younger pilots could successfully fly jets in combat. The Air Guard's pilot force, however, was almost entirely composed of World War II combat veterans. According to the Guard Bureau's own estimates in 1950, it needed six hundred to eight hundred new pilots annually to meet future Air Force requirements. Yet, on the eve of the Korean War, it was getting practically none at all. Because of a tight budget, the Air Force was unable to provide the Air Guard with adequate spaces in its pilot training programs.

The situation in the Guard's aircraft control and warning squadrons was even worse. The Air Force recognized that these units had mostly obsolete equipment and inadequate training aids. Only a few of them had been able to obtain long range radar sets. The remainder had to settle for lightweight, portable Army and Navy "hand-me-downs" suitable only for local ground control intercept operations. It was even more difficult to recruit adequate numbers of skilled personnel to man these unglamorous radar units. Consequently the states were reluctant to participate in the aircraft control and warning unit program.[112]

The Soviet Union's explosion of an atomic bomb in 1949 radically changed Air Force thinking about air defense.[113] The Air Staff argued that the United States faced a potential disaster if it continued to rely on Air Guard fighter units for seventy percent of its interceptor resources. Previous air defense plans had assumed that Air Guard units would have several months of postmobilization training to bring themselves to full operational capability in the event of a national emergency. This assumption was no longer valid now that the United States faced the potential catastrophic possibility of a surprise Soviet atomic attack. General Whitehead, CONAC's Commander, supported this Air Staff assessment in February 1950. He believed "that the atomic explosion in Russia . . . altered the problem [air defense] from an M–Day [one] to one of H–Hour D–Day."[114]

The Air Force recognized that active air defense of the United States was far from a reality in early 1950. Top ranking officers, including Generals Vandenberg and Whitehead, had no confidence in the Air Guard's ability to perform its assigned air defense mission. Studies at CONAC and Air Force Headquarters had concluded that the Air Guard's system of dual state-federal control was ineffective. Air Force officers were defensive about Air Guard charges that many of the Guard's problems were an outgrowth of the active duty establishment's shortcomings in handling reserve programs. Some feared that Air Force rebuttals "would merely add fuel to the contentious spirit already rife between the Guard people and ourselves."[115]

Early in January 1950, a meeting was held in the offices of Gen. Muir S. Fairchild, Air Force Vice Chief of Staff, to discuss this situation. Representatives from CONAC and the Air Staff were present. Air Guard officials were excluded. The participants agreed that the United States could no longer jeopardize the nation's safety by continuing to rely on the Air Guard as its primary air defense force. The Guard's archaic command arrangements, obsolete aircraft, aging pilots, and low operational readiness ratings indicated to the conferees that it was ill-suited to achieve a high degree of readiness. They suggested switching the Air Guard to less critical missions. Alternate possibilities discussed for the Air Guard included ground support, troop carrier, transport and liaison.[116]

General Vandenberg approved these suggestions and forwarded them to Secretary of the Air Force Symington on February 13, 1950. His memo stressed that:

> the Air National Guard cannot perform a D–day air defense mission because its personnel cannot leave their civilian jobs for a sufficient number of days to prepare themselves and their units to go instantly into combat. In addition the Air National Guard is not deployed and because of dependence of its personnel upon civilian jobs in specific localities cannot be employed at all times in those positions best suited to meet the potential attack.[117]

Vandenberg suggested that Symington should discuss with the Secretary of Defense switching the Air Guard to a less critical mission. Recognizing the dangerous political ramifications of this idea, Vandenberg noted that Congress and the public were then "under the erroneous impression that our National Guard units are a potent force . . . and would be capable of employment to defend the nation against a sudden atomic attack."[118] He implied that this false picture of the Air Guard's operational capabilities could be a formidable barrier to Air Force intentions to give it a less demanding role.

Although Secretary Symington concurred with Vandenberg's assessment of the Air Guard, he was unable to gain the approval of Secretary of Defense Louis Johnson to change its mission.[119] Johnson had been instructed by President Truman to hold down the defense budget. In those pre-Korean War circumstances, it was unlikely that he would have approved a major policy innovation that could have vastly increased spending for continental air defense. Modifying the Air Guard's formal M–Day mission assignment as a fighter-interceptor force meant that the Defense Department would have had to either channel vast new resources into the creation of a viable regular Air Force interceptor force or publicly downplay the Soviet atomic threat. Given the military assessments prevalent at that time and the growing public preoccupation with the communist threat, the latter policy option must have been politically unpalatable. The National Guard, moreover, was certain vigorously to resist any effort to reduce its air component to the status of a lower priority Air Force auxiliary. The Air Guard was led by officers who were, for the most part, combat veterans of World War II. They had little enthusiasm for noncombat roles and aircraft. The more politically astute among them must have recognized that the Air Guard's claim to Air Force resources would certainly decrease with any significant reduction in the importance of its assigned missions. Maintenance of the Air Guard's position as the Air Force's first line combat reserve force meant that it would continue to enjoy priority over the Air Force Reserve. Any diminution of this status would probably have been seen by air guardsmen as the beginning of another Air Force attempt to eliminate the Guard. In any event, the Korean War killed the proposal. The Air Force was compelled to rely upon its reserve components to provide the bulk of the trained manpower needed to rapidly expand it from a June 1950 strength of 411,277 to 788,881 within a year. Some 45,000 of these personnel would be air guardsmen.[120]

The proposal to strip the Air Guard of its M–Day mission was the climax of the troubled postwar phase of Air Force-Air Guard relations. The effort to build the Air Guard into a credible first line reserve component of the Air Force had floundered badly. Although considerable progress had been made in creating an organization where none had existed before, the Air Guard in 1950 still lacked any significant and immediate combat capability. It was still seen as an organizational anomaly by the active duty establishment. The confusion and delay encountered by the Air Force in preparing the Air Guard for active service during the Korean War confirmed the low impression of the Guard's operational capabilities noted by CONAC during the 1949 operational readiness tests.

As already discussed, a variety of circumstances had contributed to the Air Guard's initial poor showing. One of the obvious problems confronting it had been the lack of adequate resources. The austere postwar defense budgets of the Truman administration were considered by many in the military to be woefully inadequate to fill even the minimum requirements of the active duty establishment. Despite its announced determination to rely heavily on the reserve programs of the military services, the administration provided neither the budgets nor the sources of trained military manpower that would have given substance to this policy objective. Surplus equipment, supplies, and aircraft also failed to bridge the gap between inadequate budgets and the Air Guard's operational requirements. Much of the surplus required extensive reconditioning. Propeller-driven tactical aircraft were rapidly approaching obsolescence in the jet age, and airfields required extensive construction to make them suitable for military operations. This shortage of resources drastically slowed the pace of initial development and was at least partially responsible for the Air Guard's lack of a significant operational capability prior to the Korean War.

Inadequate resources, however, were not the most significant factors contributing to the initial failure of the Air Guard to develop into an effective combat reserve force. Rather, the inability of the parties involved to overcome the problems associated with the Air Guard's position as a state-controlled military force lay at the heart of its difficulties. The Army Air Forces had been opposed to the creation of a dual component reserve system featuring the Air Guard. Although forced to accept it due to political considerations, the AAF, and subsequently the Air Force, had struggled fruitlessly during the 1946–50 period to gain command of Air Guard units. The logic and experience of professional Air Force officers convinced them that this was necessary because the requirements of modern aerial warfare would no longer safely permit an extensive period of post mobilization training to bring reserve combat units up to full operational readiness. Nonetheless, domestic political considerations and austere postwar defense budgets compelled the Air Force to rely on the Air Guard to provide the bulk of its tactical fighter capability. Almost every effort of the Air Force to obtain greater authority over the Air Guard had been frustrated by the National Guard's politically potent allies in Congress, the states, and the National Guard Association. The resulting confrontations had created a climate of animosity which further delayed resolution of the problems that plagued the Air Force-Air Guard relationship.

Rather than directly command its primary combat reserve force to properly prepare it for its wartime role, the Air Force had been compelled to settle for a complex, inefficient, and confusing set of administrative arrangements. Logistical and administrative matters were handled through the Guard Bureau. Training supervision and annual inspections were conducted first by ADC and then CONAC, acting through their numbered Air Forces and air instructors assigned to individual Air Guard units. Command authority remained firmly lodged with the state governors and their military representatives, the adjutants general. Air Guard training was not standardized across the various states according to rigorous Air Force standards. Ineffective commanders could not be removed by the Air Force. Yet, in a national emergency, the Air Force would suddenly find itself responsible for the operational performance of these units. Air Force officers had experienced continual frustration in dealing with this basically unmanageable military command system. Their prevailing negative opinion of the Air Guard reflected the historic antimilitia bias of American professional soldiers. They argued that the Guard must be divorced from the "weed roots" of local politics and made a purely federal reserve organization before it could become truly effective.[121]

The Air Force itself had to shoulder a considerable portion of the blame for the Air Guard's inadequate development prior to the Korean War. Neither of its two reserve programs had received the attention and support they required. The prevailing attitude toward the reserve was at best apathetic and indifferent. General Whitehead put the matter in sharp focus in a valedictory letter to General Vandenberg on December 13, 1950 prior to assuming command of the resurrected Air Defense Command. Faced with an impending reorganization of CONAC which would have a significant impact on the air reserve forces, Whitehead wanted to bring problems affecting those programs to Vandenberg's attention. Based upon his eighteen months of service as CONAC's Commander, he wrote:

> Basically, the weaknesses of our Reserve Forces programs stem from a planning deficiency which still has not been corrected. We do not have a proper Reserve Forces Troop Basis. We do not have a USAF Mobilization Plan. . . . We do not know our requirements. . . . This deficiency is, in my best judgment, the one factor which has contributed most to the creation of Reserve Forces problems and difficulties.[122]

Whitehead noted that Air Force supervision of existing reserve programs had been inadequate. Neither proper organizational structures nor adequate resources had been devoted to that complex task. Turning specifically to the Air Guard, Whitehead contended that "we have permitted our lack of direct control to act as an excuse for insufficient effort."[123] He recognized that "acceptance of the present organizational status of the ANG [i.e., its status as a state-commanded reserve of the Air Force] appears inescapable."[124] Interjecting a note of pragmatism and political realism that had seldom characterized confidential Air Force appraisals of the Air Guard, Whitehead noted that this fact of life must be recognized and accepted. He also charged that the Air Staff's major divisions were inadequately aware of reserve problems and inclined to shrug off their responsibilties in that area.[125] The resultant neglect and poor planning had harmed the development of reserve programs prior to the Korean War. He urged Vandenberg not to overlook the political significance of well managed reserve programs. "The Reserve Forces," Whitehead emphasized, "can and should be the best public relations medium available to the Air Force. . . . To date we have not taken advantage of this fact and our program has been such as to hurt the Air Force."[126]

Courtesy Air Force Association

As CONAC Commander, Lt. Gen. Ennis C. Whitehead worried that the Air Guard was unprepared for its air defense mission.

Whitehead argued that the best interests of the Air Force could no longer permit this situation to continue. Instead, it must develop realistic and properly administered reserve programs based on sound military requirements. The Air Force must spend the necessary money and revise its organizational structure. Furthermore, every member of the regular establishment had to be made aware of the importance of the reserves and the necessity to create a team. Reservists must also be made to understand this. Whitehead concluded his memo on a note of deep personal concern for the future of the Air Force if these problems were not constructively addressed.[127]

Although professional military logic was on its side, the Air Force had achieved little success in its efforts to assert command authority over the peacetime Air Guard. Concentration on the federalization issue had generated hostility and political opposition. This had obscured the need to recognize the realities of American politics and to proceed with pragmatic solutions. Some of the more astute regular officers had recognized this fact. They also knew that the Air Force had used the Air Guard's problems and status as an excuse for inattention and poor planning.

Because of inadequate funding, poor planning and the inconclusive federalization struggle, on the eve of the Korean War the Air Guard was little better than a collection of flying clubs. Its tactical units, although filled with veteran combat fliers and experienced noncommissioned officers, were not prepared to function on short notice as cohesive fighting teams. It would take an enormous amount of post mobilization work to prepare them for combat operations. Only a few guardsmen were willing to concede that the Air Guard was in no condition to play its intended M-Day role. Most professional Air Force officers, hostile to the concept of a separate Air Guard from the beginning, were prepared to downgrade the entire organization. Their unsuccessful struggle to attain command authority over the Air Guard and its low operational capabilities seemed to confirm their skepticism. Yet, the interests of the Air Force and national security required strong air reserve programs. The Air Guard was too powerful politically to be eliminated.

The Air Force, because of the debacle associated with the haphazard partial mobilization of its reserves during the Korean conflict, would be forced to recognize these realities in the early fifties and proceed with the task of building an effective Air Guard. This pragmatism would be largely forced on the regular establishment by civilian defense officials as well as air guardsmen and their political allies.

Chapter III

Rejuvenation, 1950–1953

On June 25, 1950, North Korean troops invaded South Korea and quickly overwhelmed the South's armed forces. The attack caught the United States government by surprise. Assuming that the invasion was Soviet-inspired, and convinced that a failure to respond militarily would encourage future communist aggression, President Truman ordered intervention by American air, naval, and land forces. He rejected atomic retaliation because of the risk of inciting nuclear war with the Soviet Union and the danger of using America's relatively small stock of such weapons against a minor power. The limited U.S. conventional response however, proved extremely frustrating to U.S. military commanders and deeply disturbing to the nation since it was at variance with the familiar total war strategy that had characterized American participation in World War II.[1]

The outbreak of hostilities on the Korean peninsula found America's armed forces poorly prepared for combat. U.S. occupation troops in nearby Japan proved to be neither physically nor psychologically prepared for war. Like nearly all U.S. Army formations in mid–1950, their units were understrength. Infantry regiments consisted of only two rather than the standard three battalions. Their combat skills and even some of their equipment were inferior to that of the North Koreans. American 75mm bazooka rockets could not penetrate Soviet-made T–34 tanks used by the North Koreans. American heavy tanks had to be brought from the United States because Gen. Douglas MacArthur's force in Japan had been restricted to light tanks. Poor field communications and inadequate lower level leadership forced senior officers to play the roles of lieutenants and sergeants. The North Koreans captured Maj. Gen. William F. Dean, Commander of the 24th Division, as he attempted to make his way back to U.S. lines. Only overwhelming American air and naval power prevented U.S. ground troops from being completely ejected from the Korean peninsula in the summer of 1950.[2]

With its Army hard pressed, the United States was forced to resort to a partial mobilization. Ultimately, the Army mobilized 2,834,000 men and twenty divisions. Of this total, national guardsmen numbered 138,600 while 244,300 were Army reservists. The rest were volunteers and draftees.[3] In mid–1950 the Air Force found itself desperately short of trained manpower. As mentioned, budget restrictions mandated by the Truman administration had limited active duty strength to just over 400,000. This allowed the Air Force to man only forty-eight combat air groups, well below its post World War II goal of seventy groups. The Korean War eliminated the curb on Air Force expansion and ruptured the ceiling of Truman's military budget. Within a year, Air Force strength had soared from 411,277 to 788,381. It reached a Korean War peak of approximately 977,500 by June 30, 1953. Initially, the vast majority were members of its air reserve components who either volunteered or were recalled to active duty. In April 1951, for example, seventy-two percent of the officers in the Far East Air Forces, the major air command directly involved in the war, were reservists. In Korea itself, a Fifth Air Force study revealed that approximately eighty percent of its personnel were recalled air guardsmen and Air Force reservists. After the regulars had helped to stymie the initial North Korean thrust, the major portion of the Air Force's burden in the Far East fell upon its poorly prepared reserve components.[4]

Korea was the Air Guard's first war. Sixty-six of its ninety-two tactical flying squadrons were called to active duty. Numerous ground support and technical units were also mobilized. Some 45,000 air guardsmen, approximately eighty percent of its total strength, saw active duty from 1950 through 1953. Air Guard units performed a variety of crucial missions. Two fighter wings were sent to the Far East and compiled excellent combat records. Three other fighter wings were assigned to strengthen North Atlantic Treaty Organization (NATO) air power against the threat of a Soviet attack. One fighter wing trained jet air crews to man the rapidly expanding aircraft inventory. The sixteen remaining activated wings augmented the Tactical Air Command, the Strategic Air Command, and the Air Defense Command in the continental United States. Air guardsmen (and their supporters) were convinced that their performance during the Korean War vindicated their organization's existence. They argued that it won the respect of the active duty establishment and resulted, for the first time, in a sound working relationship with the Air Force which set the stage for the Guard's development as a true first line combat reserve component.[5]

Korea marked a crucial turning point in the Air Guard's short history. Its authorized troop strength, limited by prewar budgets to 44,728, was increased to a postwar goal of 67,000. Appropriations changed dramatically after the war, climbing from $106 million in fiscal year 1953 to $223.44 million in fiscal year 1960. High level Air Force attention to the Air Guard, as well as the Air Force Reserve, increased. Strenuous efforts were made to insure that the composition and strength of both air reserve programs were tied directly to the actual requirements of Air Force war plans. Reservists and air guardsmen were given greater opportunity to influence effectively the planning process. Aircraft and equipment

Three Air National Guard fighter wings were mobilized to strengthen NATO forces in case of a Soviet attack on Europe.

(Above) Members of the 117th Tactical Reconnaissance Wing prepare a trans-Atlantic shipment of machinery and supplies.

(Right) Preparing a B–26 Invader for shipment to Europe are: (top to bottom) SSgt. Weslie W. Teczar, SSgt. Harry E. Greene, and TSgt. Jerry C. James of the 126th Light Bombardment Wing.

(Below) Night maintenance on a RF–80 jet. The ground crewmen of the 117th Tactical Reconnaissance Wing are (left to right) Pfc. Rudolph J. Tipotsch, Cpl. Hugh J. Phillips, Pfc. Glenn W. Reese, and TSgt. C. B. Harris.

were upgraded. Air Guard units began to participate in exercises with the active duty armed services. Air Guard flying units augmented the Air Force's air defense alert program, including runway alert.[6]

Despite these advances, there was little evidence to suggest that the Air Guard's performance actually had a significant impact upon the willingness of the Air Force establishment to allocate additional resources. Most Air Force officers, including members of the Air Staff, remained indifferent to the Air Guard. The most crucial factors behind the post Korean War emergence of the Air National Guard were domestic politics and budget constraints rather than military performance.[7] Congressmen, executive branch officials, reserve association representatives, and individual reservists were far more important initially than professional Air Force officers in redirecting the course of the Air Guard. They noted the problems, confusion, and inequities surrounding the haphazard mobilization of reserve forces during the Korean War and pressured Congress, the Department of Defense, and the military departments to institute a series of reforms intended to correct these deficiencies. The reforms, together with the Eisenhower administration's determination to hold down defense expenditures and to rely heavily on reserve forces, were crucial to the Air Guard's growth. The Air Force, to its credit, responded constructively during and after the Korean War to these pressures for better reserve programs.

Mobilizations in 1950 and 1951 revealed problems in the air reserve structure. The concepts and assumptions underlying the reserve programs had been designed for another protracted World War II mobilization. The Air Guard was intended to be an M–Day force able to augment the active duty establishment after a relatively short period of post mobilization training. The Air Force and the Air Guard, according to this scenario, would, if given sufficient strategic warning, absorb the initial shock of an air attack. Meanwhile, the Air Force Reserve and the rest of the nation would mobilize for total war. Neither of the air reserve components was capable of playing such roles. Soviet explosion of an atomic device in 1949 had challenged the assumptions behind the Air Guard's M–Day air defense role, while the limited war faced by defense planners in July 1950 differed from anything they had anticipated. Further complicating matters, the planners feared that the North Korean attack might actually be a feint to draw U.S. attention away from military moves by the Soviet Union in Europe. The war that reservists were called upon to fight was a "police action" in an obscure corner of Asia. It involved a partial, rather than the expected total, mobilization. Consequently, the callup of air reserve components was hastily conceived and poorly executed. The Air Force was compelled to draw on its reservists because they were the only readily available source of at least partially trained manpower. Reservists were used, in effect, as a temporary solution to the Air Force's urgent requirements for a rapidly-expanded active duty force. They fought much of the war in Korea and met other vital operational commitments while the bulk of the career establishment devoted itself to an enormous expansion.[8]

The Air Force in 1950 was clearly unprepared for a large mobilization. It lacked the facilities needed to train large numbers of additional personnel. Air Force headquarters had not completed work on its first detailed mobilization plan (AF MOP 2–51); it was completed in April 1951. Once the war started, the uncertain political, as well as the military situation, periodically reshaped authorized manpower ceilings of the active duty armed forces. The Air Force consequently undertook a series of hastily improvised expedients intended to meet its growing manpower requirements.[9]

Shortly after the war began, President Truman authorized the Air Force to augment its fiscal year 1951 manpower ceiling of 416,000 by an additional 50,000. On July 7, 1950, the Air Force launched a voluntary recall of reservists. This recall was designed only to meet the immediate need of the Far East Air Forces for individual replacement "fillers" and to augment organizations in the U.S. supporting the war in Korea. Top Air Force officials had yet to identify a requirement to mobilize Air National Guard units. These officials, and their Army counterparts, reportedly spurned an urgent request from National Guard officials for total mobilization of the Guard. Guardsmen were told at that time that Korea was going to be fought by strictly regular servicemen. However, by July 19 it had become apparent that the Air Force would have to initiate an involuntary recall of reservists to rapidly attain its initial augmentation goal.[10]

The Air Force was also compelled to mobilize some of its organized reserve flying units. The first recalled to active duty were two Air Force Reserve units, the 452d Bomb Wing (Light) and the 437th Troop Carrier Wing (Medium). Both outfits were mobilized on August 10, 1950 and saw extensive combat service in Korea beginning that fall. Two Air Force Reserve troop carrier wings, the 375th and the 433d, were mobilized in October 1950. The 375th remained in the continental United States while the 433d was sent to Europe to help strengthen NATO.[11]

The first major permanent Air Force expansion was not authorized by Congress and the President until September 1950. With that authority to expand from forty-eight to fifty-eight wings, the Air Force called upon the Air Guard. Five Air Guard wings were alerted in early September for mobilization the following month. On October 10, these five wings plus fifteen of their fighter squadrons and assorted support units were ordered to active-duty with the Tactical Air Command. This limited mobilization was viewed as only a temporary expedient. Gen. Nathan F. Twining, Air Force Vice Chief of Staff, emphasized this point in a memo to the Secretary of the Air Force late in October. He wrote that "present planning indicates that we can phase out the first of our Air National Guard units by next April [i.e., 1951]."[12] Further underscoring this point, involuntary recalls of reserve airmen were stopped by October 24 because of better than expected

President Harry S. Truman authorized large-scale mobilizations of air guardsmen and reservists to augment UN forces in Korea and NATO forces in Europe.

recruiting for the active duty establishment. Involuntary recalls of officers were limited to those whose skills could not be obtained by other means. The Air Force was apparently satisfied that it could meet its manpower requirements without a long-term mobilization of the Air Guard or the rest of the Air Force Reserve.[13]

Events in the Far East soon shattered these assumptions. In November, massive Chinese communist forces entered the Korean War, dashing hopes for early allied victory. President Truman responded on December 16, 1950 with a declaration of national emergency. He authorized expansion of total U.S. military strength to 3.5 million by June 30, 1951. The Air Force, which had already been given authority to proceed with a second major expansion to sixty-eight flying wings and 651,000 personnel, now geared itself to a ninety-five wing program. This dramatic buildup was scheduled to raise its active duty manpower from approximately 539,000 in mid-December 1950 to a planned ceiling of 1,061,000 no later than June 30, 1952.[14]

At this point, CONAC was finally permitted to use Air Guard units to strengthen U.S. air defenses. Responsible for this mission until ADC was re-established as a separate major air command on January 1, 1951, CONAC possessed only twenty-three regular Air Force fighter-interceptor squadrons in June 1950. Sensitive to the weakness of America's air defenses, CONAC had, on July 20, 1950, requested mobilization of twenty Air Guard fighter suqadrons. Air Force headquarters, however, rejected CONAC's proposal because it wanted to assign newly-formed regular fighter squadrons to the air defense mission as soon as they became available. In September, CONAC proposed that it be given

63

authority to federalize Air Guard units in the event of an emergency. The Air Force again refused. The Secretary of the Air Force wanted to retain that authority. In November and early December, CONAC reiterated its request that certain Air Guard units be mobilized for air defense duty. Its repeated requests were not approved until the President's declaration of a national emergency.

On December 15, the Office of the Secretary of Defense approved a request of the Joint Chiefs of Staff to augment U.S. air defense forces by calling certain Air Guard units into federal service. One aircraft control and warning (ACW) group, three ACW squadrons, and a radar calibration detachment were mobilized on January 8, 1951. They were joined the following month by five more Air Guard wings including eighteen fighter squadrons and attached support units. All of these units, with the exception of one wing and three fighter squadrons which were assigned to train Air Force jet aircrews, joined ADC.[15] Their mobilization was still seen as only a temporary expedient. According to one official ADC history, the federalized Air Guard units would "buy time" until additional regular Air Force squadrons could take their places.[16]

Short-term mobilizations of Air Guard units, however, were abandoned by the Air Force after President Truman's declaration of a national emergency. Between December 16, 1950 and January 11, 1951, the Air Staff developed a manning policy and general reserve call-up procedures. Following Department of Defense approval of its proposed mobilization plan, the Secretary of the Air Force approved its implementation in mid-January. Air guardsmen and Air Force reservists totalling 150,000 were to be ordered to active duty beginning on March 1. Involuntary recalls of reserve airmen were resumed. Recruiting was intensified. The governors of the affected states were notified that twelve more Air Guard wings, thirty-three flying squadrons as well as a number of support and technical service units were to be ordered to active duty in March and April. The bulk of these were distributed to major air commands within the continental United States. SAC initially received six Air Guard wings and seventeen flying squadrons. Four of these wings and their flying squadrons—all tactical fighter units—were later reassigned to TAC. Three wings and six flying squadrons went to ADC. Three wings and ten flying squadrons were allocated directly to TAC. Five wings and eighteen fighter squadrons remained under the control of the states. The Air Force anticipated that they too would eventually be mobilized and assigned to ADC; they were, however, never called to active duty.[17]

Air Guard unit mobilizations for the Korean War were completed during fiscal year 1952 when an additional eight aircraft control and warning squadrons and five tow target flights were called to active duty. The first Air National Guard units called into federal service had been liable for twenty-one months of service under the provisions of Public Law (PL) 599 enacted by the 81st Congress on June 30, 1950. This period of service was later extended to twenty-four months by PL 51 enacted by the 82d Congress. According to the Guard Bureau, 45,594 air guardsmen entered federal service during the Korean War. This represented approximately eighty percent of the Air Guard's total strength.[18]

Mobilization of reserve forces during the Korean War dramatized crucial deficiencies and created an enormous political controversy. The air reserve programs were deeply involved in the resulting uproar. Air Guard tactical units required from three to six months of intensive post mobilization reorganization, reequipping, and retraining before the Air Force considered them combat ready. The length of time varied according to personnel, training status, and whether aircraft conversion was required. Many air guardsmen and Air Force reservists had assumed that they would never be called into active service again in any contingency short of a massive national mobilization. Korea did not fit this assumption.

The Air Force's recall quotas and policies seemed to change on a daily basis. One Air Staff officer, dismayed at the apparently haphazard order in which Air Guard flying units had been mobilized, characterized the entire process as "rather mystifying."[19] Organized reserve units were frequently broken up to fill the regular establishment's requirements. Even Air Guard flying units, technically immune to this fate, frequently found their ranks depleted by transfers of pilots and other key personnel to regular Air Force units. To cite an extreme example, the 137th Fighter Bomber Wing had experienced a ninety percent turn-over when it departed for Europe in May 1952 following eighteen months of active duty training in the United States. One hundred-thirteen Air Guard support units were inactivated after their entry into federal service. Shifting policies also adversely affected unmobilized air guardsmen and reservists. Facing possible recall to active duty, they were often denied civilian employment or promotion opportunities. Some even lost their jobs because of their uncertain military status.[20]

Maj. Gen. Winston P. Wilson, then a colonel, represented the National Guard Bureau's Air Force Division at Air Staff meetings where Air Guard units were allotted to the various major air commands. Wilson, a career air guardsman whose active affiliation with National Guard aviation had begun in 1929, castigated the process of dividing up the Air Guard as the "great cutting up of the pie as the Air Force called it."[21] Like other air guardsmen, he could see no rationality to the process whereby existing organizations above the squadron level were split apart and distributed to TAC, SAC, and ADC. National Guard Association officials, worried by Air Force efforts to recruit individual guardsmen and its reluctance to mobilize any Air Guard units during the war's early months, were even harsher in their criticisms. They bitterly denounced what they saw as another attempt by the regulars to destroy their organization. Some charged publicly that the Air Force, as well as the other military services, was "cannabalizing" Reserve and National Guard units of key personnel to speed the promotions of regular officers.[22]

The Department of Defense and the individual services denied these charges. They maintained that mobilization policies were based on the need to provide trained individual replacements for hard-pressed American forces in the Far East. In that context, retention of unit integrity and equity for World War II combat veterans were not pressing considerations. Brig. Gen. Harlan C. Parks, Director of Personnel and Planning at Air Force Headquarters, addressing public criticism of the Air Force's mobilization policies, told the 1951 National Guard Association conference: "We did not know whether we were facing the so-called police action in Korea or whether we were on the brink of the big adventure [i.e., war with the Soviet Union]."[23] Regardless of the merits of these positions, the controversies and problems of reserve mobilization helped create a domestic political climate receptive to fundamental changes in reserve policies.

Official Air Force histories documented the problems encountered by newly mobilized Air Guard units in 1950–51. Integration of these units into the active establishment was a difficult and time-consuming process. The organizational structure of Air Guard wings differed from their active duty counterparts. Air Force wings were organized in what was known as a combat-wing structure which featured a highly-centralized support unit operation at the wing headquarters level. Most Air Guard flying units operated from municipal airports, far removed from their parent wings, and were organized in a structure that placed tactical and support groups at each operational location. Although the Secretary of the Air

Members of the 137th Fighter-Bomber Wing board the USMS *General Ballou* at New Orleans for the trip to Chaumont AFB, France. The Louisiana Air Guard unit lost ninety percent of its original personnel to active duty units while training for deployment to Europe.

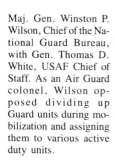

Maj. Gen. Winston P. Wilson, Chief of the National Guard Bureau, with Gen. Thomas D. White, USAF Chief of Staff. As an Air Guard colonel, Wilson opposed dividing up Guard units during mobilization and assigning them to various active duty units.

Force in 1948 had approved a suggestion that the Air Guard adopt the standard Air Force combat-wing structure to speed mobilization, financial and operational constraints had delayed the change. The National Guard Bureau and some adjutants general had opposed the reorganization. They felt that the combat-wing plan did not take into account the realities of their widely dispersed state air units. The Korean War quickly removed all blocks on Air Guard reorganization.[24]

By November 1, 1950 all Air Guard tactical wings had converted to a modified combat-wing structure which took into account their decentralized operating locations. Conversion to the new structure increased the total authorized Air Guard strength from approximately 49,500 to a wartime goal of approximately 78,000. All units were permitted to recruit to full strength. Authorized air technician spaces were increased. And, authorized flight training was increased from 110 to 125 hours per year for all tactical pilots.[25]

The legacy of postwar neglect and poor planning, however, continued to plague the mobilization of Air Guard units. Hard pressed to provide air support for allied troops in Korea during the summer of 1950, the Air Force had stripped Air National Guard units of 296 propeller-driven F–51 fighters. Consequently some units reported for active duty with severe shortages of tactical aircraft. Others lost their aircraft during their initial active duty training cycles when they made the transition to jet fighters. Many of the Air Guard's twelve light bomb squadrons were assigned other aircraft and missions. Extensive quantities of equipment and supplies, including uniforms, were also taken from Air Guard inventories to meet the requirements of the active duty Air Force early in the war. Supply problems were further complicated by the Air Guard's internal system of unit supply accounting which differed from the Air Force's and had to be changed upon mobilization.[26]

Beyond organizational changes and an increased authorized strength, Air Guard units suffered from serious personnel problems. Budget restrictions had limited their actual manning to approximately eighty percent of full authorizations. Large numbers of personnel were eligible for active duty deferments, such as family hardship and medical, and some units lost up to ten percent of their people. The gaps caused by these conditions had to be filled by recruiting youths with no prior service and assigning individuals from the Air Force Reserve. As with supply accounting, the Air Guard's system for classifying the job specialties and skill levels of its personnel did not coincide with the Air Force's and had to be changed. The actual job skills and proficiency ratings of many air guardsmen frequently failed to correspond to those shown in their records. Many of those ratings had either been simply carried over from World War II or arbitrarily awarded by individual Air Guard units. Consequently, reclassification boards had to be established to award skill ratings on the basis of actual ability. Extensive reassignment and retraining was necessary within individual units because of these deficiencies in the personnel classification system as well as the changes in the table of organization and equipment associated with adoption of the combat-wing structure. Most of this retraining was accomplished within individual units. These problems were exacerbated by frequent transfers of key personnel to assignments in higher Air Force headquarters or other tactical units.[27]

Flying proficiency and aircraft maintenance were below Air Force standards. Together with inadequate gunnery and unsatisfactory bombing proficiency, they were the most significant initial problems delaying full operational readiness of Air Guard aircrews. The Air Guard's extremely limited access to bombing and gunnery ranges prior to mobilization accounted for many of the latter problems. The Guard sorely lacked spare parts for its F–51s and P–47s. Premobilization Air Force inspections within at least one of CONAC's numbered air forces revealed that most Air Guard aircraft maintenance at the unit level was of an unknown standard. The resulting low aircraft in-commission rates slowed badly needed flying training programs.[28]

Air Guard tactical flying units mobilized during the Korean War fell far short of the combat-ready M–Day force goal originally established for them in 1945. Units mobilizing in October 1950 underwent an initial ninety-day period of intensive reorganization reequipping, personnel augmentation, and training with Tactical Air Command prior to operational assignments. Some fighter units, reequipped with jet aircraft, were placed on a second ninety-day training cycle. Others simply had not progressed far enough in their training to be reassigned. Not surprisingly, TAC's overall impression of its first batch of mobilized Air Guard units was extremely poor; it characterized the guardsmen as "Sunday Soldiers."[29]

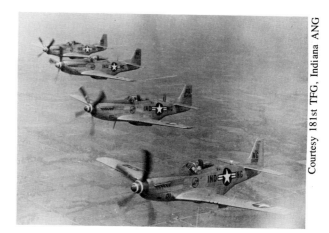

(Right) Formation of F–51s from Stout Field, Indiana, ca 1953. Many ANG units lost their F–51s to active duty organizations during the early months of the Korean conflict.

Courtesy 181st TFG, Indiana ANG

A recruiting office on wheels, used by the 111th Composite Wing in 1951 to attract new recruits and bring the Pennsylvania Air National Guard unit up to full strength.

The first Air Guard unit assigned to the Far East, the 136th Fighter Bomber Wing, did not begin arriving in Japan until May 18, 1951. After an intensive period of advanced training with pilots from the Air Force's 27th Fighter Escort Wing, the 136th's pilots saw their first combat action on May 24, over seven months after the wing had been called to active duty. The only other Air Guard organization to see combat in Korea as a unit, the 116th Fighter Bomber Wing, arrived in the Far East in July 1951. Like the 136th, the 116th had been mobilized the previous October. Both wings had originally been alerted for transfer to Europe.[30]

69

Contrary to Air Force expectations, experience, not youth, proved to be the decisive factor determining the effectiveness of jet fighter pilots in Korea. Older pilots, drawing on their World War II combat experience, scored a disproportionate number of MiG kills. Air Guard pilots, almost all of them World War II combat veterans, performed extremely well. Years later, Brig. Gen. Paul E. Hoover, Ohio's Assistant Adjutant General for Air, discussed the importance of this experience and maturity. Reflecting on his own combat service in Korea as an air guardsman assigned to the Air Force's 49th Fighter-Bomber Squadron, he emphasized that:

> When we first got to Korea, we had a lot of youngsters, Air Force types that had been put through [pilot] training rather rapidly and they were losing quite a few. Then, as the reservists and the Air Guard got there, the average age climbed quite a bit. With the experience of these individuals, our loss rate decreased rapidly. We didn't make silly mistakes like making three or four passes on the same target and we plotted our entries into target areas more efficiently than they did in the early days. They were young and not aware of what could happen. Many of us that got over there came from that World War II experience and we applied some of that experience in Korea. It reduced our losses considerably.[31]

Despite their initial mobilization problems, the Far East Air Forces' two Air Guard fighter wings compiled fine combat records in Korea. Although primarily based at Misawa to strengthen the air defense of northern Japan, the 116th maintained one of its three jet fighter squadrons in South Korea on a rotational basis so its pilots could gain combat experience. The 136th completed movement of its entire organization to Korea in September 1951. Although its three jet fighter squadrons participated in a variety of air operations over the entire peninsula, interdiction and close air support were their primary missions.

Following completion of their legally mandated twenty-one months of active duty, both Air Guard wings were relieved from federal service on July 10, 1952. Members of the two organizations plus individual air guardsmen serving with other Air Force units flew 39,530 combat sorties in Korea. They flew virtually every type of tactical aircraft from jet interceptors to conventionally-powered medium bombers.They destroyed 39 enemy aircraft and damaged another 149. They dropped 44,000 bombs, launched 31,000 rockets and fired over 16,000,000 rounds of .50–caliber ammunition.

Guardsmen were awarded over 1,300 medals and citations, four guardsmen became aerial aces. An Air Force spokesman reported that the two operational Air Guard wings in the Far East Air Forces had been assigned "very high combat efficiency indices and actual operations have demonstrated that they can effectively meet combat circumstances."[32] The price, however, was 101 guardsmen either killed or missing in action.

Like TAC, other major air commands in the continental U.S. had not been initially impressed with the Air Guard units assigned to them. For example, Air Guard units assigned directly to the Air Defense Command in the 1951 mobiliza-

Courtesy Paul E. Hoover

Lt. Col. Paul E. Hoover, Ohio ANG, with Col. James S. Coward. Looking back on the Korean conflict, Hoover attributed the success of Air Guard pilots to their experience in combat flying during World War II.

tions "didn't immediately assume an air defense capability commensurate with that of the regular Air Force squadrons" according to one official ADC history.[33] Rather, they required an intensive four-month organizational and training period after mobilization to achieve acceptable levels of operational efficiency. Only four of the fourteen squadrons mobilized to augment the Air Defense Command were initially jet equipped. Consequently, relatively few of their pilots were checked out in these high performance aircraft; neither were most of their pilots well versed in ground control intercept procedures. General Whitehead, ADC's commander, was quite blunt about the limited capabilities of the Air Guard fighter units assigned to him. In May 1951, he stated "We have found that most of the Air Guard units are not in a position to do what is expected, and the units above the squadron level [i.e., the wing headquarters] are not capable of doing their jobs."[34]

Air Guard units assigned to the Strategic Air Command experienced especially difficult transitions to active duty. Four of the six Air Guard wings assigned to SAC in the spring of 1951 were fighter units. After brief service as escorts for the command's bombers, they were reassigned to TAC that summer so that their experience and training could more readily fill immediate operational requirements. Two other units, the 106th and the 111th Light Bomb Wings, remained with SAC until they were returned to state control in December 1952 and January 1953 respectively. Neither wing was prepared for the command's demanding requirements. Their aircrews had flown short range and tactically-oriented B–26s prior to entry on active duty. They had virtually no experience with either B–29s or B–36s, the aircraft they eventually received. The technical qualifications and general experience level of all personnel was poorly suited to strategic bombing and reconnaissance missions. An official 15th Air Force history summed up the situation by noting that "by and large, the qualifications of individuals coming to duty in these two [Air Guard] units were very low."[35]

Neither SAC Air Guard wing ever achieved fully combat-ready status prior to its return to state control. However, they did serve as organizational cadres around which SAC built two of its permanent active duty bombardment wings. The 106th was equipped with B–29s and became a medium bomb wing. Reorganized as a strategic reconnaissance wing, the 111th was first equipped with RB–29s and later RB–36s.

Training of inexperienced Air Guard and other personnel in these SAC missions was extremely slow. Early shortages of aircraft, spare parts, tools, and supplies and excessive personnel turnover exacerbated the situation. Many individuals were lost to Air Force quotas for overseas units or technical schools. Many of the aircrews as well as technical specialists were transferred into these two units from elsewhere in the Air Force. The 106th Bomb Wing, for example, experienced a personnel turnover rate of 183 percent from July through December 1951. Initial unit cohesion and the distinctive Air Guard character of these organizations were obliterated. These problems resulted in lowered morale and delayed operational readiness. Many problems associated with the low morale of guardsmen and reservists were solved by reassignment or other administrative action including early release from active duty. Very few chose to remain in the Air Force once these units were returned to state control.[36]

Despite these severe problems and the questions they suggest about the Air Force's use of Air Guard resources in SAC, the guardsmen of the 106th and 111th wings made a significant contribution. Upon their return to state control, all Air Guard units left their aircraft, equipment, and supplies with the active Air Force. In many instances, they also left behind functioning military organizations that simply acquired new unit designations and remained as part of the greatly expanded permanent active duty establishment.

The pattern of Air Guard tactical unit experiences during the Korean War was fairly consistent. Upon mobilization, these units underwent an extensive period of reorganization, retraining, reequippage, and personnel augmentation. Some acquired entirely new aircraft and missions during this phase of their federal service. The duration of this initial training cycle varied from three to six months depending upon the gaining air command, the status of the Air Guard unit upon mobilization, and whether or not they had to adapt to new aircraft after they were called to active duty. Units were trained by their major air commands (including TAC, ADC, and SAC) after an extremely short transition to active duty under CONAC. The initial impression made by these Air Guard units upon the active duty Air Force establishment was almost uniformly poor. Air Force personnel, however, had little appreciation of the history of neglect, poor planning, and political controversy that contributed to the Air Guard's unsatisfactory initial showing.

On the whole, the Air Force did a good job preparing most Air National Guard units to eventually take their places beside their active duty counterparts. With that training and the fortunate circumstance that most members were World War II veterans, Air Guard units and individuals were able to make a substantial contribution to a variety of crucial operational commitments during the Korean War. These ranged from combat in the Far East to strengthening NATO air power in Europe. Stateside, Air Guard flying units augmented both SAC and ADC. The Guard's support and technical resources augmented the Air Force's aircraft control and warning, meteorological, construction, communications, and a host of other functions. Over eighty percent of the Air Guard, more than 45,000 individuals, was called to duty during the war. It also contributed equipment worth an estimated $500 million to the Air Force. This represented a major augmentation of the active duty establishment.

The Korean War reversed the pattern of hostility and neglect in the Air Guard-Air Force relationship. The Guard's budgets, manpower, and operational capabilties grew steadily throughout the remainder of the 1950s. It flourished because the political uproar generated by the improvised 1950–51 mobilizations compelled the Department of Defense and the armed services to give serious attention to revitalizing reserve programs. This pressure found a receptive audience in a small influential group of Air Force officers, including General Twining, Vice Chief of Staff, who realized that the Air Force could no longer afford to pay the political, budgetary, and military costs of neglecting the air reserve. Growing Air Force budgets during the 1950s and the availability of surplus aircraft provided the means to implement official policies emphasizing more effective reserve programs.

Individual hardships and inequities caused by recalls during the Korean War had created political pressures on Congress and the Truman administration. The burden of recalls to active military duty had fallen most heavily upon World War II veterans. They were angered that their lives were being placed in jeopardy for a second time, while draft-eligible youths who had never worn a uniform, and other reservists, who had drawn drill pay for participating in organized units, remained at home. Organized reserve units were mobilized piecemeal and then frequently cannibalized to fill the manpower and equipment needs of the rapidly expanding regular military services. Virtually all of them required extensive post mobilization training and re-equipping. It was quite evident by early 1951 that America's military reserve programs and the governmental policies affecting them were in need of a major overhaul.[37]

Tennessee guardsmen change markings on aircraft transferred from the ANG to the Air Force, Municipal Airport, Memphis, April 1951.

Pilots of the 127th Fighter Group, recently mobilized, discuss aerial maneuvers following a training flight at Luke AFB, Arizona.

(Right) A member of the 127th Fighter Group says goodbye to his family following the unit's recall to active duty at Detriot-Wayne Major Airport, Michigan. For many World War II veterans, the call-up for Korea marked the second separation from their family.

(Below) Edwin H. Burgess of Baltimore, Maryland, is sworn in as Chairman of the Civilian Components Policy Board by Secretary of Defense Louis Johnson (right). Retiring chairman William T. Faricy (left) and Mrs. Burgess look on.

Congress and the Department of Defense bore the brunt of public criticism generated by the badly managed recalls. The Defense Department was inundated with complaints from congressmen, reserve organizations, and thousands of individual reservists. Politically sensitive, President Truman directed Secretary of Defense George C. Marshall to remedy these problems. On October 27, 1950, Secretary Marshall announced that a special subcommittee of his Committee on

Civilian Components would study the mobilization problem. The eight-member committee was headed by Edwin H. Burgess, Vice President of the Baltimore and Ohio Railroad; the remaining seven were either regular or reserve officers from the various services. Marshall instructed the committee to study the problems involved in using reserves to carry out the long range buildup of the armed forces after the Korean War. He emphasized the need for policies that would be fair to reservists and their employers. In the meantime, he had already ordered the armed forces to release all reservists and national guardsmen who were on active duty involuntarily as soon as they could be replaced by draftees and volunteers.[38]

In January 1951, Marshall announced a new series of long range policies. These policies were largely the result of recommendations made by the special subcommittee, which had conferred with various veterans' and reserve organizations as well as with the military departments and the Department of Defense. The burden of future involuntary recalls would be shifted from the shoulders of men who had already fought in two wars.

The subcommittee in its recommendations also sought broad public and political support for reserve programs. Addressing himself to the reservists and the American people, Marshall noted:

> The establishment and maintenance of an effective and dynamic reserve force will be accomplished only by the full acceptance of responsibilities by all concerned. The military department must provide appropriate plans and programs. The Reservist must exercise his right and meet his obligation to participate actively in those programs. Necessary support must be made available by the Congress, and the interest, approval, and cooperation of the public is a prime prerequisite to success.[39]

Thirty-nine policies were set forth in Marshall's announcement. These included:

> Each military department would have an Assistant Secretary who would have the primary responsibility for reserve component matters.
>
> Each military department would have a military office that would serve as a focal point for supervising reserve programs and as an expediter of staff action relative to reserve problems.
>
> Advisory committees would be established in all military departments similar to the separate Air Staff Committees on Reserve and Air Guard policy.
>
> The organization, administration, training, and supply of the reserve forces of the three military departments, except as otherwise provided by law, would be completely integrated with the similar functions for the regular services.
>
> The strength and organization of the National Guard, both ground and air, would be assured. Whenever Congress determined that military units were needed for the national security in excess of the regular components, the National Guard would be ordered to active duty.
>
> An assured flow of trained manpower would be supplied to the active and reserve forces through the proposed system of Universal Military Training and Service if Congress approved.
>
> To eliminate the confusion and uncertainty that had marked the reserve mobilizations early in the Korean War, the priority and vulnerability of reservists to future recalls was

specified. Each military department was directed to establish three categories of reserve programs, Ready, Standby, and Retired. The top priority for recall would go, so far as possible, to units and individuals in the Ready Reserve. They could be involuntarily recalled to active duty by either the President or the Congress in the event of war, national emergency, or as otherwise provided by law. Second priority for recall would go to units and individuals in the Standby Reserve. The third category of reservists, the Retired Reserve, wasn't expected to see further service short of an extreme national emergency.

To provide incentives for active reserve participation, individuals who had either satisfactorily completed thirty-six months of training with the Ready Reserve or four years or more of active duty with the regular military services would be transferred to the Standby Reserve for the remainder of their eight-year military obligation. Those who had fulfilled their entire eight year obligation could be discharged from the reserve forces if they desired.

All reserve forces personnel would receive a medical examination at least every four years, or more often if their military department head deemed it necessary. Those unable to pass the examination would be dropped from the program.

Promotions for reservists were to be based upon opportunity and procedures similar to those in the regular establishment.

Policies affecting the reserve forces had to be widely publicized.[40]

Early in 1951 the Air Force began developing its own "Long Range Plan for Reserve Forces."[41] The plan was the work of a board of officers—Air Staff members, reservists, and guardsmen—convened by Secretary of the Air Force Thomas K. Finletter. Called the Smith Committee after its chairman, Brig. Gen. Robert J. Smith, an Air Force reservist, the board was to determine the make-up and the missions of the air reserve forces and the relation of these forces to the active Air Force.[42] The views of the major air commands were solicited and on August 9, the final plan was approved by Finletter. Twelve days later, Eugene M. Zuckert, Assistant Secretary of the Air Force, announced it at the fifth annual national convention of the Air Force Association.[43]

The "Long Range Plan for Reserve Forces" followed the general outline of the reserve policies announced in January by the Secretary of Defense. It also reiterated what the Air Force had pledged itself to in both *Approved Policies, 1945* and President Truman's Executive Order 10,007 in 1948. The plan was designed to provide a dependable and immediately available supply of trained individuals and units for partial or total mobilization. Assistant Secretary Zuckert would assume primary responsibility for reserve matters within the Department of the Air Force. The Air Force would continue to maintain the Office of the Special Assistant to the Chief of Staff for Reserve Forces as the Air Staff contact responsible for coordinating and expediting reserve matters. Committees on the Air Force Reserve and Air National Guard would continue, as authorized under the amended National Defense Act of 1916. Each staff office within Air Force Headquarters would have the same planning responsibilities for the air reserve forces it had for active duty forces. CONAC's responsibility to train the air reserve forces was reemphasized.

On the sensitive issue of the Air Guard and its relation to the Air Force, the legal status remained unchanged. When not called into federal service, the Air Guard was still an autonomous military force controlled by the states and territories. Its organization, administration, and composition would continue to be managed through the National Guard Bureau, which would continue to function as an administrative and reporting channel between the adjutants general and the Air Force Chief of Staff.

Many of the plan's commitments, however, had been made before and it remained to be seen whether they would be implemented now that sustained political pressure was being applied to revitalize reserve programs.[44] Significant innovations within the Air Force's 1951 plan for its reserve components suggested that the reserves might be placed on a more realistic footing. For the first time reserve missions and personnel strengths were tied to the Air Force's master war plan. Organized flying units were to be given definite missions by wing, and were to be earmarked for specific air commands in the event of mobilization. Unlike the situation which prevailed in June 1950, each wing would be given one standard aircraft type. All units would maintain up-to-date organizational structures in accordance with major air command requirements. The programmed postwar Air Guard troop strength would be approximately 67,000, up 7,500 from the prewar ceiling. The size of the air technician program would be substantially increased to support this larger organization. The Air Guard's tactical structure would be maintained at twenty-seven wings with eighty-four combat flying squadrons. All Air Guard units would be included in the Defense Department's proposed Ready Reserve. The Air Force Reserve was to have fourteen flying wings, all of which would fall in the Ready Reserve category. Responding to one of the bitterest complaints of reservists, the Air Force promised, insofar as possible, to maintain the unit integrity of organized reserve units during future mobilizations. On another complaint the Air Force committed itself to providing its reserve units with a full supply of first-line equipment. The plan was to be implemented over a six-year period extending through 1958.[45]

Improved public relations was a vital aspect of these reserve policies. Assistant Secretary Zuckert, arguing in December 1951 for the necessity of maintaining requested levels of air reserve program funds, noted: "We [i.e., the Air Force] are very much on trial . . .with Congress, with the public, and with the reservists themselves, this being our last chance to show them we are going to have a Reserve program and will support it."[46] Zuckert, as well as others, had clearly been troubled by the negative political consequences of the failure to build sound reserve programs prior to the Korean War. The inequities and uncertainties experienced by reservists during the war's first year had created a serious public relations problem which had brought on the demand for an overhaul of the system.

Zuckert's predecessor, Harold Stuart (appointed in 1948), had recognized the negative implications of the Air Force's troubled relationship with the Air Guard.

Secretary of the Air Force Symington had given him the principal civilian responsibility for reserve affairs within the Department of the Air Force. In April 1950, Stuart had attempted to launch a new era of cooperation with the Air Guard by a conciliatory speech at the annual meeting of the Adjutants General Association. He said the Air Force was dropping its demands for establishment of separate Air Guard staffs in the states to parallel the existing ground force-oriented organizations under the adjutants general. The Air Force would develop new tests to evaluate the combat efficiency of Air Guard units; such tests would no longer be conducted away from the units' home stations. There were other, lesser points of friction, which the Air Force was considering in an equally conciliatory manner. However, the issue of federalization of the Air Guard was not included.[47]

Stuart continued his campaign to improve relations with the Air Guard until the end of his tenure as Assistant Secretary in the spring of 1951. He had held a number of meetings with various representatives from NGAUS and NGB. Largely at his insistence, as well as that of General McConnell, the Adjutant General of Arkansas, Brig. Gen. Earl T. Ricks was brought to Washington to take over the troubled Air Force Division of the National Guard Bureau. Ricks brought Lt. Colonels Winston P. Wilson and I. G. Brown with him. These three members of the "Arkansas Connection" ran the Air National Guard for the next twenty-three years. During this period it emerged as a formidable reserve component of the Air Force.[48]

During Stuart's tenure, the separate Air Staff Committees on Air Force Reserve and Air National Guard Policy were merged and their membership upgraded. These committees, authorized under the provisions of the National Defense Act of 1916 as amended, were composed of equal numbers of reserve components and regular Air Force officers. Separate committees on the Air Guard and Air Force Reserve had been established in 1948. They were charged with advising the Air Force Chief of Staff and the Secretary of the Air Force on all proposed plans and policies which might affect their respective components. These committees were frequently ignored and their regular Air Force membership seldom contained the most influential professionals. The rapid expansion of the active duty establishment, however, caused the Secretary of the Air Force to direct a joint meeting of the Air Staff Committees on Air Guard and Air Force Reserve Policy in August 1950. These joint meetings were designed to provide the Air Force with an improved mechanism for obtaining advice concerning the most effective ways of using the air reserve forces during the Korean emergency. The meetings were quite popular with committee members and were continued throughout the war. Evidence of a growing Air Force commitment to strengthen this advisory mechanism was given in November when four regular Air Force general officers were added to the committee's membership.[49]

The Department of Defense and the Air Force made a determined effort to enhance their standing with both reservists and the general public. In large measure, the reserve policies they promulgated in 1951 were aimed at this objective. Top Air Force military and civilian officials publicly lauded the performance of mobilized reservists and air guardsmen at annual meetings of influential groups such as the National Guard Association, Reserve Officers Association, and the Air Force Association. According to National Guard Association observers, General Twining's remarks to the Adjutants General Association in February 1952 demonstrated a genuine acceptance of the Air Guard's role as an integral and vital part of the Air Force:

> The contribution of the Air National Guard to the Air Force since Korea has been essential to the degree of success the Air Force has met in its global commitments . . . [and] handicaps and difficulties experienced in the past have been overcome and need not arise again because the efforts of your governors and yourselves [i.e., the adjutants general] have proven the feasibility of making your air units available to the Air Force in a timely and effective manner.[50]

General Twining's speech was indicative of a much improved atmosphere for reserve forces within the upper levels of the Air Force. General Reckord, Maryland's venerable and influential Adjutant General, cautiously remarked that the relationship between the Air Force and the National Guard "now excelled that which could be expected and that the Air National Guard wanted to be most cooperative with the desires of the Air Force."[51] He contrasted the atmosphere to that prevalent during General Quesada's regime, warning that relations would

Col. I. G. Brown. Brought to the National Guard Bureau as a lieutenant colonel by fellow Arkansan Brig. Gen. Earl T. Ricks, Brown eventually became a major general and Director of the Air National Guard.

Courtesy Air Force Association

continue to improve up to the point of any future effort to modify the basic state character of the organization. A three-day conference at the Pentagon in October 1952 involving the state adjutants general and their air chiefs, representatives from Air Force Headquarters, and the National Guard Bureau underscored the improving relationship between the Air Force and the Air Guard. Air Guard spokesmen commented that the central message of the conference was that the Air Guard had demonstrated its value as a first line reserve and stood high in the Air Force's esteem. On a more substantive note, the *National Guardsman* announced after the conference that the Air Guard had finally been included in all Air Force planning and programming documents.[52]

Inadequate planning and administration of the air reserve forces had been a continuing problem for the Air Force during its brief history. Theoretically, these responsibilities had been distributed throughout the directorates of the Air Staff. In practice, however, that had seldom been the case. Reserve matters were frequently neglected or relegated to a low priority. The Office of the Special Assistant to the Chief of Staff for Reserve Forces, created by a Presidential Executive Order in 1948 to help coordinate and expedite reserve matters in the Air Staff, had consequently been forced to attempt to carry the burden of these neglected planning and administrative functions. This improvised effort to function as an "action" agency had not been especially successful.

In the spring of 1951, Stuart and Twining became convinced that action was required to insure that all sections within the Air Staff exercised their full range of responsibilities for air reserve programs. In a March 13 memo to the Air Staff, Twining criticized its members for failing to discharge their responsibilities. He directed them to rectify this situation immediately. The following September, he reemphasized the necessity for all Air Staff offices to integrate reserve programs, plans, and policies with similar activities for the regular military establishment. To underscore his determination to achieve these objectives, Twining announced that the Office of the Special Assistant would be reorganized to function under a new charter. This new charter emphasized its advisory functions and forcefully restated the Vice Chief's intent that Air Staff agencies would assume all "operating" and "action" responsibilities for reserve programs within Air Force Headquarters. These changes were to be completed by October 1, 1951.[53]

Air Force actions in 1951 fell short of the objectives. In July 1953, Air Force Chief of Staff Twining was compelled to establish yet another top level board of regular and reserve officers to investigate continuing problems with the air reserve programs, especially the Air Force Reserve. Not coincidentally, his appointment of a Reserve Program Review Board corresponded with increased concern by reserve components' associations, the press, Congress, high officials of the Eisenhower administration, and the President himself.[54]

The Eisenhower administration clearly viewed an increased reliance on reserve programs as a method of holding down defense expenditures. Initially this was part of a planned reduction of the active duty Air Force from 137 to 120 wings. On June 8, 1953, Secretary of the Air Force Harold Talbott told a Senate subcommittee that:

> Reduction in programmed [active duty Air Force] wing strength [would] be substantially offset by continuing fighter aircraft production as scheduled to the requirements of the 143 wing program, and [by] making modern fighter aircraft available to the Air National Guard and [Air Force] Reserve to the extent that regular tactical wings [were] not added. [This would] result in greatly increased strength and readiness of the Guard and Reserve.[55]

Although this planned reduction of the active duty Air Force was abandoned when the "New Look" was announced in the autumn of 1953, the Eisenhower administration remained determined to strengthen military reserve programs as a hedge against contingencies requiring the extensive use of conventional military forces. Studies conducted by the Senate Armed Services Committee, the President's National Security Training Commission, and the Office of Defense Mobilization during 1953 and 1954 underscored the weaknesses of these programs. These studies set in motion a chain of events which culminated in congressional passage of the Reserve Forces Act of 1955.[56]

The Reserve Program Review Board was headed by CONAC's commander, Lt. Gen. Leon W. Johnson. The board's seven members included two representatives from the regular Air Force, three from the Air Force Reserve, and two from the Air National Guard. Five of these officers were generals. The "Johnson Board" was told that the revitalization of reserve programs was General Twining's first planned project during his tenure as Air Force Chief of Staff. General Thomas D. White, the new Vice Chief of Staff, told board members that the Air Force had lost ground with Congress and the public because of an ineffective reserve program. He indicated that the "board should write their own ticket" with respect to its findings and recommendations on strengthening air reserve programs.[57]

Subsequent proceedings of the Johnson Board highlighted both the enormous improvement in Air Force-Air Guard relationships and the relatively serious problems of the Air Force Reserve. Air Guard representatives, testifying before the board, emphasized progress in rebuilding the Air Guard after its demobilization as well as the cooperative spirit which now prevailed between the Air Staff and the Air Force Division of the National Guard Bureau. Col. Mark H. Galusha, NGAUS legislative liaison officer, delivered high praise to the Air Force for its cooperation in rebuilding Air Guard units as they returned to the control of the states after periods of active federal service. An outstanding example of this cooperation was the speedy Air Force approval of an Air Force-National Guard Bureau proposal to create air base squadrons at flying facilities vacated by federalized Air Guard units during the Korean War. These squadrons would serve as holding cadres to form the basis for reconstituting Air Guard units once they were released from active duty. The Air Staff had approved this and associated ideas for returning Air Guard units

to state control. By way of contrast, discussions of the Air Force Reserve emphasized problems that had plagued the program since its formation after World War
II. These included difficulties in obtaining satisfactory levels of participation by
qualified personnel, inadequate facilities and equipment, and unrealistic training
programs.[58]

The Johnson Board heard testimony from many sources, including the Air
Staff, representatives of reserve components' associations, and the Army and
Navy. On August 24, 1953, after approximately six weeks of work, it forwarded its
final report to General Twining. The report concluded that the Air Force plan for its
reserve forces, developed by the Smith Committee in 1951, was basically sound
but was not being effectively implemented by the Air Force:

> It repeatedly became evident that in general the active establishment had not, and does
> not now, understand or appreciate the Reserve Program. . . . [It] does need understand-
> ing, appreciation, and implementation at all levels in the Air Force. In this connection, it
> [the board] believes that emphasis must be placed more exactly on quality rather than
> quantity and it must realistically approach the Air Force's present ability to equip,
> recruit, and train its Reserves.[59]

The board had placed the onus for failing to implement sound reserve
programs squarely on the shoulders of the active duty establishment. The board's
other significant general finding was essentially political. Assessing the impact of

Accompanying Senator Leverett Saltonstall, (third from left) Chairman of the
Armed Services Committee, on a visit to Camp Drum, New York, are several
prominent guardsmen and active duty officers: (left to right) Maj. Gen. Edward D.
Sirois, Commanding General, 26th Infantry Division; Col. Mark Galusha,
USAF; Maj. Gen. Edgar Erickson, Chief of the National Guard Bureau; Maj.
Gen. William H. Harrison, Jr., Adjutant General of the Massachusetts National
Guard; and Col. Alfred DeQuay, Massachusetts National Guard.

inadequate reserve programs it noted: "Weakness of a Reserve plan and program is more serious to the entire [active duty Air Force] establishment than just the loss of trained individuals and units. Such weakness can result in a lack of influence and support for the entire Air Force by the public and the Congress."[60] The nonmilitary consequences of the bungled 1950–51 reserve mobilizations had not gone unnoticed within the Air Force's higher echelons. The growing appreciation of these consequences and the emphasis placed upon improved reserve programs by the Eisenhower administration were crucial factors in the Air Guard's subsequent development. Twining and White strongly supported better reserve programs. They knew what Congress was saying even if many of their subordinates did not.[61]

The Johnson Board concluded that, of the Air Force's two civilian components, the Air Guard "is working to greater effectiveness than the [Air Force] Reserve."[62] Its report emphasized that: "No fundamental facts were established to show that the comparable parts of the Air National Guard and the Reserve (i.e., organized units) could not be trained and developed on an equally effective basis, provided that each had the same or comparable facilities and equipment."[63]

The board recommended continuation of the Air Force's existing reserve program for the next five years. Rejecting universal military training, it strongly endorsed continued reliance on voluntary participation in training programs. However, the board did recommend certain modifications of the air reserve programs. To increase emphasis upon reserve programs within the Air Staff, it suggested creation of an Office of Assistant Chief of Staff, Reserve Forces, with an authorized rank of lieutenant general and membership on the Air Force Council, Air Force Budget Advisory Committee, and the Air Force Installations Board. This office would replace the Office of the Special Assistant to the Chief of Staff for Reserve Forces. The board also recommended continuation of the concept of integrated regular and reserve forces action within Air Force headquarters, and noted that individuals leaving the active duty establishment would benefit from a more affirmative and conscientious program of information concerning opportunities in the reserve forces. It called for the simplification of the existing organizational structure for administering Air Force Reserve training programs and suggested that the Air Force Reserve adopt the Air Guard's practice of hiring civilian technicians to supervise its flying organizations. It further recommended expansion of the Air Guard's tactical squadron structure within existing air reserve program objectives. Concerning facilities, the board urged quick review and approval of the existing construction program for the Air Force Reserve, while administratively, it suggested that CONAC be the only field agency discharging the Air Force's responsibilities toward its reserve components—the major air commands had conducted the annual field training of reserve units since July 1952. Finally, the Johnson Board urged that the contents of its final report be made known to the civilian reserve associations prior to its release.[64]

The Air Staff responded favorably. Many of the Johnson Board's recommendations were approved and implemented: upgrading the emphasis on reserve matters within the Air Staff; simplifying the administration of Air Force Reserve training programs; retention of integrated staff planning for active duty and reserve forces' matters; and adoption of a technician program for Air Force Reserve flying units.[65]

The significance of the Johnson Board involved neither administrative nor policy changes. Rather, it was the growing awareness by top officials that the Air Force would pay an unacceptable price, both military and political, for its failure to develop effective reserve programs. The basic problem appeared to be continued inadequate support and appreciation of the reserve programs by the active duty establishment itself. These perceptions, emerging from the Korean War experience, represented a significant shift in top level attitudes. The Air Force was beginning to realize the importance of improving reserve programs. The crucial lessons of Korea had been political and budgetary. If the Air Force was going to maintain the positive relations with Congress and the public which adequate support of its active force programs required, then it would have to develop and implement more effective reserve programs. Furthermore, these reserve programs, as the Korean emergency had demonstrated, could also help to bridge the gap between military requirements and active force capabilities.

The political ramifications of reserve programs were illustrated by growing congressional involvement with reserve components' policy during the Korean War. Despite the changes which the Defense Department and the individual armed services had made in their reserve programs in 1951, Congress and the reserve components' associations pressed for new legislation. Hearings had been initiated by a subcommittee of the House Armed Services Committee in early Janury 1951. These hearings, chaired by Representative Overton Brooks of Louisiana, were the political result of the poorly handled Korean War mobilizations.[66]

The reserve associations asked Congress to rejuvenate reserve programs through a system of universal military training and service. They also wanted Congress to protect and strengthen their position within the national security establishment by enacting a legislative charter for the reserve components. In essence, they wanted Congress to mandate the size, strength, and composition of the civilian components of the armed forces. The attitudes underlying these demands were reflected in the "Annual Report of the Special Air Advisory Committee of the National Guard Association."[67] In his speech to the 1951 NGAUS conference, Brig. Gen. Errol H. Ziztel of the Ohio Air Guard reported that his committee was:

> firmly convinced that a charter or constitution in the form of a legislative enactment should be provided to control the Department of the Air Force in its relation to the Air National Guard and civilian components . . . [We are] unalterably opposed to a condition permitting. . . . the Air National Guard to be controlled by the varying policies of the Department of the Air Force or the regulations thereof.[68]

Brig. Gen. Melvin Maas, a former congressman, Marine Corps reservist, member of the Secretary of Defense's committee on civilian components, and Chairman of the Reserve Officers Association's legislative committee, articulated similar attitudes in his testimony before Brooks' subcommittee. Maas advocated congressional enactment of a charter for reservists which would ensure equal treatment for them regardless of their reserve component.[69] When asked by the subcommittee why the Department of Defense was mobilizing individual reservists instead of units, he responded that:

> there is a general feeling in the Army and pretty much in the Air Force Reserve [and the Air Guard] that the reason that they want to strip units is to get junior officers and enlisted men and not have to call field grade officers, thereby saving for themselves an opportunity for an accelerated promotion by regulars into these field grades.[70]

Early in 1951, Congress and the reserve components associations had pressured the Defense Department to submit legislative proposals designed to build an effective military reserve system and remedy inequities in the existing one. They were not satisfied with the largely administrative remedies already promulgated by the Department of Defense. These, they argued, could be altered or neglected at the whim of civilian and military officials. The eventual product of their pressures were two major pieces of legislation enacted by the 82d Congress, the Universal Military Training and Service Act of June 19, 1951 and the Armed Forces Reserve Act of July 9, 1952.[71]

The purposes of the Universal Military Training (UMT) and Service Act were:

> first to raise immediately the manpower necessary to build and maintain an armed force of the size determined by the Joint Chiefs of Staff to be our minimum security requirement, and, secondly, to provide for the maintenance of an adequate force of trained Reserves for the future security of the United States.[72]

The permanent active duty personnel strength of the armed forces was set at 2,005,882. However, this limit was suspended to allow building of a wartime force of five million. (Peak military strength of 3,685,054 during the Korean War was reached on April 30, 1952.) The act provided that every young man between eighteen and twenty-six years of age should register for military service. Each man inducted after June 21, 1951 was required to serve two years active duty in the armed forces and, after his discharge, six years in a reserve component. The service secretaries were authorized to provide that any person who entered organized units of the National Guard, Air National Guard, and other reserve components could be released from service in the regular armed services. The act also provided that, should universal military training (i.e., the National Security Training Corps) be initiated, trainees who served for six months would be obligated for an additional seven and one-half years of service in a reserve component. However, Congress never authorized universal military training because it was too controversial and there was never any pressing military need for it. In the early

Courtesy U.S. Marine Corps

Courtesy 121st TFW, Ohio ANG

Brig. Gen. Melvin J. Maas, USMCR, criticized mobilization policies that, he believed, discriminated against Reserve and Guard units.

Brig. Gen. Errol H. Ziztel, Ohio National Guard, chaired the Special Air Advisory Committee of the National Guard Association.

1950s, the Congress believed that a large active duty Air Force had more relevance to the atomic era than UMT.[73]

The Armed Force Reserve Act of 1952, the so-called "Magna Carta" of the reserve components, was based upon the proposals initially developed by the Department of Defense's Civilian Components Committee. These recommendations and the resulting legislation were designed to rejuvenate the armed forces' reserve components. The act sought, as had the War Department's *Approved Policies 1945*, to create readily available trained units and qualified individuals to augment the regular armed forces. It codified many existing statutes relating to the reserve components and provided various benefits and equalization measures for individual reservists regardless of their component. Each of the armed forces was required to maintain a ready, a standby, and a retired reserve. The ready reserve force was authorized a strength of 1.5 million. The act also limited the exposure of Korean veterans to future recalls.[74]

The Armed Forces Reserve Act of 1952 also strengthened the influence of reserve officers in the service planning process. Each service was required to maintain a top level reserve affairs office within its military staff structure in Washington. These offices would be responsible for expediting and coordinating reserve components' planning and administration within each service. Further-more, each of the armed forces was required to have reserve officers on active duty in the nation's capital to participate in the preparation and administration of all policies and regulations affecting their respective reserve forces. Consequently, Air Guard and Air Force Reserve officers were assigned to active duty with the major divisions of the Air Staff. The act also required top level civilian administra-tion of reserve component programs within the Department of Defense and the individual military departments by assistant secretaries whose principal duties would include reserve matters. These provisions of the law strengthened reserve forces administration by granting statutory authority to several existing admin-istrative arrangements.[75] All Air Guard units were included in the nation's highest priority military reserve category, the ready reserve—a position they had, in fact, if not in law, held since 1946. Under the 1952 act, their legal status was finally affirmed and enhanced.[76]

The Korean War marked a turning point in the history of the Air Guard. The conflict reversed the downward slide of the Air Force-Air Guard relationship. It signaled the beginning of the Air Guard's development as a sound reserve compo-nent of the Air Force. This transformation was initially the product of political expediency and budgetary limitations rather than military performance or chang-ing national security requirements. Although Air Guard units and individuals had made substantial contributions to the expansion of the Air Force and its global missions during the Korean War, available evidence strongly suggests that this military performance had virtually no impact on the organization's post-Korea rejuvenation. Rather, the inequities and weaknesses that evolved in reserve pro-grams during the Korean War unleashed a flood of public indignation and con-gressional criticism. The Department of Defense and the armed forces, fearing political consequences and recognizing the serious military shortcomings of their existing reserve programs, took steps to strengthen these programs. They also launched a vigorous public relations campaign designed to placate reservists and the public. Top Air Force officials, especially civilian policy-makers, were clearly convinced that unless effective reserve programs were developed, the active duty establishment would lose the public and political support it needed to maintain its own programs. Furthermore, they believed that properly handled reserve programs could significantly enhance air strength at a fraction of the cost of comparable active duty forces. They were supported by a small but influential number of professional Air Force officers. The work of the Smith Committee in 1951 and the Johnson Board in 1953 reflected this growing determination to develop effective reserve programs.

Congress encouraged these initiatives by holding extensive hearings and enacting controversial legislation. This legislation, principally the Armed Forces Reserve Act of 1952, had little immediate impact upon the Air Guard. However, it did signify the political dangers of neglecting reserve programs. Moreover, it had a significant long range impact by strengthening the influence of reserve officers, including air guardsmen, on the top level planning processes. This legislation also resulted in the designation of assistant secretaries, within each military department and the Department of Defense, who bore legal responsibility for reserve matters.

The Korean War compelled the Air Force to overcome its own deeply ingrained professional prejudice against the Air Guard's citizen-airmen. Guardsmen were one of the few available sources of trained manpower. Political necessity and budget constraints forced civilian officials to concentrate upon developing a productive working relationship with the Air Guard. Although they were joined in this effort by a small number of top Air Force officers, the initial impetus for the changed attitude toward the Air Guard clearly came from outside the uniformed military establishment.

The Air Guard itself had not performed auspiciously during the early stages of the Korean mobilization. Although its units contained a reservoir of talented World War II veterans, they had not been welded into effective combat teams. The flying clubs of that postwar era had operated as state air forces without benefit of standardized supervision from the active duty establishment. Mobilized Air Guard units had required extensive personnel augmentation as well as reorganization, retraining, and resupply. They were unprepared because of the extreme sensitivity of the states to federal encroachment on their military prerogatives; the disinterest and even hostility of the active duty establishment; and the inadequate military budgets of the immediate post World War II era. However, air guardsmen had overcome their initial mobilization deficiencies and had demonstrated that, if properly trained and equipped, they could effectively augment the active Air Force in a broad range of important missions. More significantly, their leadership recognized that in the post Korean War era only realistic training for legitimate military missions, effectively supervised by the active duty establishment, could guarantee the Air Guard's future. They were willing to permit increased Air Force control of the Air Guard and to shoulder a portion of the active duty establishment's mission responsibilities in exchange for increased federal support. The post Korean War modus vivendi between the Air Guard and the Air Force reflected a mutual appreciation of these political, budgetary, and military facts of life.

One of the first F–80s acquired by the Air National Guard. During the 1950s jet fighters replaced propeller-driven tactical aircraft such as the veteran F–51s.

Chapter IV

Integrating with the Active Force, 1953–1960

The Eisenhower administration marked a new era in the short history of the Air Guard. From 1953 through 1960, the Air Guard experienced dramatic growth and modernization accompanied by an increasingly closer integration with the active duty Air Force. Buoyed by official praise of their performance in Korea and aggressive new leadership in the National Guard Bureau, veteran air guardsmen shed the negative image associated with their late 1940s reputation. Generals Ricks and Wilson, both having served as Chief of the National Guard Bureau's Air Force Division, were confident that Air Guard units could develop the high operational readiness demanded by the Air Force. They firmly believed that those same units could compete against their active duty counterparts in a variety of missions and eagerly sought opportunities to expand the Air Guard's missions and demonstrate its operational competence in competition with regular units. During the late 1950s, the Air Guard made noticeable progress toward becoming the well-prepared first line combat reserve force originally envisaged in the War Department's *Approved Policies 1945*.[1]

The confidence of veteran air guardsmen was well-founded. By 1960 the Air Guard's personnel strength had reached 71,000, an increase of 26,272 over its pre-Korean War level. Reflecting this growth and the increasing technological complexity of equipment, the number of technicians had expanded from 5,814 to 13,200. Air Guard appropriations had more than doubled, growing from $114.69 million in Fiscal Year 1950 to $233.44 million in Fiscal Year 1960. The number of Air Guard flying squadrons had been expanded from 84 to 92. Their federal missions, almost exclusively concerned with air defense in the early 1950s, had been greatly diversified. By 1960 missions included tactical fighter and reconnaissance, troop carrier and heavy airlift, and aeromedical evacuation. Although still largely dependent on excess or obsolescent aircraft, the Air Guard's flying inventory had increased. By 1960 all of its fighter aircraft were jet-powered. Some units had been equipped with century series fighters, including the F–100 and the

F–104. Others were flying the all-weather, nuclear-capable F–89J fighter interceptor. Air Guard units augmented the Air Force with a real, albeit limited operational capability, which had been conspicuously absent in 1950.[2]

Air guardsmen were regularly involved in the everyday business of running the Air Force. Air Guard officers, assigned to the Air Staff and the major air commands on extended active duty tours, participated in the formulation of policies, plans, and programs that affected their reserve component. Chiefs of the Air Force Division of the National Guard Bureau had assumed the added role within the air staff of Deputy for Air National Guard Affairs under the Assistant Chief of Staff for Reserve Forces. They were effectively promoting the interests and military capabilities of the Air Guard. Guard aircrews were beginning to participate in Air Force exercises and gunnery meets on an extremely limited basis. Its aircraft control and warning squadrons and other technical units provided technical support to the active duty establishment.

Fighter interceptor squadrons were actively augmenting the Continental Air Defense Command's runway alert force around the clock on a year-round basis. By 1960, twenty-two Air Guard fighter interceptor squadrons were participating in this highly successful program that had been initiated in 1953 as a limited experiment with only two squadrons. Air guardsmen were convinced that the growing capabilities demonstrated by their successful augmentation of the air defense program and participation in other peacetime missions had created an environment within the Air Force amenable to an even more significant allocation of resources and responsibilities.[3]

For its part, the Air Force abandoned any serious effort to eliminate the state character of the Air Guard. Federalization was a dead issue because of the potential political damage. Moreover, the Air Force discovered that the Air Guard was increasingly responsive to its requirements. New leadership in the National Guard Bureau convinced the states of the long term advantages of permitting their Air Guard units to function as Air Force reserves rather than as state air forces. They were willing to exchange a measure of state autonomy for increased levels of federal support and supervision. They were convinced that this would enhance the Air Guard's performance, thereby buttressing the argument for its continued existence as a reserve force with a distinctive state character.

In this context, the issue of the Air Force's command jurisdiction looked less crucial than it had in the late 1940s. Air Force leadership grudgingly accepted the necessity to develop the Air Guard into a sound program despite its state-federal status. Chagrined by the political and military costs of the Korean War mobilization, nourished by abundant defense appropriations under the nuclear-oriented "New Look," and sensitive to the Eisenhower administration's initial enthusiasm for strong reserve programs, the Air Force sought to implement the recommendations of the Smith Committee and the Johnson Board. The Air Force's commitment to the Air Guard and the Air Force Reserve was also encouraged by its growing appreciation of their ability to help bridge the gap between operational commitments and available resources.

Unlike the Korean War era, significant innovations in management and utilization of reserve programs originated within the Air Force and the Air Guard during the 1953–60 period. These innovations, as noted before, included the Air Guard's participation in the air defense runway alert program in 1953; upgrading reserve forces representation within the Air Staff in accordance with the Johnson Board's recommendations that same year; and adoption of the 1959 Reserve Forces Review Group recommendation of the gaining command concept of reserve forces management in 1960. (The latter, discussed in detail later in this chapter, was particularly significant.) The concept transferred responsibility for supervising the training and inspection of reserve programs, including the Air Guard, from CONAC to the major commands that would actually employ them in another emergency. This was a functional rather than a geographic approach. It provided a major incentive for Air Force commanders to train and equip reserve forces up to operational standards. With these innovations, as well as the emphasis upon force modernization and the peacetime support roles of the Air Guard, the Air Force evolved what later became known as the total force policy.[4]

Rebuilding demobilized units was the most pressing task during the closing stages of the Korean War—a task comparable in some respects to the challenges associated with development of the Air Guard after World War II. Having been stripped of their aircraft and equipment prior to leaving active federal service, Guard units returning to state control in 1952 and 1953 were frequently little more than skeleton organizations. By June 30, 1953, the Air Guard's eighty-two authorized flying squadrons had only 250 tactical aircraft.[5] Many of these were obsolete World War II propeller-driven fighters. Many guardsmen, especially young enlisted men, had terminated their military affiliations when their units were demobilized or were planning to do so as soon as they were eligible to transfer to standby reserve status under the provisions of the Armed Forces Reserve Act of 1952. Some officers had elected to remain on active duty. By the end of June, 1953, the Air Guard's personnel strength had shrunk to 35,556, well below its programmed ceiling of 52,500.[6] The most critical shortage was with qualified fighter pilots—their annual attrition rate was twenty percent. Since the Air Force still had not set aside adequate flight training positions for the Guard to compensate for these annual losses, the shrinking pilot force continued to rely heavily on World War II veterans. Vacancies in certain specialties such as weatherman and air controller were also difficult to man with fully qualified personnel. Consequently, many in these jobs were inexperienced youths recruited directly from civilian life and trained on the job.[7]

The Air Guard was also short of suitable airfields. With few exceptions, Air Guard flying units were to return to the airfields they had occupied prior to mobilization. All of these units were scheduled to be equipped with jet fighters.

Many of their airfields, however, could not handle jets. Some lacked adequate facilities, especially runways. Others encountered strong local opposition to the prospect of noisy and dangerous jet operations.[8] An extensive and costly construction program had begun during the war to expedite conversion to an all jet fighter force. Eight pre-Korean War Air Guard airfields could not be modified for jet fighter operations. Consequently, units at these airfields were converted to airlift missions. Displaced fighter squadrons were relocated at bases able to handle jets.[9]

Despite these challenges, air guardsmen approached the task of rebuilding with self-confidence and enthusiasm. Reflecting this optimism and the growing integration with the active force, a veteran Guard officer later commented:

> It [Korea] gave us extreme confidence in our ability to train up to a level where we would be ready to go at any time. . . . After we got into Korea and came back, we developed our capability by an increase in technicians. . . . We finally realized that we could react with a minimum of notice and that was because we began to work more closely with Air Force units. . . . We were tested more and actually became competitive with the Air Force.[10]

State officials also reflected this confidence. By the end of the war, thirty-eight states had requested that the Air Force authorize them to organize an additional sixty-six flying units beyond those already programmed. Although these requests were consistent with the Johnson Board's recommendation that the Air Force take advantage of the Air Guard's ability to expand its tactical unit structure, they were never implemented.[11]

The Air Force's failure to approve an expansion of the tactical structure in 1953 was a minor disappointment. It failed to dampen the optimism of the Air Guard's leadership. The Air Guard had finally been included in the Air Force's war plans. Each flying unit had been given a definite mobilization assignment. Officers serving on active duty with the Air Staff and major air commands participated in the planning process as it affected their reserve component. General Ricks, Chief of the National Guard Bureau's Air Force Division, and his assistant, Col. Wilson, had built an atmosphere of cooperation and harmony between the Air Force, the states, and Air Guard leaders. Their political skills were complemented by an excellent grasp of Air Guard matters that made them effective advisers to the Air Force leadership. Because of them, the National Guard Bureau got what it had been denied in the past, an effective voice in the policy process at the highest levels of the Air Force.[12]

Under Ricks and Wilson, the foundations were established for a realistic post-Korean War training program. Each wing organization was scheduled to receive standard type aircraft, assigned a definite mission, and allocated to a major air command for mobilization. Training programs were keyed to a mission. To save money, units were provided with a minimum of supplies and equipment. In the event of an emergency, they would be brought up to full operational readiness after mobilization. Compensating for the chronic shortage of training funds, material and locations, nine permanent Air Guard field training sites were selected. Each site contained the facilities, supplies, and equipment the units needed to conduct their field training. Units were to be rotated through these sites for two weeks of training each year.

The bureau anticipated conversion to an all jet force by the mid-fifties. During the Korean War, it initiated a program to lengthen runways at civil airports housing Air Guard tactical squadrons. Conversion to jets had significantly raised the accident rate of some units in the early fifties. A more intense and controlled flying training program was needed to compensate for the increased difficulty of flying these high performance aircraft. The bureau proposed an additional thirty-six annual flying training periods for all Air Guard jet pilots. In March 1956, the Defense Department approved a similar proposal, applicable to both guardsmen and Air Force reservists, that had been submitted to the Air Staff by its Committee on National Guard and Reserve Policy. Finally, the Air Guard adopted a plan for concentrating its unit training on weekends. Prior to the Korean War, most units had met two hours each week for training, and pilots flew as individuals when they had the time available. This approach had drastically limited teamwork. To overcome this problem, the Air Guard adopted the practice of concentrating all of its training during one weekend each month.[13]

During the latter stages of the Truman administration, the Air Force continued to implement its commitment to build stronger air reserve programs. General Twining, upon becoming Chief of Staff in June 1953, emphasized that one of his first planned projects was the revitalization of those programs. Planning was elevated to a higher level within the Air Staff in October 1953. Consistent with a recommendation of the Johnson Board, Twining dissolved the Office of the Special Assistant to the Chief of Staff for Reserve Forces and replaced it with the more powerful Office of the Assistant Chief of Staff for Reserve Forces. The Assistant Chief of Staff was directly responsible to the Chief of Staff for coordinating and expediting reserve matters in the Air Staff. He was also given a seat on the Air Force Council, the Air Staff's top collective policymaking body. Furthermore, he was represented on the Budget Advisory Committee and the Air Installations Board. This reorganization reflected the Air Force's increased emphasis on reserve programs at the highest decision-making levels.[14]

A far more important initiative in upgrading reserve programs was launched on an experimental basis in the spring of 1953. At the suggestion of the NGB and Maj. Gen. George G. Finch, CONAC's Deputy for Air National Guard Matters, the Air Force began to use air guardsmen to augment the Air Defense Command's runway alert program. Concerned by the absence of realistic training programs for the units under state control, Finch had suggested in May 1952 that better use might be made of them if a ". . . small number of pilot officers at each strategically

Maintenance training at Holman Field, St. Paul, Minnesota, 1953. Holman was a summer training site for Minnesota ANG units.

placed ANG unit [were placed] on active duty with the unit for the purpose of performing . . . air intercept missions."[15]

Gen. Leon W. Johnson, CONAC's Commander, was Finch's superior. He liked the proposal and approved it. General Johnson had taken over CONAC in February 1952. At that time, General Vandenberg, Air Force Chief of Staff, had told him to "get up there [to CONAC] and straighten out that god-damn can of worms."[16] The "can of worms" referred to by Vandenberg was the enormous public dissatisfaction of reservists and guardsmen as well as members of Congress with the continuing absence of effective and meaningful reserve training. Recognizing that the Air Guard was too firmly entrenched to be eliminated, Johnson felt that CONAC's job was to make the program work despite its shortcomings rather than to waste energy in a counterproductive effort to assert command jurisdiction. He needed to find realistic missions and establish effective training programs for the politically-potent but still militarily-underdeveloped Air Guard. Its active participation in the air defense runway alert program promised to help accomplish these objectives.[17]

At first the Air Force did not embrace the proposal. Its Judge Advocate General ruled that the proposal was illegal under existing statutes. The Air Staff

Courtesy Air Force Association

(Above) Lt. Gen. Leon Johnson (left) receives a commendation from Maj. Gen. Ellard A. Walsh, NG, ret., (center) President of the National Guard Association of the United States. The resolution praised General Johnson for his personal interest in Air Guard activities during his tenure as CONAC Commander. Air Force Vice Chief of Staff Gen. Thomas D. White is at right.

(Below) ADC Commander Gen. Benjamin W. Chidlaw initially opposed using guardsmen to augment the runway alert program. But facing problems of insufficient funding and personnel shortages, he later embraced the proposal.

97

was convinced that the idea was impractical. ADC's commander, Lt. Gen. Benjamin W. Chidlaw, initially rejected the proposal in a long letter to Johnson. Chidlaw later changed his position. Faced with insufficient funding and the inability of the Air Force to retain enough experienced fighter pilots, ADC could neither adequately perform its air intercept mission, nor provide sufficient simulated fighter interceptor attacks for the Strategic Air Command to train its bomber crews. The gap between mission and capability could be partially closed if the pilots the Air Force was unable to retain on active duty could be induced to participate, on a part-time basis, in the proposed Air Guard runway alert program.[18]

ADC submitted a plan to Air Force Headquarters to implement the Air Guard runway alert concept. The Air Staff remained unconvinced. However, faced with continuing political pressure to revitalize reserve programs and unwilling to allocate appreciably greater resources to air defense at the expense of the Strategic Air Command, the Air Staff agreed to give the plan a trial run.[19]

The experiment commenced on March 1, 1953. Two Guard squadrons—the 138th Fighter Interceptor Squadron at Syracuse, New York and the 194th Fighter Interceptor Squadron at Hayward, California—were selected to augment ADC's runway alert program. Each squadron maintained two aircraft and five aircrews on alert status from one hour before sunrise to one hour after sunset seven days a week. They were to be scrambled within five minutes of notification. Pilots served short tours of active duty while ground crews remained in their civilian status.[20]

The experiment was an outstanding success. ADC was enthusiastic about the results. It reported that the performance of Air Guard aircrews was close to that of their regular Air Force counterparts. ADC requested retention and expansion of the program. It wanted thirteen more Air Guard squadrons to participate. The request was approved, but the National Guard Bureau had to postpone implementation because of a shortage of aircraft and equipment. The Air Guard's eighty-two tactical flying squadrons possessed only 250 combat aircraft at the end of Fiscal Year 1953. The National Guard Bureau insisted on distributing these few fighter resources as widely as possible to maintain at least minimal flight training in its tactical units. As late as March 1954, each Air Guard fighter unit possessed, on the average, only five or six tactical aircraft. Many of them were still World War II propeller-driven F–51s, inadequate for operations in the mid-1950s. The Air Force's inability or unwillingness to provide the additional manpower spaces needed to expand to a full-fledged operational program also remained a problem.[21]

Developments outside the Air Force soon overcame these barriers. The new Eisenhower administration was committed to a fundamental reassessment of national security policies. The President was an economic conservative who believed that deficit spending by the federal government posed a serious threat to the nation's economic health. Eisenhower was convinced that the struggle against communism would be a protracted one. Success would depend as much upon economic as military strength. He was convinced that, if the communists were unable to beat the U.S. militarily, they would attempt to bankrupt her. Eisenhower was alarmed by the inflation that had accompanied the huge increase in U.S. military spending during the Korean War. It seemed to confirm his fears about the dangers of oversized defense budgets.[22]

Eisenhower took office with his own ideas on American strategy based on his conservative economic views. The President was determined to hold down defense spending while maintaining military superiority over the Soviet Union by greater reliance on atomic air power. This was coupled with an emphasis upon developing military technology and building strong allied forces around Russia's periphery. Although advisers like Secretary of the Treasury George Humphrey and Secretary of State John Foster Dulles were influential, Eisenhower dominated the strategic policy process.[23]

To implement his ideas, the President installed a new set of Joint Chiefs who would presumably be more amenable to defense budget reductions than the holdovers from the Truman era. The Joint Chiefs developed a national security strategy that incorporated Eisenhower's assumptions. National Security Council "NSC"–162, issued in May 1953, helped to establish the design of the new strategy by endorsing the Truman administration's containment policy. However, unlike Truman's policy of developing balanced land, air, and naval forces, NSC–162 stressed an increased reliance upon strategic nuclear forces. The preliminary strategic plan of the Joint Chiefs, offered in August 1953, proposed a further buildup of the strategic air forces as well as a stronger air defense. Defense budgets would be reduced by scaling down the size of overseas garrisons and creating a mobile strategic reserve in the United States. This would be coupled with an increased reliance upon allies.[24]

Eisenhower endorsed NSC–162/2 in October 1953. American military expenditures were to be reduced to between $33 and $34 billion by Fiscal Year 1957. Military strength would drop from 3,403,000 in December 1953 to 2,815,000 by June 1957. The Army was scheduled to carry the brunt of this reduction, from 1,481,000 to 1,000,000 men. The number of divisions would be reduced from twenty to fourteen. The Navy would be cut from 765,000 men and 1,126 combat vessels to 650,000 men and 1,030 combat vessels. The Marine Corps would go from 244,000 men in three divisions to 190,000 men in three reduced strength divisions.[25]

The Air Force was the big winner. It would expand to 137 wings from its earlier interim goal of 120 wings. The former goal was to be achieved by the end of fiscal year 1957 with a projected Air Force personnel strength of 975,000. The planned 137–wing Air Force was to be oriented toward strategic deterrence. Its projected strength included fifty-four Strategic Air Command wings. To further strengthen deterrence, the number of air defense wings was set at thirty-four, an increase of five above the Truman administration's plans. The principal reduction

President Dwight D. Eisenhower boards his aircraft at Dow AFB, Maine. Under Eisenhower's administration, the Air Force was spared sharp budget cuts and emphasized strategic nuclear forces.

from Truman's 143–wing goal was in air transport. Despite theoretical emphasis on building a mobile strategic reserve force in the United States, the Eisenhower administration planned to reduce the number of transport wings from seventeen to eleven. This defense strategy, with its growing reliance upon the Air Force's nuclear deterrent, became known as the "new look."[26]

One element of the "new look" that has often been neglected was its emphasis upon strengthened reserve forces. Early in the administration, Secretary of Defense Charles E. Wilson indicated that he intended to reduce defense costs and maintain the nation's military strength through a revitalization of the reserves and reduction of the size of the active duty establishment. Wilson made this intention known when he submitted the administration's first defense budget to Congress. A revision of the Truman administration's Fiscal Year 1954 proposals, the Eisenhower budget called for a $5 billion cut in the requested Air Force appropriation for the coming fiscal year. It sliced the Air Force flying unit program from 143 to 120 wings. In his testimony before a subcommittee of the Senate Armed Services Committee Wilson stressed that increased Air Guard and Air Force Reserve combat strengths would counter the projected reductions in the active duty Air Force. Secretary of the Air Force Harold E. Talbott supported Wilson's testimony. On June 8, he told the same Senate subcommittee that:

> reduction in programmed [Air Force] wing strength [would] be substantially offset by continuing fighter aircraft production as scheduled to meet the requirements of the 143

wing program, and [by] making modern fighter aircraft available to the Air National Guard and [Air Force] Reserve to the extent that regular tactical wings [were] not added. [This would] result in greatly increased strength and readiness of the Guard and Reserve.[27]

This proposal contemplated shifting 1,200 more aircraft into the Air Guard and Air Force Reserve than they would have had under the Truman administration's budget for Fiscal Year 1954. Beset by complaints from reservists about continuing weaknesses and inequities, Congress was sympathetic to the administration's announced intent.[28]

Reserve programs were still shot through with inequities. The burden of reserve service still fell largely upon veterans, both World War II and Korea. Young pilots and other skilled technicians were in short supply. Age and rank structures were out of balance. Unit cohesion and proficiency were seriously undermined by high annual personnel turnover. According to the Department of Defense, the most glaring deficiency of the reserve system was the reluctance of enlisted reservists, except national guardsmen, to participate in training programs. Only twenty-eight percent of those enrolled in the reserve components were receiving drill pay at the end of Fiscal Year 1954.[29]

President Eisenhower was determined to revitalize the reserve forces. Following extensive studies by the National Security Training Commission and the Office of Defense Mobilization, the Defense Department, and the individual services were asked to make comments. The resulting recommendations were presented to the NSC in June 1954. Evidently this was the first time in the Council's seven-year history that a meeting had been convened specifically to deal with reserve programs. The recommendations were further revised after consultations within the executive branch. Briefings with the various reserve component associations followed, and a final presentation was made to the NSC in November. It was approved and presented to the Congress as the National Reserve Plan.[30]

The National Reserve Plan was introduced into Congress as House Resolution (H.R.) 5297. It sought direct recruitment and training of youths for the reserve components within a universal military training system while, at the same time, retaining the draft to help the regular armed forces fulfill their manpower needs. Other significant features of the plan included: changes in the reserve forces structure; transfer of trained personnel into the National Guard if voluntary recruitment failed; and insured participation in reserve training activities once basic training had been completed. H.R. 5297 had serious shortcomings and stirred enormous political controversy on Capitol Hill. Universal military training was especially unpopular with voters. Congress had shied away from several similar proposals to implement it since the end of World War II. Universal training's prospects for passage were dim in 1955. Despite the objective of evenly distributing the burden of military service, the bill was inherently inequitable. It would permit youths to either serve two years of extended active duty with the regulars under the draft or six months of military training followed by seven and one-half years of reserve service.

Cost was another problem. The administration estimated that the program would cost $2 billion a year by 1959. Although this estimate was probably far too conservative, it did emphasize the squeeze such a grandiose program would make on the funds available for the regulars. Finally, the bill failed to address adequately the fact that each of the armed services had separate reserve problems to contend with. The Air Force, like the Navy, relied on the recruitment of longterm volunteers. It feared that the National Reserve Plan's universal military training and reserve service alternatives could have a ruinous effect on enlistments. Furthermore, it felt that a more basic failing of the National Reserve Plan was its failure to recognize the degree to which an effective reserve program must rely on the participation of individuals with previous military service. The plan envisaged reserve forces primarily composed of individuals without such experience. The Army, unlike the Air Force, stood to benefit from the National Reserve Plan by gaining an assured flow of trained non-prior service youths into its reserve components, particularly their combat units.[31]

The National Guard Association also fought passage of H.R. 5297. The Association opposed mandatory basic training for the National Guard's non-prior service recruits and rejected the idea of involuntary assignment of trainees to its all-volunteer ranks. With respect to the Air Guard, General Walsh, the National Guard Association President, told the Senate Armed Services Committee that the Air Force had already solved the basic training problem. It permitted Air Guard recruits without prior service to attend eleven weeks of training with the active duty establishment. An amendment to H.R. 5297 offered by Representative Adam Clayton Powell, barring racial segregation in the National Guard, killed the bill. An alternative proposal, H.R. 7000, was then introduced in the House. At the insistence of the Guard Association and its allies, the new proposal omitted the provisions set forth originally for the National Guard.[32]

The 84th Congress eventually enacted two significant pieces of legislation designed to address the weaknesses in military reserve programs highlighted by the National Reserve Plan and subsequent legislative proceedings. First, the 1955 Amendments to the Universal Military Training and Service Act extended authority to induct men into the armed forces until July 1, 1959. Second, the Reserve Forces Act of 1955 amended the Armed Forces Reserve Act of 1952 and the Universal Military Training and Service Act of 1951. The Reserve Forces Act of 1955 increased the size of the Ready Reserve from 1.5 million to 2.9 million men; authorized the President to mobilize up to one million ready reservists in a declared emergency; reduced the total obligation for active and reserve military duty from eight to six years; required all those who entered the armed forces after August 9, 1955 to participate in reserve training following completion of their active service, and authorized specific sanctions for those who failed to participate; provided for direct enlistments in the reserve forces of nonprior service youths; and established a system of continuous screening for members of the ready reserve to ensure their availability for active duty. The act did not include provisions authorizing universal military training, mandatory basic training for National Guard recruits, or authority to induct men into the reserves if sufficient numbers could not be obtained voluntarily. Although gravely concerned by these omissions, President Eisenhower, at the strong urging of the Secretary of Defense, signed the bill into law on August 9, 1955.[33]

The Reserve Forces Act of 1955 had a minimal direct impact on the legal status, size, and composition of the Air Guard, but it was significant. It reflected continued concern about the health of reserve programs. Sensitive to this political climate and the desire of the Eisenhower administration to hold down defense budgets by emphasizing stronger reserve programs, the Air Force had already taken important steps to strengthen its reserve programs. In January 1955, General Twining had established a requirement that air reserve tactical flying units be trained and equipped to achieve an immediate combat capability upon mobilization. This goal, subject to budget and other limitations, applied to fifty-one Air National Guard and Air Force Reserve combat flying wings. It marked a significant departure from earlier policies that had emphasized the necessity for substantial post mobilization refitting of air reserve units.[34]

The Air Force's ambitious objectives for its reserve forces, however, were partially thwarted by the Eisenhower administration's changing budget priorities. When the administration reversed its early 1953 decision to cut the active Air Force flying program to 120 wings and authorized 137 wings instead, the pace of the Air Guard's aircraft modernization program was drastically curtailed. The projected conversion of the Air Guard to an all-jet force fully equipped with modern aircraft by 1956 was delayed several years. By June 30, 1955, the Air Guard had received 2,054 aircraft from the Air Force. Although this represented seventy percent of the aircraft to be assigned under the 27 wing Air Guard program, most of them were not modern, first line fighter aircraft. Only 1,097 were jets. The remaining fighters were prop-driven F–51s. The last F–51 was not eliminated from the Air Guard flying inventory until December 1957. Shortages of equipment, supplies, and qualified airmen further limited the Air Guard's development. Poor ammunition storage facilities and the lack of suitable ground gunnery ranges were also problems. However, inadequate airfields posed an even more fundamental barrier to the Air Guard's transformation into a modern combat reserve force. The Air Force estimated early in 1954 that twenty-three of the Air Guard's eighty-one flying locations would not be able to handle jets by the end of Fiscal Year 1955. These factors seriously inhibited the pace of the Air Guard's development. They precluded its evolution into a combat-ready force capable of immediate deployment in a crisis situation.[35]

A1C Dennis Ellsworth and A2C Monty Ellsworth load a 50–caliber machine gun of an F–51 during their summer encampment with the California ANG, 1953. Air Guard units were still flying the propeller-driven F–51s as late as 1957.

Nevertheless, the Air Force had been moving to make the Air Defense Command's runway alert experiment a permanent feature of the Air Guard's force structure and training program. Encouraged by the outstanding success of the 1953 experiment and the resultant clamor of the Air Guard for its expansion as well as its own inadequate air defense resources in the face of what it believed to be a serious Soviet bomber threat, the Air Force prepared to place a limited number of Air Guard squadrons on permanent alert duty at critical locations around the country. This use of air guardsmen to augment the active Air Force in its peacetime missions was a revolutionary innovation in air reserve programs which dominated the evolution of the Air Guard through the remainder of the decade. It established a precedent for increased participation of air reserve forces in a slowly expanding circle of Air Force missions. Although it was implemented on an extremely limited basis prior to the 1960s, this growing integration of reserve forces with the active duty establishment established the foundations of what later came to be known as the Department of Defense's total force policy.

In 1953, concrete steps had been taken to convert the runway alert experiment to a permanent program. The Air Force had scheduled seven Air Guard fighter squadrons to receive F–94A/B all-weather interceptor aircraft by the end of fiscal year 1954. These were the first specific air defense aircraft ever assigned to the Air Guard. The Air Force also increased the authorization of active duty personnel for the Air Guard from seventy-five to ninety for that same fiscal year. In November 1953, primary mobilization assignments for all Air Guard fighter squadrons were shifted from TAC to ADC. This increased the number of Air Guard fighter units potentially available for air defense in an emergency from fifty-two to seventy squadrons. However, only seventeen of these squadrons were scheduled to participate in the runway alert program on a continuing basis, and only nineteen were actually equipped as interceptor units. The remaining fifty-one squadrons were equipped with fighter-bombers. They were unrealistically required to train for both the interceptor and fighter-bomber roles. In reality, only the seventeen Air Guard fighter-interceptor squadrons scheduled to participate in the runway alert program on a daily basis had a significant air defense capability. The other fifty-three squadrons, designated to augment ADC in the event of an emergency, added little to the nation's actual air defense capabilities. Extensive reequipment and post mobilization training would have been required to make them a viable air defense force. This was slow in coming due to the demands of the active duty establishment under the 137–wing program.[36]

Eight Air Guard fighter squadrons took their places beside their regular Air Force counterparts in the first permanent augmentation of ADC's runway alert program on August 15, 1954. Each squadron furnished two jet fighter aircraft and five aircrews to man them fourteen hours per day on a year-round basis. Pilots were voluntarily recalled to active duty for short periods to participate in the program. Participating squadrons rotated this duty among all their pilots. The initial eight units were joined by nine more on October 1, 1954. Air Force Headquarters and the National Guard Bureau approved an ADC plan in 1955 to place nineteen Air Guard fighter-interceptor squadrons on permanent alert and augment them with forty-eight additional squadrons on rotating alert in groups of sixteen. Actual implementation of the plan, scheduled for July 1, 1956, floundered because of inadequate funding and the difficulty in obtaining skilled personnel at some Air Guard locations.[37]

By mid–1957, ADC's Air Guard fighter-interceptor force had grown to seventy-six squadrons. Twenty of these squadrons actually participated in the runway alert program. Although the total Air Guard interceptor force was quite large, it was generally poorly equipped by modern air defense standards. Ten of its squadrons flew modern first-line jet interceptors including the F–94C, F–86D, and F–89D. Forty-two squadrons flew day fighters. The remaining twenty squadrons operated second-line interceptors including the F–89B/C and the F–94A/B. Unit and individual training levels frequently left much to be desired. CONAC complained that Air Guard squadrons were not receiving the advisory service and close liaison with ADC that their mission required. This complaint arose because, although these Air Guard units participated in ADC's alert program and would augment its forces in an emergency, CONAC was still responsible for supervising their training.[38]

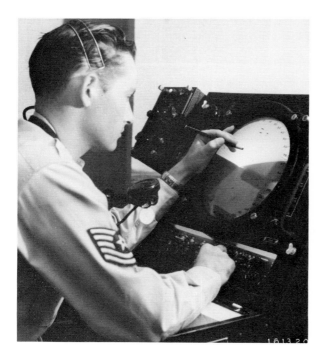

Guardsmen on the air defense team. (Above) Air National Guard pilots on runway alert get instructions from an ADC control center. Their mission was to intercept and identify suspect aircraft. (Left) A member of a Guard aircraft control and warning squadron scans his radar scope.

Despite the successful integration of a limited number of Air Guard aircraft and aircrews into ADC's air defense network, the program generated a predictable amount of tension between the regulars and the guardsmen. Many professional Air Force officers, including some in ADC, considered Air Guard participation in the air defense alert program to be strictly an augmentation of the active force. In their view, the Air Guard was still strictly a "second team" outfit participating in air defense primarily for training purposes. More significantly, some regulars feared that the politically powerful Air Guard would try to run off with the lion's share of the increasingly significant air defense mission and its considerable resources. As early as December 1954, a top ADC staff officer assured his counterpart at Air Force Headquarters that any further expansion of the Air Guard alert program would be carefully considered from this perspective. Nevertheless, ADC continued to press for an expansion of the Air Guard's role in air defense until 1956 when Congress reduced the funds available for that increasingly expensive mission. ADC, which had previously recommended that all Air Guard fighter-interceptor squadrons be equipped with all-weather jet interceptors, reversed its position in November 1956. It recommended that no more than thirty percent of the Air Guard's flying squadrons be equipped with all-weather fighters while another thirty would be equipped with modern fighters like the F–100. The remaining Air Guard flying units, according to this particular ADC recommendation, should be reequipped for air rescue and transport missions. Responding to an ADC request to reduce the size of the Air Guard's interceptor force and reductions in its projected budget for FY 1958, the Air Force reduced the Air Guard interceptor force from seventy-six to fifty-five squadrons by the end of 1957. This force had been reduced to forty squadrons by June 1960.[39]

Vigorously defending its own prerogatives and resources, ADC had strongly opposed the Air Guard's pressure to be included in the Bomarc air defense missile program in 1958 and 1959. The Guard's pressure evidently provoked ADC's Commander, Lt. Gen. Joseph H. Atkinson, to make a bitterly hostile attack on the Air Guard that threatened to puncture the still fragile framework of official Air Force-Air Guard harmony that had prevailed since the Korean War. Atkinson, in a letter to Gen. Thomas D. White, Air Force Chief of Staff, clearly expressed some of the underlying tensions that had strained relations between professional officers and citizen-soldiers through much of American history. He asserted that:

> Reserve forces should have no role in the air defense fighting forces. . . . I vigorously oppose equipping them with first line weapons. . . . This demands immediate response to command . . . 'command' by negotiation, persuasion and state politics will not do the job. I put little dependence on the Air National Guard as an emergency interceptor augmentation. Reserve forces belong in minimum cost, minimum support missions which do not materially compete with us for resources. I recommend a concerted effort to so employ them.[40]

General White, in his reply, patiently explained the political and military facts of life to ADC's Commander. He wrote:

> I must also consider that the administration and the Congress expect our reserve forces to perform active functions in U.S. defense. Any action to completely deny Air National Guard participation in air defense with newer weapon systems would meet with considerable opposition.[41]

The exigencies of domestic politics clearly required the regulars to moderate or at least mask their fears about the challenge that reserve programs posed to their control of military missions and resources.

General Atkinson was not alone among the Air Force's top uniformed leadership in harboring serious reservations about the Air Guard. Gen. Curtis E. LeMay, the outspoken Air Force Vice Chief of Staff, caused a minor political uproar in October 1959 when he indicated publicly that he was unhappy with existing air reserve programs. LeMay's concerns, however, were quite different from Atkinson's. LeMay feared the military weaknesses of those programs rather than their political strengths. Speaking at a reserve forces seminar in Washington, D.C., he asserted that he did not think that the present Air Guard and Air Force Reserve would make much of a contribution if war came. He opposed separate organizations with the same general aims. Reminding his audience that his remarks represented only personal views, General LeMay called for an amalgamation of the Air Guard and Air Force Reserve. The Vice Chief of Staff also forecast a decreasing tactical role for "weekend warriors" in the future. Arguing that modern weapons were becoming too technical to be adequately mastered by amateur military men, LeMay noted that:

> One element of the overall Air Force program which we are looking at is the present and future roles of the air reserve forces. As weapons complexities continue to increase, the possibility of their being maintained and operated with a high degree of efficiency by other than members of the active establishment will decrease. I can see the tactical role for our reserve forces diminishing. . . . Looking ahead, I can see the need for only one air reserve component.[42]

The National Guard Association, meeting at its annual conference, immediately passed a resolution demanding reevaluation of LeMay's qualifications and usefulness in light of his remarks about the air reserve components. The Secretary of the Air Force, James H. Douglas, Jr., moved quickly to calm this political storm. He telegraphed the President of NGAUS at the association's annual conference in San Antonio, Texas. Douglas sought to "clarify" LeMay's remarks by asserting that they had been made to stimulate "dynamic thinking." He noted that LeMay had:

> . . . recently approved the appointment of fourteen highly qualified officers to conduct a study of long range missions and requirements for the reserve forces. . . . Its members will consider future roles for the Air Force Reserve and Air National Guard in the light of revisions in military equipment, methods, and techniques.[43]

Douglas assured that Air Force policy was that both the Air Force Reserve and Air Guard were valuable to the overall program of aerospace power. He emphasized that, as Secretary of the Air Force, he supported this policy.[44]

Courtesy Air Force Association

Lt. Gen. Joseph H. Atkinson, ADC Commander, opposed the Air National Guard's increasing involvement in the air defense mission.

Air Force speakers at the National Guard Association's conference reiterated the Secretary's position. Lt. Gen. William E. Hall, CONAC's Commander, praised the ". . . truly astonishing combat readiness of the Air National Guard."[45] Dudley C. Sharp, Under Secretary of the Air Force, noted the future missions of the air reserve forces were under review by the Air Staff and a special board of officers. Addressing the anxieties of the assembled guardsmen, he assured them that:

> . . . there is no second team in the Air Force. Active units, [Air National] Guards and [Air] Reservists jointly form one first string deterrent force now. . . . [The Air Guard] is an integral part of the entire defense team.[46]

Public praise notwithstanding, the skepticism about reserve programs voiced by Atkinson and LeMay in 1959 may very well have been widespread within the Air Force's top professional military leadership. Their enthusiasm for these programs was often grudging. General White had commented in October 1958 to his Deputy Chiefs of Staff that ". . . the reserve forces were here to stay and that it was our job [i.e., the Air Staff's] to find ways for them to best serve and take some of the load off the regular establishment."[47] However widespread such private skepticism about the air reserve programs may have been, it was impolitic to voice it publicly.

General LeMay's critical comments about the air reserve forces and the political furor they generated represented more than lingering professional military skepticism about amateur airmen. The political minitempest LeMay precipitated in 1959 was an outgrowth of a series of Air Force reassessments of the size

Secretary of the Air Force James H. Douglas promptly denied that the Air Force favored establishing a single air reserve force.

Courtesy Air Force Association

and missions of its reserve programs. The first of these formal reviews had been initiated in November 1956 under the chairmanship of Lt. Gen. Charles B. Stone III, CONAC's Commander. General Stone had written Gen. Nathan F. Twining, Air Force Chief of Staff, in August, suggesting the need for such a review. Stone, concerned by impending cuts in the Air Force budget, believed that air reserve forces could be better employed to augment the active Air Force than current concepts and policies permitted. He had suggested that a reappraisal of their composition and missions ". . . would result in a realignment of functions which would make it possible for the regular Air Force to concentrate on the performance of these tasks not at all practical for the reserve."[48] A little more than a month later, General White, Air Force Vice Chief of Staff, had replied for General Twining. White had approved Stone's suggestion, noting that budgetary and manpower limitations demanded the maximum utilization of every available resource, and had appointed Stone chairman of the Air Reserve Forces Review Committee. Besides Stone, the committee's membership had included General Hall, Assistant Chief of Staff for Reserve Forces, General Wilson, Chief of the National Guard Bureau's Air Force Division, five representatives of Air Force Headquarters, as well as representatives from SAC, TAC, ADC, the Military Air Transportation Service, and the Air Materiel Command. Supporting research for the study was done by CONAC, Air Force Headquarters, and the Air University. The Stone Board had submitted its final report to the Chief of Staff on February 12, 1957.[49]

The Stone Board's principal recommendation was expanded utilization of the air reserve forces through their active participation in a number of peacetime support functions. The board's final report analyzed twenty-three Air Force peacetime support functions, grouping them in accordance with their perceived suitability for reserve forces participation. It concluded that five of the twenty-three functions could be handled as well by reserve forces as by the active duty establishment and at appreciably lower costs. These five included: aircraft control and warning, air evacuation, tow target, certain logistical functions, and unspecified defense missions. The reserves could be of substantial assistance in nine other functions: ADC manned fighters, troop carrier and airlift, air rescue, fighter-bomber and tactical reconnaissance, tactical control, radio relay, communications construction, and communications maintenance. In six areas, peacetime reserve participation did not appear to be practical. These were: aerial resupply, weather service, airways and air communications, air terminal augmentation, personnel processing, and medical services. No committee position could be established on strategic missiles. Base support functions could be augmented by individual reservists but not units, and the ground observer function could be performed by reservists but no real savings were anticipated.[50] The report also recommended ". . . that the Air Staff review the validity of the wartime requirements of all Reserve Forces units" and that existing reserve units with no substantial peacetime utility be ". . . evaluated for program retention."[51]

The Stone Board's recommendations challenged the prevailing logic behind the Air Force's reserve programs. That logic assumed that since preparation for D–Day missions was expensive and the active force was unlikely to ever get all the resources it wanted, the reserves must be relied upon to bridge part of the resulting gap. The Stone Board recommended that the conception of reserve forces' roles be broadened whenever possible to support the active force in its peacetime functions as well as augment its preparations for D–Day. The board's recommendations were approved in part by the Assistant Chief of Staff for Reserve Forces and then by the Chief of Staff. However, their implementation was sidetracked, at least for several years, by a substantial Defense Department budget and manpower retrenchment ordered by President Eisenhower in 1957. Nevertheless, the board's recommendations are extremely significant. They represented the first official Air Force recognition that growing pressures on its budget might necessitate the adoption of a much broader conception of the use of reserve forces and a closer integration of these forces with the everyday activities of the active duty Air Force.[52]

A major retrenchment ordered by President Eisenhower in the fiscal year 1958 defense budget struck the Air Force hard. In July, the President approved a 100,000–man reduction in active duty military strength to be completed before January 1, 1958. The Air Force's share of this reduction was 25,000 of its approximately 919,000 personnel. Additional manpower reductions were planned which would reduce the Air Force's active duty strength to 850,000. These reductions were to be accompanied by substantial budget cuts. In August, the Air Force was directed to limit its fiscal year 1958 expenditures to $17.9 billion, almost $1 billion below its estimated requirements. The Air Staff decided that those portions of the Air Force with missions directly related to air defense and retaliatory capabilities or missile development projects would sustain the minimum budget reductions under the revised program.[53]

The Fiscal Year 1958 budget retrenchment was also shared by the Air Guard and Air Force Reserve. All further expansion of these components was ordered halted by the Chief of Staff in August 1957 pending yet another study of reserve programs. The Secretary of Defense had directed the Air Force on March 1, 1957, to reduce the size of its ready reserve and place more emphasis upon their wartime roles. Consequently, Air Force Headquarters directed its reviewers to assume that the Air Force would only program those reserve units needed from D–Day to D–plus–thirty days in a general war and, as practical, those units having local war utility. On August 16, the Chief of Staff approved a proposal to reduce the air reserve forces' flying programs. Twelve of their fifty-one wing headquarters were scheduled for elimination, three from the Air Guard, and nine from the Air Force Reserve. Three Air Guard and ten Air Force Reserve flying squadrons were also scheduled to be cut. Furthermore, the entire air reserve fighter program was to be given to the Air Guard. The Air Force Reserve was to specialize in the unglamorous and less costly troop carrier mission. These cuts also reduced the Air Guard's total personnel authorization from 92,797 to 81,000. Actual Air Guard strength by June 30, 1957, had reached 67,950. The entire Air Force retrenchment project was dubbed "Streamline 3."[54]

General Wilson, Chief of the National Guard Bureau's Air Force Division, painted a grim picture of the future for air guardsmen assembled at the annual National Guard Association conference in October 1957. The Air Guard's appropriation had been reduced by $20 million for fiscal year 1958. It would have to deactive three wing headquarters and three flying squadrons. The money squeeze, he implied, was hurting the availability of flying hours. The annual Air Guard quota in the Air Force's pilot training programs had been reduced from 500 to approximately 155. The Air Guard had been a growing organization prior to 1957; now it faced a situation where its strength was rapidly approaching its shrinking personnel ceiling. There was, however, a bright spot in this picture. Wilson noted that a number of Air Guard squadrons had been converted to certain unspecified new missions that the regular Air Force could no longer perform because of reductions in its strength. Furthermore, the Air Guard would be receiving newer and more modern aircraft twelve to eighteen months earlier than expected due to reductions in the active Air Force's flying inventory.[55]

David S. Smith, Assistant Secretary of the Air Force, predicted that the Air Guard's operational role would increase as military spending was reduced.

Courtesy Air Force Association

Largely because of Streamline 3, there were some striking improvements in the Air Guard. By June 30, 1958, its jet inventory had increased by 362 aircraft; and its overall aircraft inventory included 792 all-weather fighter-interceptors, approximately 1,000 day fighters, and 140 reconnaissance aircraft. It had begun to receive the F–100 and the RB-57. All sixty-nine Air Guard fighter squadrons had air defense designated as their primary mission. However, eleven of those squadrons, equipped with F–84Fs, were instructed to practice a secondary mission, the delivery of tactical nuclear weapons. The public announcement of this new mission emphasized that none of these squadrons would actually train with nuclear weapons nor would such weapons be stored at Air Guard bases. Addressing other positive aspects of the Air Guard program, Wilson noted that aircrew readiness had increased from twenty-seven to thirty-three percent while aircraft operational readiness had grown to sixty-three percent during the first six months of 1958. Finally, he emphasized that, although the Air Guard had lost three wing headquarters as scheduled, only one fighter squadron had actually been eliminated.[56]

David S. Smith, Assistant Secretary of the Air Force for Manpower and Reserve Affairs, emphasized the Air Force's need for increased reliance upon its reserve components as a result of reductions in the Air Force budget. He explained to the guardsmen:

> Clearly, with the requirement on one hand, and with the urgent need to control and reduce expenditures on the other, the Air Force cannot afford a full-time force to handle every risk ahead of it. We must place a large share of our defense burden on you and your fellow guardsmen throughout the nation. . . . In the past, our reserve forces concept included a large training mission but today our concept requires that the unit program constitute a force in being with very high standards of readiness. . . . [Our new reserve structure] will constitute in a very real sense, an extension of our active force ready for mobilization in any future conflict. . . . You are nearer to being an integral component of the active Air Force than at any time in the past.[57]

Smith emphasized that the Air Guard would be concentrating upon the following operational tasks: air defense runway alerts, early warning, airborne sampling of nuclear clouds, as well as tactical fighter and reconnaissance operations in local wars. The official emphasis was shifting from growth and training to increased operational readiness and closer integration with the active duty force. Paradoxically, this shift was to be accomplished while the Air Guard sustained a substantial budget cut.[58]

The Eisenhower administration's budgetary retrenchment received a rude jolt from the Russians in October 1957. Sputnik, the earth's first artificial satellite, shattered some comfortable national assumptions about American military, technological, and educational superiority. The Department of Defense responded with $1.5 billion in added budget estimates for fiscal year 1959. These included funds for accelerated missile development and a reduction in planned cuts in the Army budget. The previously announced Air Force budget cuts were also reversed. Total Air Force obligations for fiscal year 1958 actually were over $23.8 billion, a rise of $5.9 billion beyond its projected spending ceiling under the administration's discarded austerity budget. This also represented a growth of $5.3 billion over the Air Force's total obligations for fiscal year 1957. The Air Guard budget profited modestly from Sputnik. Its total obligations for fiscal year 1958 were some $257.5 million. This was a growth of approximately $8.2 million over its fiscal year 1957 obligations.[59]

In late 1959, new budget constraints forced another formal review of the air reserve programs. The Under Secretary of the Air Force in June had rejected a request from the Chief of Staff for an increase of 10,000 paid drill spaces for the Air Force Reserve. He had also directed that "a complete and searching review be made of the entire program with the objective in mind of fully justifying a realistic existence of the reserve program and active establishment support thereto."[60] Air Force budget estimates for fiscal year 1961 had also entered the picture that summer. The Defense Department had directed the Air Force to submit estimates of $18.8 billion and $18.3 billion. These estimates were well below the $19.3 billion the Air Force considered essential. Following its Sputnik-induced $23.89 billion peak in fiscal year 1958, total Air Force obligations had shrunk to $20.28

billion in fiscal year 1959 and would shrink an additional $1.93 billion in fiscal year 1960. Active Air Force bases were being closed and tactical units were being eliminated. These shrinking budgets had led to the Under Secretary's request that the Air Force undertake yet another formal reassessment of the organization and missions of its reserve forces. General LeMay's public criticisms of the air reserve forces in September 1959 alluded to this forthcoming Air Force review.[61] In response to these pressures, a Reserve Forces Review Group was convened in the Pentagon on October 19, 1959. It was chaired by Maj. Gen. Sory Smith, Commander of CONAC's 4th Air Force. The membership also included representatives from the Air Guard, Air Force Reserve, Air Staff, CONAC, Continental Air Defense Command, Air Materiel Command, Military Air Transport Service, SAC and the Tactical Air Command. They assessed the Air Force's needs throughout the upcoming decade and how the reserve forces should be configured to support those needs. After thirty days of deliberations, the review group produced its report, "The Air Reserve Forces: New Roles in a New Era."[62]

Generally, the report strongly endorsed the continuing need for existing air reserve forces. It was satisfied that they were capable of meeting the same high standards as regular Air Force units. However, it was extremely critical of the obsolescent aircraft given the Air Guard. The release of aircraft to the Air Guard had been forecast at such a limited rate that the Guard had been forced to carry fighters such as the F–89D/H and the F–86D/C well beyond their anticipated obsolescence. These aircraft, the report concluded, would be hopelessly mismatched with the most probable threat. It emphasized that budget restraints had forced the Air Force to rely on equipping its reserve forces with aircraft dropped from the active force's inventory. Since there would not be enough high performance aircraft available to equip most Air Guard units outside the Air Defense Command, the report recommended that they be converted to other missions like troop carrier. It recommended the concentration of aircraft in the Air Guard that would have assured roles in both peacetime and war. The report also recommended reserve forces participation in new mission areas. These included nuclear attack survival and recovery; operation of alternate bases for the SAC and ADC; and off-base storage of war readiness materials. It also urged the Air Force to defer reserve force participation in the operation of defensive missiles until regular units had obtained considerable experience with them. It further suggested that the reserves might operate one of the Air Force's basic flying schools. The Air Guard was already operating its own jet instrument school.[63]

The most significant recommendation of the report called for a substantial restructuring of the Air Force's system of reserve force management which later became known as the gaining command concept. In order to save administrative overhead ". . . the group recommend [ed] that CONAC Headquarters, its immediate supporting structure and its subordinate numbered Air Forces be disestablished."[64] It proposed that CONAC's responsibilities be shifted to the major air commands which would gain mobilized reserve units in the event of a war or other emergency. The office of the Assistant Chief of Staff for Reserve Forces would be given responsibility for the budget allocations, coordination, and supervision of all reserve forces. The report carefully added that no changes should be made in the internal Air Guard administrative structure except that inspection and supervision of its training would be shifted from CONAC to the gaining major air commands. The board cautioned that:

> . . . these proposals can succeed only if the highest Air Force officials insist that the Air Staff and the major air commands conscientiously and understandingly accept their responsibility for imaginative, objective, and enlightened guidance of the reserve forces.[65]

The review group had good reason to insert this caveat. The NGB had urged adoption of a similar approach to reserve forces management beginning in 1954, but ADC and Air Force Headquarters had strongly resisted the proposal. An Air Staff proposal along those lines had gone nowhere in 1957. In that instance, the proposal was quietly shelved when the major air commands failed to concur with it. For the most part, the major air commands had not been eager during the 1950s to take full responsibility for training and inspecting the air reserve forces.[66]

Some of the review group's proposals were quite controversial. CONAC, naturally enough, was opposed to being eliminated. It had a powerful ally in the Reserve Officers' Association (ROA). The ROA, which had played a pivotal role in sponsoring the Armed Forces Reserve Act of 1952 and the Reserve Forces Act of 1955, had emerged as an effective champion of the federal components of the reserve forces during the 1950s. The Reserve Officers' Association publicly opposed the Air Force's gaining command concept of reserve forces managment, erroneously citing the 1945–50 period as an experiment of that sort which had failed. ROA believed that the interests and preparedness of reserve components would be best served by continuation of CONAC, a major air command primarily concerned with their training. However, the Air Force Association and the National Guard Association endorsed the proposal. The Air Staff, which had conducted its own study of the air reserve components concurrently with that of General Smith's review group, continued to mull over various proposals through January 1960. A special meeting of the Air Staff's Reserve Forces Policy Committee was called in late January to advise on the merits of the review group's report, primarily its suggested changes in reserve forces management. However, the policy committee could not agree on the merits of the proposed new concept of reserve forces management. It recommended return of the review group's report to the Air Staff for further study. The Secretary of the Air Force disregarded this advice and approved the gaining command concept and a proposed reserve force structure on February 2, 1960. Two days later, General White, the Chief of Staff, added his formal approval.[67]

The plan, originally announced to the press on February 6, differed significantly from the original recommendations of the Reserve Forces Review Group. CONAC was not eliminated. It would continue to be responsible for the logistic, administrative, and budgetary support of the Air Force Reserve. CONAC would also continue to administer training programs for Air Force Reservists who served as individual mobilization augmentees rather than members of organized units. Minor modifications of the plan were made in light of comments received by Air Force Headquarters. The Chief of Staff approved the plan in its final form on May 17, 1960. The essential feature of the gaining command concept remained intact. The major air commands would assume, effective July 1, 1960, responsibility for inspecting and supervising the training of all Air Guard units assigned to them in contingency plans. They would also exercise the same functions with respect to Air Force Reserve units. Henceforth, the commanders of the major air commands would be directly accountable for the training and operational performance of those reserve units assigned to them. The training and management of reserve units would be organized on a functional basis similar to that long enjoyed by active Air Force units.[68]

The Air Guard retained its basic twenty-four wing flying unit structure. However, there were some significant changes in its aircraft inventory and missions. Six wings, three each from the air defense and tactical fighter forces, were converted to the long range transport mission. They were reequipped with C–97 aircraft and assigned to support Military Air Transport Service (MATS). The C–97 was the first four-engine, prop-driven aircraft operated by the air reserve forces. Further aircraft modernization was also scheduled. Both Congress and the Reserve Program Review Group had been highly critical of the obsolescence of the Air Guard's aircraft. Century series fighters had been introduced in only three squadrons by May 1960, but the National Guard Bureau had plans to convert additional fighter units to F–100s, F–104s, and F–102s during fiscal year 1961. The pace of conversions to more modern aircraft accelerated considerably with the deactivation of ten of the Tactical Air Command's forty-five tactical flying wings during fiscal year 1959. Fifty-five Air Guard flying squadrons underwent these conversions between July 1, 1959, and June 30, 1961. By the latter date, the Air Guard had 2,000 aircraft, all of them jets except for a limited number of support aircraft and transports flown by the twenty-six squadrons participating in non-tactical missions.[69]

The Air Guard's entry into the long range air transport field illustrated some of the most significant factors that have shaped its force structure and missions. According to General Wilson:

> We had six air defense units that we didn't have any missions for. . . . And, all at once, I saw where they were disbanding or modernizing the active Air Force. They were putting forty-eight C–97s into the boneyard. Well, I started a paper to convert six fighter-

interceptor squadrons to transports. . . . The Air Force turned it down . . . Mendell
Rivers found out about it . . . and directed that the Air Force keep the C–97s in the
inventory. . . . I put in my paper through the Air Staff and it got a non-concurrence.[70]

General Wilson explained that the Air Staff had argued that air guardsmen,
drawn from various occupations and training only one weekend each month, could
not be formed into effective teams to maintain and fly complex, multi-engined
aircraft like the C–97s. Secretary of the Air Force Douglas overruled the Air Staff
and authorized transfer of the transports to the Air Guard after reading Wilson's
paper and discussing the issue with him personally.[71]

The Air Guard still had to overcome ingrained professional skepticism in the
late fifties. This skepticism largely ignored the enormous skill and experience of
the cadre of ex-Air Force flyers and maintenance personnel who constituted the
heart of the Air Guard program. These individuals could maintain advanced levels
of military proficiency on a part-time basis. The C–97 episode illustrated the fact
that the Air Guard continued to rely upon its political influence and the availability
of surplus or obsolescent Air Force aircraft to modernize its flying inventory.
These factors, more than any other, molded the Air Guard's force structure and
missions through the fifties. In one form or another, they had dominated the shape
of National Guard aviation since 1920. Although legitimate military uses could
almost always be found for aircraft made available by this process, it imposed

A formation of Texas ANG F–102 Delta Daggers flies over Kelly AFB and Lackland AFB,
Texas.

substantial limitations upon the mission assignments and operational potential of Air Guard flying units.

Adoption of the gaining command concept in 1960 marked the beginning of the Air Guard's integration into the Air Force's operational structure on an across-the-board basis. It also signaled the beginning of broad-gauged Air Guard support of the Air Force's peacetime functions which the air defense alert program had foreshadowed and the Stone Board had explicitly recommended. These developments contributed significantly to upgrading the operational readiness of Air Guard units by providing Air Force commanders with direct personal incentives to enhance their performance. Air Guard leaders, anticipating diminished future requirements for manned fighter aircraft, had encouraged these developments throughout the late 1950s by pushing for a diversification of the Air Guard's missions, greater peacetime support of the Air Force, and elimination of its ties with CONAC. They correctly foresaw that diversification would make the Air Guard far less vulnerable to future program shifts.[72]

Significant changes in the Air Guard-Air Force relationship were soon evident with the adoption of the gaining command concept. Closer ties between the Tactical Air Command and the thirty-six Air Guard flying squadrons assigned to it in 1960 led to their frequent use in firepower demonstrations and reconnaissance missions. They also began actively participating in joint Army-Air Force exercises. Although the Air Guard's air defense mission was downgraded in terms of total numbers, the quality of its participation improved. By June 1960, its fighter-interceptor force had shrunk to forty squadrons, down considerably from the unwieldy force of sixty-nine squadrons assigned to ADC in 1958. This slimmed down force had, on the whole, much better equipment than its larger predecessor. Prompted by reduced estimates of the Soviet bomber threat and the increased availability of all-weather interceptors, six Air Guard fighter-interceptor squadrons had expanded their alert program participation from fourteen to twenty-four hours a day in mid–1959. Two years later, twenty-five Air Guard fighter-interceptor squadrons were participating in the alert program on this around-the-clock basis. Nine of these squadrons, flying F–89J interceptors, were equipped with nuclear rockets in 1961 and 1962. Three squadrons actually stood alert with the rockets by late 1962. General Atkinson, ADC's Commander, was much happier with the closer supervision of Guard squadrons his command had acquired in July 1960. He emphasized that Air Guard squadrons should, so far as possible, be trained to the same level of proficiency as their regular Air Force counterparts.[73]

The Air Guard had enjoyed a period of enormous growth, modernization, and increasing intergration with the active duty Air Force establishment from 1953 through 1960. By the latter date, its personnel strength had reached 71,000, well above the 35,556 reported in June 1953 as the Air Guard began to rebuild following its participation in the Korean War. Its technician complement had been expanded to 13,200 to handle the increasingly sophisticated technology its units were called upon to operate. The Air Guard budget had more than doubled since Fiscal Year 1953. Total obligations during Fiscal Year 1960 stood at some $232.61 million. This represented only 1.3 percent of the total Air Force budget for that year. The Air Guard's share of the total Air Force budget had remained fairly constant during this period, ranging from 1.1 to 1.4 percent of the total obligations each fiscal year.

The total number of Air Guard flying squadrons had been expanded to ninety-two by 1960, an increase of eight over its pre-Korean War level. The missions of these squadrons, although predominantly oriented toward air defense during much of the 1950s, had been enormously diversified. By 1960, air guardsmen were participating in tactical fighter and reconnaissance, air transport and aeromedical evacuation, as well as air defense missions. Their aircraft inventory, although still dependent on the fallout of excess or obsolescent aircraft from the active Air Force inventory, had been substantially improved. Their F–51s and B–26s had been replaced by F–84s, F–89s, F–100s, F–104s, and C–97s. Although still manned and equipped on a training basis, they possessed limited operational capabilities that had been conspicuously absent in 1950. In effect, integration of the Air Guard's training with the daily operations of the Air Force and the concomitant emphasis upon air reserve forces' peacetime support of a broad range of active force missions, marked the beginning of what later became known as the total force policy.

The Air Guard and the Air Force had gradually evolved a productive working relationship. For political and budgetary as well as military reasons, the Air Force had tacitly agreed to ignore the Air Guard's anomolous state status. Federalization was no longer a live issue. The contentious bickering over command authority that had troubled Air Guard-Air Force relations prior to the Korean War was almost entirely absent. Top Air Force leaders, encouraged by the Eisenhower administration's initial enthusiasm for stronger reserve forces and comforted by the lion's share of defense budgets under the "new look," grudgingly accepted the pragmatic necessity of building a strong Air Guard program.

The Air Guard, led by officers who recognized that their organization's future ultimately depended upon its development of high level operational capabilities, proved to be extremely responsive to Air Force direction. Organizational, training, and operational readiness requirements were standardized in accordance with the directives of Air Force commanders. Air guardsmen achieved an effective voice in the development of policies, plans, and programs related to their particular reserve component at the Air Staff and major air command levels. In this context, arguments over formal command jurisdiction were far less compelling than they had been in the late 1940s. The Air Force achieved the objectives of command authority because of the willingness of the Air Guard leadership to accept increased federal control and supervision of training. Guardsmen had done this to achieve the improved operational performance that would, in their view, help guarantee the Air

Guard's future as an Air Force reserve component with a distinctive state character. They had exchanged a measure of state autonomy for higher levels of federal support and closer integration with the active Air Force to insure their own survival. The growing mutual accommodation between the Air Force and the Air Guard transformed the Guard into a viable component of the active duty establishment between 1953 and 1960.

Chapter V

The Cold Warriors, 1961–1962

John F. Kennedy's inauguration as President in January 1961 signaled the beginning of a fundamental shift in U.S. national security policies. The new President was committed to an activist foreign policy backed by usable conventional military power. Although he accelerated the deployment of land and sea-based intercontinental ballistic missiles, Kennedy considered the Eisenhower administration's emphasis on nuclear forces dangerous and ineffective. His emphasis on nonnuclear military forces, taken in conjunction with the increasingly close integration of the active Air Force and its reserve components under the gaining command concept, eventually transformed the Air Guard into a highly proficient element of the total force.

Before these programs could be fully implemented, however, the Air Guard was tested in a new role. Between October 1961 and August 1962, nearly thirty-three percent of its strength was mobilized to help serve as a diplomatic counterweight to Soviet efforts to eject the western powers from Berlin. Part-time airmen became full-fledged cold warriors. Nearly three hundred Air Guard aircraft were sent to Europe in the autumn of 1961. However, their success was limited and the product of brilliant improvisation rather than sound reserve forces policy and planning. The Berlin mobilization revealed many shortcomings in the Air Force's reserve programs. Air Guard tactical units deployed to Europe displayed limited operational capabilities and required extensive active force support. Their shortcomings were a product of Defense Department-imposed manpower and equipment limitations as well as faulty Air Force planning. Although the Air Guard was able to perform far more impressively in 1961 than it had done ten years earlier during the initial Korean War mobilizations, the Berlin Crisis showed that its tactical units were still not M–Day forces. They had been manned, organized, and equipped for training rather than immediate operational roles. The Air Force lacked concepts and well-developed plans for using reserve units in situations short of a general war. Problems associated with the Air Guard's performance during the

122

Berlin mobilization resulted in changes that rectified many of the planning and management deficiencies. Resource deficiencies, however, continued to be a major barrier until Secretary of Defense Robert S. McNamara moved to create a selected strategic reserve force in 1965.

President Kennedy and Secretary of Defense McNamara were concerned by America's heavy reliance on nuclear weapons. The massive retaliation doctrine had long been under attack by certain Army officers and influential civilian intellectuals who specialized in national security issues. Essentially these critics, including retired Gen. Maxwell D. Taylor and Dr. Henry A. Kissinger, argued that massive retaliation was a dangerous doctrine that stripped the U.S. of usable military power in most of the conflict situations it was likely to face. During the Eisenhower administration, the nation's conventional ground, naval, and air forces had been allowed to atrophy. The bulk of Eisenhower's defense budgets had gone to the strategic retaliatory and continental air defense forces as well as into research and the development of new weapons. However, several international crises, including Suez, Taiwan Straits, and Berlin, had demonstrated that the U.S. could not use its nuclear-armed, strategic retaliatory forces to meet low-level challenges to its security interests. Furthermore, America's allies lacked both the will and the ability to fill the gap in conventional military forces that Eisenhower's emphasis on massive retaliation had created. The Soviets were beginning to develop a formidable strategic nuclear force of their own. Consequently, when President Kennedy took office in 1961, he believed that he faced an increasingly unpalatable choice between nuclear war or inactivity in future international crises.[1]

The Kennedy administration moved rapidly to rectify what it perceived as dangerous shortcomings in its predecessor's security policies. Defense spending grew significantly. Total Department of Defense obligations under Kennedy's fiscal year 1962 budget were $51.5 billion, an increase of over $9.1 billion above the Eisenhower administration's fiscal year 1960 defense obligations.[2] Although existing strategic weapons programs such as Polaris and Minuteman were accelerated, much of this increase was devoted to upgrading the strength and readiness of America's conventional military forces.[3] The President signaled his determination to rebuild the nation's conventional military forces in his first special defense message to Congress. In the message, delivered on March 28, 1961, he declared:

> Our defense posture must be both flexible and determined. Any potential aggressor contemplating an attack on any part of the free world with any kind of weapons, conventional or nuclear, must know that our response will be suitable, swift and effective.[4]

Kennedy was calling for creation of a broad spectrum of military power that could be used in situations short of a nuclear confrontation.

The Kennedy administration's approach to national security came to be known as the doctrine of flexible response. It sought to reduce the threshold of nuclear war and restore the link between diplomacy and military power. Individual situations could be met with a specifically tailored combination of diplomacy and military force rather than with dangerous threats of massive nuclear retaliation. The President intended to reinvigorate American foreign policy. Conventional military power became one of his prime instruments for achieving that objective.

(Below) President Kennedy visiting Det. 1, 152d Tactical Control Group, Roslyn Air National Guard Station, Roslyn, N.Y. The Commander-in-Chief favored a buildup of conventional forces. Secretary of Defense Robert S. McNamara (left) shared the President's objection to relying on nuclear forces for national defense.

Underscoring this emphasis upon the creation of strong non-nuclear forces, Kennedy called General Maxwell Taylor, retired Army Chief of Staff and critic of the Eisenhower administration's security policies, into the government as his military adviser.[5]

The Kennedy administration also launched a crash study of the armed forces' reserve components. Assistant Secretary of Defense Carlisle P. Runge was placed in charge of the Reserve Forces Task Force that had been directed to complete this study by April 1, 1961. The Runge group inherited a Defense Department/Joint Chiefs of Staff study of the reserves launched during the last year of the Eisenhower administration. By 1961, that administration's initial enthusiasm for the reserves had cooled considerably. The President's budget request for Fiscal Year 1961 had called for a ten percent reduction in the Army's reserve components. National Guard Association and Reserve Officers' Association officials were alarmed by a published report that Runge's group was considering a more extensive role for the reserves in civil defense while downgrading their combat functions. They also feared that it might be sympathetic to the Eisenhower budget proposals. The House Appropriations Committee began questioning Defense Department and reserve association officials in executive session about the Kennedy administration's plans for the reserve forces. In late March 1961, the National Guard and Reserve Officers' Association publicly called upon Congress to block the proposed cuts in the Army's reserve components carried over from the Eisenhower administration. This pressure achieved its objectives. The Eisenhower proposals were quietly shelved. Although the Runge report was never released to the public, the Pentagon announced in June 1961 that the Army's reserve components were to be bolstered as part of the Kennedy administration's highly touted efforts to strengthen America's limited war capabilities. Earlier, the Department of Defense had revealed that all reserve forces would be maintained at levels previously established by Congress for fiscal year 1961.[6]

With its mix of fighters and transports, the Air Guard was potentially well-suited to the new emphasis upon conventional military forces. When President Kennedy took office in 1961, the Air Guard's personnel strength was just under 71,000. Its flying organizations included thirty-two interceptor, twenty-two tactical fighter, twelve tactical reconnaissance, sixteen transport, and ten aeromedical evacuation squadrons. These units were supplemented by various technical and support organizations. Twenty-one Air Guard interceptor squadrons continued to participate successfully in the air defense runway alert program. Other units supported TAC and the Army in various exercises.[7] Although still seriously handicapped by obsolescent aircraft, shortages of spare parts, and Department of Defense personnel ceilings, Air Guard units had benefited from closer ties with the active Air Force following adoption of the gaining command concept of air reserve forces management in July 1960. The Tactical Air Command's official history for January–June 1961 reported that ". . . in general it may be said that their [i.e., the

Air Guard's] readiness was high— of thirty-eight ANG units [reported in a May 1961 summary] thirty-five had maintained C–1 or C–2 ratings [i.e., fully or nearly fully combat ready]."[8] The Defense Department's annual report for fiscal year 1961 noted that approximately sixty-six percent of all the Air Guard's flying units were rated combat-ready.[9] Although these estimates of the Air Guard's operational capabilities in mid–1961 were greatly exaggerated, they suggested that the Air Guard could play a valuable role in the Kennedy administration's flexible reponse doctrine.

Before the Kennedy administration could implement its buildup of conventional active-duty and reserve forces, the Soviet Union mounted a major diplomatic challenge in Europe. Premier Nikita Khrushchev renewed the Soviet campaign to force the western powers out of Berlin. At a June 1961 summit meeting with President Kennedy in Vienna, Khrushchev presented a fresh statement of Soviet proposals on Germany and Berlin. He demanded the speedy conclusion of a German peace treaty and conversion of West Berlin into a so-called "free city" with the termination of western access rights. If the western powers failed to comply, Khrushchev threatened to sign a separate peace treaty with the German Democratic Republic that would cancel all existing western rights in Berlin. He raised the possibility of war if the western powers sought to interfere with any unilateral Soviet settlement of the German question. Shortly after the Vienna summit the Soviet Premier set a year-end deadline for compliance with those demands.[10]

The Kennedy administration had begun to consider its Berlin policy shortly after taking office. In March, the President had asked former Secretary of State Dean Acheson to examine the problems of NATO and Germany. Secretary of Defense McNamara had reviewed existing Berlin contingency plans. Early in May, McNamara informed the White House that those plans assumed an almost immediate resort to nuclear war. The President expressed dissatisfaction with the state of planning at a July 8 meeting with his top aides. He directed Secretary McNamara to produce a plan that would permit conventional military resistance strong enough to convey American determination to stay in Berlin while encouraging the Soviets to negotiate. On the diplomatic side, he asked Acheson, who was advocating a military confrontation with the Soviet Union, to develop a political program for Berlin. Secretary of State Dean Rusk was instructed to develop a negotiating prospectus. The Defense and State Department papers outlining these options were due at the White House within ten days. Meanwhile, a fierce debate between hardliners and moderates on the Berlin issue raged within the Kennedy administration.[11]

The President spent most of July struggling through the debate to reach his own conclusions. On the evening of July 25, he presented his Berlin plan to the American people in a televised speech. "We cannot and will not permit the communists," Kennedy said, "to drive us out of Berlin, either gradually or by force."[12] Rejecting the idea of an immediate military confrontation with its high probability of nuclear war, he announced an American military buildup coupled with a renewed offer to negotiate the larger German question. The military buildup included a request for an additional $3.25 billion for the defense budget and enlargement of the civil defense program. Approximately $1.8 billion of the requested defense budget increase would be spent on conventional weapons and equipment. Draft calls were to be doubled and tripled. The Air Force delayed deactivation of B–47 bombers. The President further requested authority to mobilize certain Reserve and National Guard units.[13] He and McNamara had decided at least as early as July 19 to mobilize twenty-nine Air National Guard flying squadrons.[14] This military program supplemented the $3.4 billion increase in U.S. defense expenditures requested on May 25.[15] These moves gave substance to Kennedy's firm stand on Berlin and his determination to strengthen America's conventional military capabilities.

The administration moved quickly to implement its announced conventional military buildup. On the day following the President's speech, Secretary McNamara asked Congress for Presidential authority to order up to 250,000 ready reservists to active duty for no more than one year without a declaration of national emergency. Congress obliged. Six days later it enacted Public Law 87–117 and approved the administration's request to expand the defense budget.[16]

On August 1, the National Guard Bureau implemented procedures to mobilize national guardsmen. All discharges from the National Guard were frozen and units were urged to recruit to full manning. General Wilson, Deputy Chief of the National Guard Bureau, advised the governors that virtually all of the Air Guard's tactical fighter units and two of its tactical reconnaissance wings would be mobilized on October 1. He authorized designated priority units to increase their monthly flying hours by twenty-five hours per aircrew and to hire additional fulltime aircraft maintenance and administrative technicians on a temporary basis.[17]

An increased sense of urgency was imparted to these preparations when the Soviets escalated the Berlin Crisis on August 13. A few minutes after midnight on that date, the East Germans installed roadblocks and barbed-wire barricades between the two halves of the city. Four days later, they began construction of the Berlin Wall. The implications of these actions were not clear at the time. Some American officials feared that the wall might be part of a Soviet master plan to drive the Western powers out of Berlin. Remarking that there was now one chance in five of a nuclear war, Kennedy mobilized the decisionmaking resources of his administration. The special Berlin Task Force went into continuous session. It concluded that an accelerated American military buildup would be the most effective response to the latest Soviet challenge. The task force also drafted a formal diplomatic protest to Moscow. Increasingly sensitive to the need for more concrete American actions, the President decided to send Vice President Lyndon B.

Johnson to West Berlin. He also ordered 1,500 Army troops to move from West Germany via the autobahn to Berlin. On August 30, the President appointed Lt. Gen. Lucius Clay as his personal representative to the city. Clay was still remembered from the early days of the Cold War as the great symbol of western determination to stay in Berlin. The President also ordered some 148,000 reservists to active duty under Public Law 87–117. The Army mobilized 113,000, the Air Force 27,000 and the Navy 8,000.[18]

The Air Guard's performance during the 1961–62 Berlin Crisis was justifiably hailed as a success. The number of air guardsmen mobilized was 21,067. The Department of Defense's annual screening of ready reservists, instituted during the mid–1950s, worked well. Less than one percent of the mobilized guardsmen were lost for personal hardship or other reasons; Korea had seen a loss rate of up to ten percent. The bulk of the individuals mobilized during the Berlin crisis reported for active duty with their units on October 1. Units mobilized on that date included eighteen tactical fighter squadrons, four tactical reconnaissance squadrons, six air transport squadrons, and one tactical control group. On November 1, three more fighter squadrons were mobilized. Selected units were notified on October 9 to prepare for overseas movement about November 1. In late October and early November, eight fighter squadrons deployed overseas. They flew 216 aircraft to various bases in Europe without a single accident. Additional units, including three squadrons of F–104s and their sixty aircraft, were airlifted to Europe in late November. All of these units were in place overseas within one month of their respective mobilization days; Korean mobilization and overseas deployment had taken at least seven months. Air Guard fighter squadrons retained in the U.S. on active duty were prepared to go to Europe in a second wave when needed.[19]

The Air Guard's deployment to Europe, Operation Stair Step, was publicly praised as a great success.[20] The U.S. commander in Europe, Gen. Lauris Norstad, lauded the ". . . outstanding performance of the Air National Guard squadrons in crossing the Atlantic and taking over their bases in Germany and France and then participating almost immediately in defense tasks. . . ."[21] General LeMay praised ". . . the magnificent showing of the [Air] Reserve Forces in the face of the current threat. . . . These units [i.e., federalized Air National Guard squadrons] are generally ready. They can fight. They can be depended upon."[22] Secretary of the Air Force Eugene M. Zuckert declared that "the response to Berlin reemphasized the importance of our Reserve Forces. It put new factual evidence behind our belief in the need for and the effectiveness of our Air Reserve Forces Program."[23] Secretary of Defense McNamara, emphasizing the fundamental significance of the Berlin recall, told Congress that "I don't believe there is any action that has been taken that more clearly demonstrated the strength, the will, and the firmness of purpose than the call-up of these [reserve] units."[24]

Public praise aside, the Berlin mobilization revealed a host of problems within the Air Force and its reserve programs. Many of these problems stemmed

TSgt. Buck Slee of the 112th Tactical Fighter Squadron, Ohio ANG, prepares his aircraft for deployment overseas during the Berlin Crisis.

As a response to the Berlin Crisis, the 157th Fighter-Interceptor Squadron, South Carolina ANG, left for Moron AB, Spain on Nov. 10, 1961. Here, Military Air Transportation Service loadmasters guide a F–104 Starfighter up the loading ramp of a C–124 Globemaster.

General Lauris Norstad on his return to the states and retirement as Commander, Supreme Headquarters Allied Powers, Europe.

from the fact that the U.S. was not prepared to fight a conventional war in Europe. Secretary McNamara's review of Berlin contingency plans in May 1961 had revealed that they were virtually all predicated on the early use of nuclear weapons. The Air Force lacked an adequate supply of consumable items that could sustain conventional combat operations for any length of time. The gaining command concept of reserve forces management notwithstanding, the Air Guard was still a doctrinal orphan in the nuclear and space-oriented Air Force. The Air Force lacked the concepts, plans, and spare parts to rapidly integrate Air Guard units into its daily operations in a situation short of general war. Consequently, an enormous amount of post mobilization planning, reorganization, retraining, and resupply was required before Air Guard units could fully participate in European operations.[25]

The shortcomings of the Air Guard program had become evident in August after the state governors were notified that some of their units might be mobilized. In 1957, Air Guard squadrons had been limited to eighty-three percent of their authorized organizational strength by the Department of Defense. The resulting manpower shortages were overcome by mobilizing approximately 3,000 individual Air Force reservists and assigning them to Air Guard units. However, many of these individual fillers provided little help. Either they lacked the skills attributed to

Secretary of the Air Force Eugene M. Zuckert and General Curtis LeMay. Both leaders praised the performance of the Air Reserve Forces during the Berlin Crisis.

them in the Air Force personnel records or they arrived too late to fulfill the requirements established by continually changing Air Force personnel manning documents. These manning documents were a major source of difficulty. In an effort to adjust Air Guard unit structures to European theater requirements, no fewer than six different manning documents were presented by the Air Force after the Air Guard units had received their tentative mobilization alert notification on August 1. Consequently extensive post mobilization training of personnel was required. One official Air Force history estimated that these extensive reorganizations placed almost thirty percent of the airmen in some Stair Step units in positions for which they had not been trained. The last change in unit manning documents was imposed less than two weeks prior to overseas deployment. Complicating matters further, the headquarters of all but one of the Air Guard wings deployed overseas were split between the U.S. and Europe. This ad hoc split-wing organization was adopted so that the units sent overseas could function independently while awaiting the planned follow-on deployment of the remainder of their respective wing organizations. However well intentioned, the split-wing organizational format diluted the experienced leadership of individual Air Guard units by dividing them between the U.S. and Europe.[26]

Air Guard mobilization planning had envisaged moving mobilized units to the Air Force's main operating bases where extensive active force support would be available. However, they actually were sent to inactive dispersed operating bases in France that were far from ready to receive them. Upon arrival at these bases, Air Force and Air Guard personnel had to devote considerable time and energy to make them livable, while considerable construction and repair activity was required to adapt the facilities, designed to support World War II aircraft, to jet fighter operations. The extra pressures of extensive base renovations and intensive preparations to assume European alert commitments initially caused serious morale problems.[27]

It soon became evident that Air Guard units had not been adequately equipped for sustained combat operations prior to mobilization. Unit equipment authorizations did not meet the Tactical Air Command's requirements. Air Guard units had only been authorized seventy percent of the equipment needed for full time operations. Aircraft had to be modified to carry Tactical Air Navigation (TACAN), radio air navigation system, and racks for 750–pound bombs. Tactical flying squadrons lacked adequate flyaway kits, portable collections of spare parts and tools needed to keep their aircraft operational for thirty days without outside support. Air Guard fighter squadrons only had rudimentary kits for aging F–84Fs and F–86Fs. The Air Force in Europe was not flying these aircraft and did not maintain stockpiles of spare parts for them. Consequently, spare parts shortages became a crucial problem for Air Guard units in Europe once they began flying their aircraft on a sustained basis. Due to these shortages, units were sometimes unable to maintain a high percentage of their aircraft in an operationally ready status. For example, the Air Guard's 102d Tactical Fighter Wing noted in a news release that "as a direct result of this situation [i.e., the spare parts shortage], the wing found itself unable to maintain its operational readiness [i.e., seventy percent in-commission rate required] during several of the most important days of the Berlin crisis."[28] The most serious problems in this regard were encountered by the three F–104 squadrons which were airlifted to Europe in November. These aircraft were repeatedly grounded for maintenance or air safety reasons during the first six months of 1962.[29]

Although Air Guard pilots were generally rated as excellent individual aviators, their flying training programs had not prepared them for a transatlantic deployment. Most had only been trained for short overland flights and had never practiced aerial refueling. Few had ever flown in survival suits. Consequently, the Air Force instituted a crash program of intensive advanced flight training. Air Guard pilots flew long-range missions and practiced crash landing procedures for ice caps, fjords, and the sea. They also began to acquire the rudiments of aerial refueling skills. A substantial amount of retraining for conventional weapons delivery was also required once Air Guard units arrived in Europe.[30] The Air Force had planned to send the air guardsmen overseas as a conventional weapons augmentation force that would free regular Air Force tactical fighter squadrons for nuclear strike roles. Yet, according to an official 17th Air Force history, "all of the Stair Step units had been trained for a nuclear mission; therefore, considerable training was necessary to prepare them for a conventional role."[31]

Initially, Stair Step called for mobilizing six tactical fighter wings and one tactical reconnaissance wing on October 1. All of these units, including their twenty-eight tactical flying squadrons, were originally scheduled to be sent to Europe on December 1. Air Force Headquarters, however, set the launch date ahead to November 1. The deployment force itself was changed to include five tactical fighter wing headquarters with seven fighter squadrons, one tactical reconnaissance wing headquarters with one reconnaissance squadron, one tactical control group with two aircraft control and warning squadrons, and three fighter-interceptor squadrons. A follow-on force, of one tactical fighter wing and fourteen tactical squadrons was retained in the United States. While all of these Air Guard units were being prepared, the Tactical Air Command augmented United States Air Forces in Europe (USAFE) with eight regular Air Force fighter squadrons possessing 144 aircraft. These squadrons were dispatched to Europe in mid-September ostensibly to participate in NATO Exercise Check Mate. They were scheduled to return to the United States once the Air Guard units arrived in Europe.[32]

Despite the difficulties encountered in preparing the mobilized Air Guard units for Europe, Operation Stair Step was an outstanding success. Small advanced echelons of air guardsmen were sent to USAFE bases in mid-October to gather food, supplies, and equipment for the units in Europe. Beginning on October 29, nearly 10,000 Air Guard ground support and administrative personnel as well as tons of supplies were airlifted to Europe by the Military Air Transport Service. A steady stream of transports completed this operation within forty-eight hours. Air Guard combat aircrews and their aircraft departed their home bases on October 27. Eight squadrons with 216 jet fighters, reconnaissance aircraft, and trainers assembled at McGuire AFB, New Jersey, and Loring AFB, Maine. Their move across the North Atlantic would be the largest single jet fighter deployment in U.S. Air Force history.[33]

F–86H fighters and T–33 trainers were assembled at Loring AFB, Maine. They would island-hop to Europe via Newfoundland, Greenland, Iceland, and Scotland. Brig. Gen. Charles W. Sweeney of the Massachusetts Air Guard personally led them. The F–84s and RF–84s assembled at McGuire AFB, New Jersey. Brig. Gen. Donald J. Strait, New Jersey Air Guard, led them on a more southerly route to Europe. They stopped at Newfoundland, the Azores, and Spain.[34]

The ocean crossing was originally scheduled to begin November 1. However, because of good weather, the F–86Hs at Loring AFB left two days early. The T–33s followed on November 1. The F–84Fs and RF–84s left McGuire AFB on schedule. The deployment was conducted during daylight hours only. Each squadron flew in formations of four aircraft, launched at fifteen minute intervals. The pilots

In Operation Stair Step, tactical fighter units were deployed overseas in order to bolster U.S. military strength in Europe. (Above, left) F–84s of the Ohio ANG over Etain AB, France, 1962. (Above, right) Among the cargo airlifted to France, a portable ground power unit is secured aboard a Douglas C–124 by a member of the 102nd Tactical Fighter Group, Massachusetts ANG. (Below) Brig. Gen. Donald J. Strait, Commander, 108th Fighter-Bomber Wing, (center) gives flight information to the ramp control officer at Lajes Field. The New Jersey unit stopped at the Azores enroute to France.

(Above) An F–86 of the 102d TFG undergoes an engine check at Prestwick Air Base, Scotland before taking off for the final leg of the journey to France. The fighters island-hopped across the Atlantic, stopping for servicing and maintenance at bases in Newfoundland, Greenland, Iceland, Scotland, the Azores, and Spain. (Right) Col. S. T. Maron, Commander of the 131st Tactical Fighter Wing, Missouri ANG, climbs out of his F–84 aircraft. The wing was activated and sent to France during Stair Step. (Below) An aerial view of the air-sea rescue landing ramp at Prestwick AB, lifeline for Stair Step pilots.

rested overnight while their aircraft were repaired and refueled. Stair Step aircraft began arriving at their assigned bases in Europe on November 2. The entire deployment was completed by November 17, two weeks ahead of the original schedule, without an accident or the loss of a single aircraft.[35]

There was considerable anxiety about the dangers associated with Stair Step within the Air Force's top military leadership. The North Atlantic crossing was considered extremely dangerous for the limited range day fighters flown by the air guardsmen. To minimize some of the risks, an impressive array of units was deployed to support the Air Guard pilots. C–54 "Duckbut" aircraft with radar monitored their flight. The Strategic Air Command supplied KC–135 tankers. These aircraft were primarily used as communication relay stations rather than as aerial refueling platforms. Coast Guard vessels and freighters were strung out beneath the flight routes to conduct rescue operations if needed. They were augmented by 10 aircraft and approximately 100 men from five Air Force Reserve air rescue squdrons who had volunteered for active duty to support Stair Step.[36]

The Commander of the Tactical Air Command, Gen. Walter C. Sweeney, monitored the deployment from his flying command post over the North Atlantic. General LeMay, Air Force Chief of Staff, also closely followed the operation. Piloting his own transport, LeMay visited every airfield used during the critical ocean crossing period. Afterwards he congratulated the Air Guard ". . . for the outstanding manner in which this difficult and important task was accomplished."[37]

Following Stair Step's completion, Air Guard flying units were stationed at five dispersed operating bases and one main operating base in France. The dispersed bases were generally in poor condition when advanced parties of air guardsmen began arriving in mid-October. Guardsmen had to repair barracks as well as administrative and maintenance facilities. Electrical power systems, which had been installed to support the flight operations of propeller- driven aircraft, were inadequate to handle jets. They had to be augmented. Munitions storage facilities had to be constructed. It took an enormous amount of work to make the dispersed bases operational.[38]

The 152d Tactical Control Group from New York went to Europe as part of Stair Step. Its primary mission was to provide radar control for USAFE aircraft on tactical offensive missions. The main body of the 152d personnel was flown to Germany between November 7 and 12. The bulk of its equipment was not airlifted to the continent until the beginning of December. It units achieved limited success in their efforts to become operational by year's end; only four of its six aircraft control and warning squadrons were close to being operational by December 31.[39]

Stair Step forces were augmented by three more Air Guard fighter squadrons in November. Beginning on November 10, sixty Air Guard F–104s from three squadrons were airlifted to Ramstein Air Base, Germany and Moron Air Base, Spain by giant C–124s from the Military Air Transport Service. The project was named Operation Brass Ring.[40] The F–104 squadrons had experienced a dramatic transition since their recall to active duty on November 1. Prior to that date, they had been fighter-interceptor squadrons participating in ADC's runway alert program. They were, however, mobilized as tactical fighter squadrons and assigned to the Tactical Air Command. This had required extensive organizational realignments within the three units on a crash basis. Although their aircraft were repeatedly grounded for maintenance or safety reasons during the first six months of 1962, these units stood their European theater alert requirements successfully from December 19, 1961 on.[41]

Stair Step forces were sent to USAFE under unilateral U.S. and tripartite contingency plans rather than NATO agreements. The U.S. wanted to avoid commitment of these forces to NATO so they could be withdrawn from Europe as the situation permitted with a minimum of political and military complications. USAFE mission concepts for Air Guard forces included conventional interdiction strikes, counter air operations, and on-call close air support for the Army in the event of a general war. They were also assigned missions within Berlin corridor access contingency plans. All tactical fighter squadrons were standing alert by December 31. Some of them had assumed alert status in November.[42]

The Air Force found that the Air Guard units sent to Europe had extremely limited operational capabilities. The 17th Air Force observed that "as the Stair Step units began to arrive, it appeared that they were not manned, trained, or equipped to assume full base operational and maintenance responsibilities."[43] Initial tactical evaluations of the Stair Step fighter wings were begun by USAFE prior to the end of 1961. Only the 7108th and 7122d Wings were rated satisfactory. Tests indicated that the 102d, 7121st, and 7131st Wings could not carry out their missions under wartime conditions. Their pilots were acceptable, but wing combat operations centers, premission briefings, ordnance handling, and aircraft turn-around times showed serious weaknesses. Nor could these wings sustain launch sequence rates called for in exercise plans. After additional command guidance and assistance, USAFE tactical evaluations rated the 102d, 7121st, and 7131st Wings satisfactory early in 1962. Subsequent USAFE operational readiness inspections concluded that all these units were in satisfactory condition except the 7121st Tactical Fighter Wing and the 152d Tactical Control Group. A second tactical evaluation rated the 152d satisfactory in May 1962. The 7121st TFW's problems included poor weapons delivery skills and inadequate aircraft availability rates. A subsequent inspection yielded an unsatisfactory rating in weapons delivery. Air Guard F–104 units were not formally evaluated by USAFE.[44]

A large force of mobilized air guardsmen remained on active duty in the U.S. after Stair Step and Brass Ring were completed. Less than half of those called up had been sent to Europe. Two wings of C–97 transports joined MATS. Those Air Guard aircraft and crews flew airlift missions to Europe, the Far East, Southeast Asia, the Middle East, Africa, South America, and Alaska. They also participated in airlift exercises within the U.S. and between the U.S. and exercise locations overseas. The Stair Step follow-on force of one tactical fighter wing and fourteen tactical flying squadrons worked closely with the Tactical Air Command to enhance their operational readiness. These units participated in TAC and joint service exercises. Fighter squadrons also conducted firepower demonstrations and flew thousands of close air support missions for Army exercises. Reconnaissance squadrons flew aerial photographic missions for TAC.[45]

In the summer of 1962, Air Guard units returned to the U.S. and demobilized along with their counterparts who had remained in the states on active duty. Air guardsmen were publicly praised for their military performance and patriotic sacrifice during ten months of service, but privately the Air Force was skeptical about the military value of the Air Guard deployment to Europe. USAFE concluded that it had required a major diversion of effort and resources within the command. Because of the extensive modification and training before the Guard units attained substantial operational capability, the command's operations staff did not consider the Guard to be potentially effective in the opening stages of a general war; however, it still believed that they might be useful in limited actions. USAFE had opposed deploying the Air Guard follow-on force from the U.S. to its European bases. It had feared that the Air Guard's obsolescent aircraft would saturate the command's bases, thereby making it difficult to either disperse its own aircraft or receive superior additional regular Air Force squadrons from TAC.[46] Consequently, it recommended "that TAC regular force squadrons be deployed in any future USAFE augmentation rather than reserve forces."[47] Clearly, the Air Force in Europe had not been especially pleased with the Air Guard's performance during the Berlin Crisis.

Privately, General LeMay was even more skeptical than USAFE about the combat capabilities of the Stair Step units. Assessing the Air Guard's performance years after his retirement in 1965, the outspoken former Chief of Staff observed:

> They flew their airplanes over there [i.e., to Europe in 1961] and they could get some airplanes up in the air. How well they could pilot them is something else again. There again [they were] better than nothing. . . . But, it wasn't the kind of outfit that we should have had in the Reserves at that point. They just weren't ready. They had equipment. It was old equipment but going downhill. . . . It would fly, but whether it would do its job in combat is something else again. If its bomb racks won't work or their guns won't shoot, why it's not good . . . . If you are not fully combat equipped, and if your crews are not fully combat trained, you haven't got a combat tool. That's what I am talking about. And, they just weren't what I would call combat ready.[48]

The Berlin mobilization demonstrated that the Air Guard's equipment and manning had been designed for training, not actual combat operations. Its organizational structure had not been compatible with USAFE's requirements. Frequent changes in manning documents prior to the European deployment had created an enormous burden and reduced the effectiveness of the units involved. Splitting veteran wing staffs between the U.S. and Europe had further complicated these problems. The Defense Department's refusal to approve Air Force and National Guard Bureau requests to lift the eighty percent drill pay ceiling on Air Guard units in the years prior to the 1961 mobilization also had significantly weakened the operational potential of Air Guard units. Obsolescent aircraft and inadequate supply inventories had further diminished the Air Guard's combat potential. Air Force planners had not expected to use Air Guard squadrons in situations short of general war. Furthermore, it appears that the Air Force had anticipated having an extensive post M–Day period to bring mobilized Air Guard units up to full operational readiness. Neither the Air Force nor the Air Guard was adequately prepared to cope with a Cold War crisis like Berlin that implied the use of conventional military forces on a limited scale.[49]

Air guardsmen saw the lessons of the Berlin mobilization in a wholly different light than the regulars. For them, it had been a great success. Working closely with active duty Air Force personnel, air guardsmen, despite the problems they encountered, prepared their units quickly for a successful overseas deployment. Their 1961 mobilization performance was far superior to the Korean War mobilization debacle. Operation Stair Step itself was a brilliant testimony to the basic flying skills of Air Guard pilots. Although mobilized units had demonstrated limited operational capabilities in Europe, they did contribute to the American conventional military buildup during the Berlin Crisis. From a diplomatic perspective, their mere presence in Europe was an important display of American resolve. On the military side, their improvised deployment had demonstrated the Air Guard's potential to become a first rate combat reserve force. Furthermore, they had provided a badly-needed interim buildup of conventional military forces as they had during the Korean War. Their veteran pilots and full-time technicians were excellent. Due to the pressures of the draft, they were backed by a highly educated body of enlisted men who could provide excellent support if properly trained and utilized.

Maj. Gen. John J. Pesch typified the positive attitude of veteran air guardsmen about the lessons of the Berlin mobilization. During 1961–62, Pesch had been an Air Guard colonel assigned to the Operations Directorate of Air Force Headquarters. Following his retirement as Director of the Air Guard in February 1977, Pesch commented:

> We had F–86H units that went to Europe. They performed well [in 1961–62]. . . . We opened up some old bases in rather austere places in France. And so here again we proved we had the ability to man and operate and function from, if not a bare base, almost a bare base. It proved again what many of us knew. We could do a job and do it professionally. I think it demonstrated to the Air Force too, to the Germans, to the French and to the Spanish that we had an augmentation force that was truly a combat capable augmentation force. . . . The [Air Force] officers and airmen we came in contact with on active duty, who later got into positions of influence, were favorably impressed. You had people who saw firsthand the professionalism of Air Guard officers and airmen.[50]

As a veteran guardsman, Maj. Gen. John J. Pesch viewed the Berlin Crisis as a confirmation of the Air Guard's professionalism.

Obviously, a vast gulf separated Air Guard and Air Force assessments of the former's Berlin mobilization. The Air Guard believed that Berlin had illustrated its emerging capabilities as a combat reserve force. The regular Air Force, focusing upon the problems encountered by Stair Step and Brass Ring units, questioned the value of mobilizing the Air Guardsmen and sending them to Europe. Most high ranking regular officers still refused to recognize any real improvement in the Air Guard program. To them, air guardsmen were still amateurs with limited usefulness in an era that demanded increasingly high standards of operational competence. They failed to recognize the limitations which obsolescent aircraft, inadequate funding and manning levels, as well as poor planning had placed on the Air Guard's operational performance.

Despite its reservations about the quality of the Air Guard's military performance during the Berlin Crisis, the Air Force worked closely with the National Guard Bureau to correct some of the problems revealed during the mobilization. In May 1962, General Sweeney, TAC Commander, directed the development of a comprehensive program to enhance the Air Guard's operational capabilities. As early as December 1961, the bureau had asked the Air Force to require its major air commands to prepare mobilization manning documents for their assigned Air Guard units in the same manner as they did for their own regular units. Air Guard units were reorganized in 1962–63 in a cellular structure that matched the manning requirements of their gaining commands. This change made it possible for the Air Force to mobilize only those portions of specific wings that would be needed in a given contingency situation. Air Guard units were also written into Air Force plans for limited wars and cold war contingencies like the Berlin Crisis. The Chief of the National Guard Bureau concluded in his annual report for FY 1962 that the manpower and organizational problems revealed by the Berlin mobilization had brought about closer and more enlightened cooperation between the Air Guard and the Air Force's gaining commands.[51]

Some fundamental Air Guard problems remained unresolved, and, indeed, were exacerbated, in the immediate aftermath of the Berlin mobilization. The Department of Defense failed to authorize full manning for Air Guard units. The Air Guard's personnel situation deteriorated as 285 of its officers, mostly pilots, volunteered to remain on active duty with the Air Force.[52] An Air Force operational survey of all Air Guard units released from active duty in August 1962 found that the Guard had experienced an average 12.5 percent personnel loss since mobilization. Demobilized units had also experienced serious losses of aircraft to the active duty establishment. In 1961, Secretary McNamara had approved expansion of the regular Air Force's tactical fighter force from sixteen to twenty-one wings as part of the Kennedy administration's conventional military buildup. The five new wings were temporarily equipped with obsolescent F–84s from Air Guard squadrons demobilized in 1962. The Department of Defense was unable to immediately provide adequate replacement aircraft for those Air Guard units.[53] As a consequence of these pilot and aircraft losses, the Air Force reported that "at the end of the year [1962]. . . Air Guard squadrons assigned to TAC for training and instruction purposes were low in capability."[54]

The Berlin mobilization was an important episode in the Air Guard's development into a proficient component of the total force. Regular Air Force skepticism aside, it demonstrated that the Air Guard's tactical flying units had made enormous progress since the Korean War mobilization. Operation Stair Step had been a brilliant improvised success. Guard units had shown a substantial capacity to rapidly adapt to unforeseen circumstances. Its pilots had demonstrated excellent flying skills. They were backed by a highly skilled cadre of full-time technicians in the maintenance, flight supervision, and administrative support fields. Inadequate planning, funding, and obsolescent equipment, however, had seriously limited the Air Guard's immediate operational capabilities. It had not been prepared for immediate deployment overseas as a tool of Cold War diplomacy in a potential limited war situation. Air Force planning had not even envisaged the Air Guard's employment in situations short of general war. Department of Defense budget limitations had insured that Air Guard units would require substantial post mobilization assistance before they could become proficient combat teams. Yet, by 1961–62 the Air Force and the Air Guard had evolved management and training systems for the latter. Inadequate resources and planning, not the Air Guard's anomalous state-federal status, were clearly the major barriers to the Air Guard's evolution into a proficient component of the total force. Many of these barriers were removed when Secretary McNamara created a selective strategic reserve force in 1965. The Air Guard was then in a position to demonstrate the operational capabilities that its ardent champions had long claimed.

Chapter VI

Vindication, 1963–1969

Following the Berlin mobilization, the Department of Defense and the Air Force made significant changes in the Air Guard. Its operational readiness was substantially improved. Its weapons were modernized. The trend toward an increased emphasis upon tactical aviation, evident in the late 1950s, was accelerated. Air defense was downgraded even further. The Air Guard was transformed from a force requiring considerable post mobilization preparation for combat to one containing units available for immediate employment in a crisis. The Defense Department's emphasis upon stronger conventional military forces under the flexible response policy and Secretary Robert S. McNamara's determination to create a select force of immediately-deployable reserve units in support of that policy provided the impetus for this transformation of the Air Guard. The growing American involvement in Southeast Asia also had an extremely important impact on the Air Guard. With the active duty establishment increasingly tied down by the Vietnam War, air guardsmen and Air Force reservists shouldered a growing share of the burden of routine Air Force operations. The Air Guard's total personnel strength continued to grow. By June 30, 1969, it had reached some 83,000, an increase of approximately 9,000 above its June 1963 level. This growth reflected the increasing technological sophistication and maintenance requirements of the Air Guard as well as its growing annual appropriations. Accelerated draft calls after 1965 made it relatively easy to fill the Air Guard's expanded personnel authorization.[1]

In 1965, Secretary McNamara intensified the Defense Department's emphasis upon reserve readiness. Frustrated by Congress in his attempts to reduce the size of the Army's reserve components and merge them into a single organization, McNamara directed the creation of a Selected Reserve Force within each of the armed forces. This force, including nine tactical fighter and four tactical reconnaissance groups from the Air Guard, would constitute America's strategic reserve while the bulk of the active duty establishment was preoccupied with Southeast Asia by the late 1960s. The Department of Defense authorized Selected Reserve Force units to draw equipment on a high priority basis, recruit to fill wartime manpower levels, and perform additional paid training. The program proved its value in 1968. Following seizure of the USS Pueblo by North Korea in January of that year, a number of Selected Reserve Force units were mobilized and sent to Asia. Among them were Air Guard tactical fighter and reconnaissance units that served with distinction in South Vietnam. Their truly outstanding performance in 1968–69 appeared to substantiate the claims of ardent air guardsmen. Mobilized units had demonstrated that, given adequate support by the Defense Department and the active duty establishment, they could achieve the high standards of performance and readiness demanded by Air Force doctrine. Thus a portion of the Air Guard finally demonstrated the operational capabilities originally anticipated by the War Department in 1945.[2]

The early 1960s saw a substantial buildup of American military strength. In the three years prior to June 30, 1964, nuclear weapons available to U.S. strategic alert forces increased 150 percent, and the strategic bomber alert force enlarged 50 percent. During that same period, Army active duty strength increased from 859,000 to 973,000. The total number of combat-ready Army divisions went from sixteen to twenty-one. Procurement of weapons and materiel for these conventional ground forces grew from $1.5 billion to $2.9 billion. The total number of Air Force tactical fighter wings in June 1964 stood at twenty-one, an increase of five since June 1961. Three more tactical fighter wings were programmed. Force modernization had also been emphasized. During fiscal year 1964, the F–105F and F–4C began entering the Air Force's tactical inventory for the first time. Improved air-ground cooperation under the newly-established Strike Command and more frequent joint service exercises further underscored the Air Force's growing conventional warfare role.[3]

The buildup of active duty military strength was accompanied by Defense Department efforts to enhance the readiness of the reserve components. The major initial focus of these efforts was on the Army National Guard and Army Reserve. Unlike their predecessors in the Eisenhower and Truman administrations, Department of Defense officials in the 1960s recognized that a prolonged and massive World War II style mobilization was no longer likely. The Berlin mobilization had underscored this point. For example, two so-called high priority Army Guard divisions, the 32d Infantry and the 49th Armored, had been recalled to active duty in 1961. Although these units had responded swiftly to their initial mobilization notice, their active duty performance had been extremely disappointing. They were critically short of fully-trained personnel, supplies, equipment, and modern weapons. Low authorized manning rates and generally substandard personnel job proficiency levels had made it necessary to recall many veterans to serve as individual fillers in those units. Although mobilized for one year, the 32d and 49th

Divisions required up to nine months of intensive preparations to achieve combat ready status. This was six months longer than their premobilization readiness schedules had anticipated. Given the speed with which the Berlin Crisis had unfolded in 1961, nine months was far too long to support U.S. diplomatic and military objectives.[4]

Secretary McNamara initially responded to this disappointing Army Reserve mobilization performance with a proposal for extensive reductions in the Army Guard. Congress, following an investigation by the House Armed Services Committee, blocked the proposed reductions in 1962. McNamara then shifted his approach. He clearly wanted a smaller reserve force tailored for a rapid response to a broad range of global contingency plan requirements. Congress had taught him that massive manpower reductions in the reserves were not politically feasible. Adequate funds were not available to bring the entire reserve force up to desired standards of readiness. Consequently, in 1963, McNamara directed the Army to create a high priority force within its existing reserve system. The Army's high priority force would consist of six National Guard divisions, eleven separate brigades, as well as an unspecified number of air defense missile batteries and support units. Units in this force were reorganized, given priority access to materiel, and manned at seventy-five to eighty percent of their full wartime strength. Their mobilization objective was full combat readiness within eight weeks.[5]

As the Vietnam War escalated, McNamara attempted to carry his program to improve Army reserve components' readiness a step further. In December 1964, the Department of Defense announced a proposal to create a single-component Army reserve system. Mindful of the failure of previous attempts to federalize or eliminate the National Guard, DOD asked Congress to authorize the merger of the 300,000–man Army Reserve into the 400,000–man Army Guard. The end result would be a 550,000–man Army Guard. All units that could not be made ready for combat within twelve to eighteen months of mobilization were to be eliminated. Approximately 2,100 units, including fifteen National Guard and six Army Reserve headquarters, were earmarked for deactivation. All units in this proposed force structure were to be fully prepared for rapid overseas deployment. A less publicized proposal to merge the Air Force Reserve into the Air Guard was also quietly approved by the Air Force. Both proposals were extremely controversial. Although they were cautiously supported by the National Guard Association, intense lobbying by the Reserve Officers' Association helped defeat them in Congress in 1965.[6]

Following the defeat of his merger proposals, Secretary McNamara announced the creation of a Selected Reserve Force in 1965. The goal of this program was to identify high priority units that could be prepared for rapid deployment overseas if needed. The Selected Reserve Force's Army component consisted of 150,000 men. It was organized in three infantry divisions, six separate brigades, and many smaller units. It was given first priority for training funds, modern equipment and manpower. Within a few months of the Selected Reserve Force's creation, its units were reportedly fully manned and equipped. They constituted the bulk of the Army's strategic reserve in the U.S. once most of the active duty establishment's strategic reserve units were sent to Vietnam in 1967 and 1968.[7]

The Air Guard's performance during the Berlin mobilization had been far superior to that of the Army's reserve components. Consequently, it had not been singled out for much special Defense Department attention early in Secretary McNamara's regime. Nevertheless, it faced significant materiel and personnel shortages during the first years of his stewardship at the Pentagon.[8]

Problems facing the Air Guard were highlighted by the report of a Reserve Forces Ad Hoc Study Group in December 1963. The group, organized by General LeMay in response to a request from the Under Secretary of the Air Force, analyzed the major problems facing the air reserve forces during the next decade. The group's members—regular Air Force, Air Guard, and Air Force Reserve officers—concluded that the basic reserve system of the Air Force was sound. However, it argued that the regular establishment still lacked adequate appreciation of the reserve forces. Interest peaked only in response to relatively infrequent stimuli like the Berlin crisis. The major air commands could, according to the study group, make considerably better use of the reserve forces available to them, satisfying the total range of Air Force requirements. Evidently, the active duty establishment still had not fully implemented the gaining command concept. This was especially important given the increasingly tight resource situation confronting the regulars.[9]

Air Guard problems highlighted by the group included an aging pilot force as well as difficulties in recruiting and retaining younger enlisted personnel. The Air Guard was hampered by the limited transfer of young pilots from the active force and small annual pilot training quotas in regular Air Force schools. During fiscal year 1964, the Air Guard pilot training quota was only 114. This was clearly inadequate to sustain the total strength as well as a proper age and rank structure for an organization with a total authorized pilot strength of 4,592 as of June 30, 1963. According to the study group, enlisted retentions had become a major problem in 1963 after the loss of large numbers of nonveteran airmen following their active duty during the Berlin mobilization. Finally, the group concluded that the principal limitation on the capabilities of the air reserve forces still was the inferior quality of their equipment. Continued adherence to the policy of supplying reserve units with obsolescent equipment no longer needed by the active duty establishment limited the full operational potential of the reserve forces. The study group recommended that the Air Force purchase new equipment directly for the reserves to overcome this qualitative deficiency. Projecting Air Force requirements through the 1964–73 period, the group correctly predicted that world conditions would confront the active duty establishment with responsibilities far in excess of its capabilities. If properly managed and equipped, the air reserve forces could help bridge that gap.[10]

Although there is little direct evidence that the Ad Hoc Study Group's report significantly influenced Air Force policy and programming, its conclusions clearly reflected contemporary Air Force thinking about the importance of maintaining reserve units in high states of operational readiness. Following the Berlin and Cuban crises, the emphasis on reserve readiness and closer integration with the active duty force was intensified. *Air Force Regulation 45–60,* published in February 1963, reflected this development. According to the regulation, the objective of air reserve programs was no longer the creation of M–Day forces that required extensive post mobilization preparation. Rather, "the objective of the Air Reserve Forces program is to provide operationally ready units and trained individuals that are immediately available to augment the active duty establishment. . . ."[11]

Although full implementation of the new policy objective was still constrained by shortages of equipment, operating funds, and qualified manpower, Air Guard training and organization were geared to achieving enhanced operational readiness. Air Guard unit structures were reorganized in the wake of the Berlin mobilization to approximate more closely the requirements of the gaining commands. Air Guard aircraft made nonstop, air-refueled deployments to Alaska and Puerto Rico for training in 1963. In August of the following year, a composite force of thirty-one Air Guard tactical fighters and reconnaissance aircraft flew to Europe for their annual field training. This was the first time U.S. reserve units had been sent to Europe for training purposes. Compared with the six-day island-hopping Operation "Stair Step" in 1961, the 1964 deployment was a model of speed and efficiency. With the aid of aerial refueling, the entire transatlantic crossing was completed in a little over nine hours. Air guardsmen were also becoming more actively involved in stateside joint service exercises. Three provisional Air Guard units, formed from sixteen separate Air Guard organizations, participated in the Joint Chiefs of Staff exercise "Desert Strike" in May 1964. Their performance was rated outstanding by active Air Force observers. Members of the Air Guard's 146th Fighter-Interceptor Group from Pittsburgh placed first in the F–102 category at the Air Force's global "William Tell" fighter weapons meet in October 1963. Special exercises and meets aside, Guard units participated in more mundane operations. For example, twenty-two Air Guard fighter-interceptor squadrons continued to provide substantial support of the Air Defense Command. In fiscal year 1965, they flew approximately 30,000 hours and completed more than 38,500 intercept sorties as an integral part of that command's operations.[12]

The Air Guard's nontactical units were also heavily involved in supporting the active duty establishment. In fiscal year 1965, Air Guard transports flew 1,469 missions overseas for the Military Air Transport Service that involved 60,840

Members of the Alabama ANG hold a last-minute briefing before an aerial photo mission at Elmendorf AFB. Deployment to Alaska gave the guardsmen realistic training.

flying hours and moved 11,388 tons of military cargo. Their destinations included South Vietnam, Japan, Germany, and Spain. In addition to their MATS missions, these transport units also carried more than 25,000 Army Guard troops to their annual training sites while flying 12,160 hours. An Air Guard C–123 unit in Alaska flew 2,919 hours while carrying more than 3,600 passengers and 950 tons of cargo in support of Air Force resupply missions in that state. Air Guard Communications Maintenance and Ground Electronics Engineering and Installations Agency units continued to train through "live scheme" projects, repairing communications and electronic equipment at Air Force and Air Guard bases. Six Air Guard fixed-site aircraft control and warning squadrons continued to conduct around-the-clock operations as part of America's active air defense system. An Oklahoma-based Air Guard airborne communications center nicknamed "Talking Bird" was sent to Puerto Rico in May 1965 to support U.S. intervention in the Dominican Republic.[13] National Guard Bureau Chief, General Wilson, testifying before a subcommittee of the Senate Appropriations Committee, summarized these recent changes in the Air Guard's status. "Largely within the past three years," he indicated, "our units have been transformed from primarily a training status to that of a ready and global force fulfilling operational missions on an almost daily basis."[14]

During 1964–1965, the process of modernizing the Air Guard's flying inventory with aircraft dropped by the Air Force and diversifying its mission responsibilities continued.[15] Fighter-interceptor units phased out the last of their F–86Ls and replaced them with supersonic F–102s. The remainder of the interceptor inventory consisted of F–100As and F–89Js. One F–86L unit had converted to an aerial refueling mission flying KC–97s while another began operating RF–94F reconnaissance aircraft. Its first tanker units had been formed during fiscal year 1962. Additional Air Guard aircraft modernization efforts in fiscal year 1965 included F–100Cs and a small number of F–105s. These two fighters were its most advanced aircraft. The bulk of its tactical fighters were still aging F–84Fs and F–86Fs. Tactical reconnaissance units were flying RF–57s and RF–84Fs. Air commando units, first established during fiscal year 1965, were flying a variety of light utility and transport aircraft including U–10s, HU–16s, and C–119s. Air Guard transport units were primarily flying C–97s and C–121s. A small number of shorter-range C–123s was also included in their transport inventory.[16]

The Air Guard's aircraft inventory and missions structure had changed dramatically between 1960 and 1965.[17] Its total aircraft strength had shrunk from 2,269 to 1,525 while being modernized. The emphasis on air defense missions had

Operation Ready Go. Minutes after this RF–84F landed at Ramstein AB, Germany, following a non-stop flight from Dow AFB, Maine, SSgt. Edward H. Gober (left) and TSgt. Starke C. Trotter were preparing it for a mission over West Germany. This marked the reserve forces' first training flight to Europe.

been replaced by a growing concern with a wide range of conventional warfare responsibilities.[18]

Escalating American involvement in the Vietnam War and the defeat of the reserve merger proposal encouraged yet another Defense Department initiative to enhance reserve readiness. On July 28, 1965, President Johnson announced his decision not to mobilize reserve units to augment the initial American military buildup in Vietnam. Acting against professional military advice, he had decided to rely upon volunteers and draftees to fill the expanded ranks of the armed forces.[19] In August, the Department of Defense announced the creation of the Selected Reserve Force program. This force would constitute a strategic reserve in the continental U.S. while active duty units were occupied in Southeast Asia. The Air Guard component of this program included nine tactical fighter groups flying 225 F–100s, four tactical reconnaissance groups flying 72 RF–84s, and one tactical control group. Within the Air Force, this program was known as "Beef Broth" and, later, "Combat Beef." Its mobilization objective was the capability to deploy reserve units overseas within twenty-four hours of a recall to active duty. By August 1966, all of the Air Guard's "Beef Broth" units were rated either fully combat ready or combat ready with minor deficiencies.[20]

The escalating war in Southeast Asia compelled the Air Force to integrate air guardsmen more fully into its routine operations. By 1965, air guardsmen had become involved in a variety of global activities that directly or indirectly supported the war effort. Air guardsmen were flying airlift missions for the Military Airlift Command (MAC) in the Pacific area by August 1965. MAC's own aircraft had been unable to meet the rapidly growing demands of America's increased military involvement in Vietnam. Stateside missions flown by guardsmen released some MAC aircrews for use in Southeast Asia. The initial sizable direct involvement of the Air Guard in Southeast Asia began in late 1965 with the airlift of Christmas gifts to U.S. military personnel in that theater. Between January 1966 and July 1967, air guardsmen flew an average of 200 overseas flights per month supporting MAC's global airlift operations. Seventy-five of these went to Southeast Asia.

Pilot shortages due to Southeast Asia operations increasingly affected the Air Guard. Small numbers of Air Guard F–102 pilots were encouraged to volunteer for temporary active duty overseas. In July 1968, twenty-four of these pilots were on active duty at bases in Holland, Germany, Alaska, the Philippines, and Okinawa. From August 1965, Air Guard aeromedical evacuation aircrews regularly flew domestic and offshore missions. These missions, although not flown to Southeast Asia, freed Air Force aeromedical units for duty there. In May 1967, the Air Force, faced with the Strategic Air Command's inability to provide enough tankers to keep European-based tactical fighter and reconnaissance aircrews proficient in aerial refueling techniques, called on air guardsmen to fill the gap. Air guardsmen, volunteering for short active duty tours in Germany, operated this highly successful project for the next ten years. And, although Air Guard tactical fighter and reconnaissance units provided no direct support to Air Force operations in Southeast Asia prior to 1968, they indirectly contributed to the war effort by supporting the Tactical Air Command's training and contingency plan requirements in the continental U.S.[21]

"Beef Broth" and support of the regulars notwithstanding, the Vietnam buildup proved detrimental to parts of the Air Guard program. Non "Beef Broth"

Guard units flew airlift missions to resupply American forces in Southeast Asia. (Left) A C–97 of the New York ANG is unloaded at Tan Son Nhut AB, Republic of Vietnam, March 1966. (Below) New York guardsman TSgt. Michael A. Measino supervises the unloading of this aircraft.

units lost considerable equipment and spare parts to support escalating Southeast Asia operations. By October 1966, aircraft losses in that combat theater had pushed back the Air Guard's projected modernization schedule by some eighteen months. Obsolete F–84s and F–86s were retained in the Air Guard's aircraft inventory to offset this delay. The chronic shortage of junior Air Guard pilots was exacerbated by the demands of the active force. Adequate quotas in the Air Force's undergraduate pilot training program were simply not available to the air reserve forces by 1966.[22]

More significant, the self-image, military utility, and political acceptability of reserve programs, including the Air Guard, again came into question. President Johnson's decision to rely on draftees rather than reservists raised questions about the expense and military utility of reserve programs. Many Americans were incensed that their sons and husbands were being drafted to risk death in Southeast Asia while men who received drill pay stayed at home. The draft-exempt status of the National Guard, as well as other reserve programs, became a major incentive to volunteer for those programs. And, although the vast majority of the volunteers proved to be skilled and conscientious, the Guard's draft haven image was painful for its leaders who regarded their all-volunteer organization as a legitimate heir of the minuteman tradition. Growing antiwar sentiment contributed to a decline in public esteem of all American military institutions including the Air Guard. Furthermore, the Air Guard's social composition began to draw criticism. In the late 1960s, its personnel were overwhelmingly white, male, and middle class. Militant civil rights organizations lambasted the Air Guard as a bastion of established privilege that systematically excluded minorities. Another source of contention was the Guard's performance in the race riots that swept through American cities in 1965–67. Guardsmen mobilized to quell these disturbances were accused of being undisciplined, untrained, trigger-happy, and ineffective. Although these criticisms were not directed specifically at the Air Guard, they threatened the broad public and political support that was the real foundation of its existence.[23]

Public criticism and simultaneous developments within the defense establishment created considerable anxiety within the Guard's top leadership. The defensive tone of remarks at the 1967 National Guard Association conference reflected this anxiety. General Wilson lashed out at critics of the Guard. He told the assembled delegates:

> We in the National Guard have nothing to be ashamed of. . . . We've taken a beating in the press lately. . . . There have been suggestions that the National Guard has been tarnished by a few unfortunate incidents in the recent past. . . . Stature, image and credibility are matters of vital importance. All 500,000 of us . . . have been damned before the American public. . . . And many believe that we are not even necessary.[24]

The President of the National Guard Association, Maj. Gen. James F. Cantwell, castigated the Air Force for planning a substantial reduction of the Air Guard's flying units while, at the same time, publicly praising its performance. According to Cantwell, eight airlift squadrons had been scheduled for elimination by July 1, 1968.[25] The July 1967 issue of the *National Guardsman* reported that the Air Guard's future role, then under review, was the subject of serious controversy within the Defense Department and the Air Force. Congressional intercession had blocked the proposed reduction of Air Guard airlift units through Fiscal Year 1967, but their long term future was in doubt. The *National Guardsman* complained that the failure to mobilize the reserve forces, the constant efforts by the Secretary of Defense to reduce those forces, and unfounded public criticisms of the National Guard had created doubt and confusion about the military reserve programs. It noted that, in an effort to resolve these uncertainties, several studies of the future of the Air Force's reserve components had been launched.[26]

One of these studies was conducted by the RAND Corporation, Santa Monica, California. The RAND study revealed a good deal about the actual condition of the air reserve programs and the nature of the policy process as it affected those programs in the 1960s. The moving force behind the Air Force request for the RAND study was Dr. Theodore Marrs, Deputy Assistant Secretary of the Air Force for Reserve Affairs. An avid air guardsman from Alabama, he had been sent to France during the Berlin crisis and on returning to the United States, had served an active duty tour in the National Guard Bureau. Later appointed to his civilian position within the Department of the Air Force, Dr. Marrs maintained a close liaison with the reserve components' associations as well as the National Guard Bureau. He championed their interests amid the anti-reserve atmosphere in the Pentagon. By 1966, he had convinced General John P. McConnell, Air Force Chief of Staff, to request a RAND study of future roles for the air reserve forces through the mid–1970s.[27]

The resulting massive ten-volume RAND study arrived at the Pentagon in late July 1967. At the request of General McConnell, political factors had been regarded as secondary by RAND's researchers. Instead, the report focused on military considerations versus the capabilities of reserve forces to effectively perform in all Air Force mission areas. Volume three, describing the air reserve tactical fighter program, was especially relevant to the Air Guard. It noted that all twenty-three reserve tactical fighter groups were Air Guard units. They comprised approximately twenty-five percent of the Air Force's total tactical fighter inventory. However, their actual combat potential, as measured by their payload capabilities for ground attack missions and their air-to-air combat characteristics, was considerably less. Air Guard tactical fighter squadrons were authorized twenty-five aircraft per unit while active Air Force squadrons were authorized eighteen. Most Air Guard squadrons were equipped at or near their authorized aircraft strength. Air Guard pilots were authorized 135 flying hours per year compared with 240 hours for their active force counterparts. During the last six months of 1966, Air Guard units had passed all but one of twenty-three Air Force operational readiness inspections. This trend had been constant since 1962.[28] The Air Force's evaluation

153

of the relative effectiveness of Air Guard and active force aircrews was summed up in the following quote taken by the RAND researchers from official classified correspondence:

> Operations personnel of the Air Staff and NGB agreed that standardization/evaluation checks, operational readiness inspection results, and differences in training times and events should amount to a five percent degradation of ANG operational readiness aircrew (sic) capability to successfully perform conventional weapons delivery missions.[29]

The researchers then addressed the crucial question of limitations upon the employment of reserve forces. They observed that there were strong management and political constraints against frequent mobilizations: for management—the difficulty of retaining people in the reserves if frequent call-ups handicapped their civilian careers; politically—the general public and foreign governments saw mobilizations as signals of grave international emergencies.[30]

Assessing the future of the reserve forces in the tactical fighter role, the RAND researchers observed that "they possess a significant capability today, and . . . it is feasible to consider them for an even stronger role in the mid–1970s."[31] Assuming a continuation of the presently programmed force, the researchers recommended that the most suitable role for the reserve tactical fighter force appeared to be close air support and battlefield area interdiction. They also recommended modernization of reserve tactical fighter forces with direct buys of A–7s for the Air Guard and retention of the current selected unit readiness policy. Responsibility for air superiority and nuclear delivery missions, however, should be concentrated in the active force.[32]

The RAND report suggested that some major shifts in the regular/reserve tactical fighter force might be contemplated on the basis of cost-effectiveness considerations alone. Since reserve units could have nearly the same combat potential as active force units in some scenarios, the report cautiously concluded that it would be in the national interest to increase the reserve mix in tactical fighter forces, but this should not be done to an extreme degree. Tactical fighter forces with a heavy mix of reserve units ran considerable risk of nonavailability in some contingencies. They would also produce fewer sorties than their active force counterparts in the initial days of war, especially if strategic warning was lacking. On the other hand, the larger total force obtained from a greater reserve mix would allow a higher daily sortie rate later in a campaign.[33]

The report's overall summary recommended neither a specific force structure nor a particular regular/reserve unit mix. It suggested:

> That part of the contingency spectrum which demands stringent mobility, frequency of use and rapid response time for deployment, these forces . . . should be in the active establishment. However, those units needed for later application to complete the force buildup and to serve as attrition fillers, can be maintained at a lower peacetime response level and are likely candidates for the reserve components. The result is attainment of the

required total cost at a lower peacetime sustaining cost than if only the active force were used.[34]

In urging expansion of air reserve forces' participation in all major mission areas except strategic nuclear delivery, the study recommended increased reserve participation in air defense, tactical fighter, tactical airlift, and tactical reconnaissance missions. This expansion should be accompanied by the earliest possible modernization of aircraft. It estimated that reserve flying units in general would cost about one-half as much as active force units if similarly manned and equipped. The RAND summary concluded that Air Force planners should consider placing a larger portion of the total force mix from most mission areas into the air reserve forces.[35]

The RAND report received favorable reviews from the Air Staff, the National Guard Bureau, and the reserve components' associations. However, its impact upon subsequent policy and programming was negligible. The Department of Defense continued to press for smaller reserve forces held in higher states of readiness. Congress reacted to this pressure with the Reserve Bill of Rights and Vitalization Act of 1967. Among other provisions, the act gave statutory sanction to Secretary McNamara's Selected Reserve Force but required Congress to approve its authorized strength annually. It also specifically precluded an Air Guard-Air Force Reserve merger. Moreover, it gave statutory protection to the Office of the Assistant Secretary of the Air Force for Manpower and Reserve Affairs. The level of top policy attention devoted to the Air Force Reserve was finally put on a par with that given the Air Guard. An Office of Air Force Reserve was created to work directly with the Air Staff on policy, roles, and missions for the Air Force Reserve. This new office replaced the Office of the Assistant Chief of Staff for Reserve Forces that had been concerned with both air reserve components. Through this legislation, Congress clearly expressed its intent to retain the basic structure of the existing reserve system and strengthen reserve policymaking machinery.

The Air Force itself, however, remained reluctant to allocate additional missions and resources to its air reserve programs in the late 1960s. The Vietnam War precluded dramatic across-the-board improvements in these programs. Modern equipment, especially aircraft, simply was not available for the reserves. More fundamental problems moreover, precluded implementation of RAND's recommendations. Direct purchases of modern aircraft for the reserves were extremely limited. Top Air Force officers were reluctant to initiate plans that would reduce the size and budget of the active force. They remained skeptical about reservists' ability to satisfactorily perform ever more demanding missions involving the operation of increasingly sophisticated equipment. Air Guard and Air Force Reserve officials still had difficulty convincing the Air Force's leadership that their units could shoulder expanded responsibilities. At best, the RAND study was another selling point that these officials could use to support their drive for broadened reserve participation in the total range of Air Force missions. The history of the RAND study demonstrated that, despite increased active force reliance on the air reserve programs due to the demands of the Vietnam War, attempts by the reserve forces to expand their own roles within the Air Force still met with considerable resistance.[36]

A stronger selling point for the Air Guard occurred in 1968. On January 23, the North Koreans seized the USS *Pueblo*, an electronics surveillance ship, as it cruised off the Korean coast. The incident shocked the United States. President Lyndon B. Johnson, already struggling to balance military commitments against inadequate resources and to hold together declining public support for the Vietnam War, did not want to be drawn into another inconclusive war for murky purposes in Asia. American military commanders in the region had advised Washington that they could not recapture the *Pueblo's* crew from the North Koreans. Low-keyed public statements by the President and other administration officials soon made it clear that the U.S. would not go beyond diplomatic means to redress the capture. The South Korean government, however, had to be reassured by some overt display of American resolve. Fearing that the *Pueblo's* seizure might be a prelude to a North Korean invasion, the South Koreans were threatening to withdraw their troops from South Vietnam. To display American resolve while minimizing the chances of an armed conflict with the North Koreans, President Johnson dispatched some 350 Air Force tactical aircraft to South Korea and mobilized approximately 14,000 naval and air reservists. The reservists, in effect, replaced regular units from the depleted strategic reserve in the continental U.S. Although no war erupted on the Korean peninsula, the communists' Tet offensive in South Vietnam soon placed additional pressures on U.S. military resources. In March, the President decided to mobilize an additional 22,200 reservists, effective May 13.[37]

The *Pueblo* crisis confronted the Air Guard with its third partial mobilization since the end of World War II. Its 1968 mobilization performance was demonstrably superior to its showing during the Berlin crisis seven years earlier. The *Pueblo* call-up came without warning on January 25, when President Johnson issued Executive Order 11392 mobilizing 9,343 air guardsmen. Within thirty-six hours approximately ninety-five percent of them had reported to their units. Eight tactical fighter groups and three tactical reconnaissance groups as well as three wing headquarters were mobilized.[38] The tactical fighter units were participants in the "Combat Beef" program. They were rated combat ready by the Air Force at the time of activation and could have deployed overseas within a few days. At least one unit, the 140th Tactical Fighter Wing, was alerted to prepare for overseas movement within seventy-two hours of its mobilization. The three tactical reconnaissance units were not rated combat ready because of equipment shortages, when activated. Within one month, however, they could have been sent into combat.[39]

For nearly three months, the fate of the mobilized air guardsmen remained uncertain. The *Pueblo* crisis was defused. In South Vietnam, the Tet offensive was a military defeat for the communists. But, despite the battlefield loss, they won a psychological victory. Tet caused American public opinion to shift against the war. The shift brought on furious debate and policy reappraisal within the Johnson administration. Meanwhile, military planners had to find new uses for the mobilized air guardsmen.[40]

While policymakers debated America's future in Vietnam and planners scrambled to define new contingency plan requirements, mobilized air guardsmen remained in limbo at their home stations. Their speedy activation followed by uncertainty about their future caused serious morale problems. Few had the time to place their personal affairs in order before the call-up. Unit commanders, acting under instructions to be prepared for immediate overseas movement, were reluctant to release their personnel to settle such matters. The changing international situation and the ongoing Vietnam policy debate in Washington effectively blocked Air Force guidance concerning the future employment of activated reserve units. In the meantime, while politically embarrassing questions were being raised about the necessity for the mobilization, air guardsmen remained at their home bases through March.[41]

Two additional factors contributed to the delay in speedily integrating the mobilized air guardsmen into active Air Force operations. Although Air Guard organization permitted selective recall of portions of each unit, the Defense Department mobilized entire units when, in fact, it only needed Air Guard flying squadrons. Many maintenance and support personnel were not needed to augment the active duty establishment. Consequently, they were eventually split from their units and individually reassigned throughout the Air Force. This was a time-consuming process that contributed to morale problems and deprived the Air Force of many smoothly-functioning maintenance and support organizations. Further complicating the situation, Air Guard units were structured differently than their active Air Force counterparts. As a result of problems encountered during the Berlin mobilization, they had been reorganized by the Tactical Air Command under a wing-group-squadron concept. The group was the key organization in this format. It consisted of maintenance and support elements collocated with a tactical flying squadron. This permitted the flying squadron to operate autonomously from its home base. In many cases these bases were located at remote airports far removed from a squadron's parent wing. Beyond reflecting the realities of non-mobilized Air Guard operations, this organizational format would permit Air Guard units to deploy intact to bare bases in future emergencies. TAC subsequently abandoned this organizational structure for its active force units. It substituted a wing-integrated squadron concept that provided centralized support services at the base level while decentralizing field maintenance at the squadron level. Hurried mobilization planning in January 1968 did not take into account either of these organizational incompatabilities or the possibility of a selective recall of needed portions of Air Guard units. Rather, to show American resolve, entire Air Guard wings and groups were hastily recalled to active duty.[42]

The experience of Ohio's 121st Tactical Fighter Group illustrates the problems associated with the poorly-handled January 1968 mobilization. The 121st remained at its home station, Lockbourne AFB, Ohio, for nearly four months before the Air Force announced that the group would be sent to South Korea in mid-June. During this interim period, the unit engaged in normal training and was rated fully combat ready by a TAC operational readiness inspection team. Just two weeks before the unit was scheduled to go to Korea, TAC reorganized the 121st into its wing-augmented squadron concept. The original 900–man 140th Tactical Fighter Group was reduced to the 410–man 166th Tactical Fighter Squadron. Surplus personnel were reassigned throughout the Air Force with reassignments based on TAC recommendations rather than those of the Air Guard commander or his staff. Other Air Guard tactical units mobilized in January had similar experiences. Such reorganization and reassignments delayed the Guard's integration into the Air Force, hurt morale, and damaged, at least temporarily, its operational effectiveness. Ironically, units like the 166th that were sent to South Korea found themselves operating on bare bases temporarily without support and maintenance personnel—the same skills that had been stripped from their units when they converted to the wing-integrated squadron organization.[43]

Fortunately, the Department of Defense and the Air Force dealt with these problems constructively prior to a second mobilization announced by the Secretary of Defense on April 11. On that date, he ordered an additional 22,200 reservists, including 1,333 air guardsmen, to active duty effective May 13. Unneeded maintenance and support personnel were not mobilized this time. Because of the advance notification, individual guardsmen were able to place their personal affairs in order before reporting for active duty, and units were able to reorganize before being mobilized. It was a much smoother operation than the January call-up.[44]

The Air Guard units mobilized in May included two tactical fighter groups equipped with F–86Hs and a medical evacuation unit flying C–121s.[45] The fighter units sent augmented squadrons to Cannon Air Force Base, New Mexico, where they trained Air Force pilots as forward air controllers and combat crewmen. The medical evacuation unit moved patients from casualty staging bases and military installations to treatment hospitals. It operated primarily in the eastern U.S., Texas, and the Caribbean area. All three units were demobilized the following December.[46]

Four of the Air Guard F–100 units mobilized in January were alerted in late April for deployment to South Vietnam. The first stage of the deployment ended on May 3 when twenty F–100s from Denver's 120th Tactical Fighter Squadron landed at Phan Rang Air Base. The remainder of the squadron's support personnel and materiel followed close behind. Its pilots began flying operational missions on May 8. By June 1, all pilots had been checked out in the theater's requirements and were flying combat missions. Meanwhile, the other three Air Guard tactical fighter squadrons—the 174th from Sioux City, Iowa, the 188th from Albuquerque, New Mexico, and the 136th from Niagara Falls, New York—arrived in South Vietnam. In addition, the 355th Tactical Fighter Squadron, an active Air Force unit, was eighty-five percent manned by air guardsmen, primarily volunteers.[47]

Air guardsmen were quickly and effectively integrated into Air Force operations in South Vietnam. Each of the four F–100 squadrons was sent into the combat theater with twenty to twenty-one aircraft and 350 men. They were assigned to regular Air Force wings at their new home bases. Approximately 200 from each squadron were then assimilated into the Air Force wing and support organizations at these bases. Many of these air guardsmen assumed top management positions in the maintenance, ordnance, supply, and service fields.[48]

Air Guard tactical fighter units saw combat in South Vietnam from June 1968 through April 1969. Pilots from the 120th, 174th, 136th, and 188th Tactical Fighter Squadrons flew 24,124 sorties and 38,614 combat hours. If the preponderantly Air Guard 355th Tactical Fighter Squadron is included, these totals rise to

Inactivation ceremonies for the 121st Tactical Fighter Group. First mobilized in January 1968, the unit was not deployed to South Korea until mid-June.

approximately thirty thousand sorties and fifty thousand combat hours. Air guardsmen flew a variety of missions including close air support, aircraft escort, and landing zone construction (i.e., bombing landing zone sites so that helicopters would have space to land). They also maintained aircraft on fifteen-minute alert status to respond to emergency requests for aerial firepower. Combat losses suffered by the Air Guard included seven pilots, one intelligence officer serving as an observer, and fourteen aircraft. Each of the five Guard-manned squadrons completed its full eleven-month combat tour without a reportable accident due to pilot, materiel, or maintenance failure.[49]

The combat performance of the air guardsmen in South Vietnam was truly impressive. The *Air Reservist* reported that the air guardsmen were:

> . . . flying more combat missions than other [i.e., regular Air Force] squadrons at their bases, and in-commission rates, bomb damage assessment, and other criteria by which tactical fighter units are judged, rate higher than other F–100 squadrons in the zone.[50]

Air Force personnel in Vietnam were similarly impressed. The 35th Tactical Fighter Wing's (TFW) official unit history reported: "Almost no problems were encountered when the 120th TFW became part of the 35th TFW. Personnel deploying with the 120th TFW were skilled and experienced enough to perform their duties in a highly professional manner."[51]

Gen. George S. Brown became the Air Force Commander in South Vietnam shortly after Air Guard units joined the Seventh Air Force. Testifying before the Senate Armed Services Committee during his confirmation hearing as Air Force Chief of Staff in 1973, General Brown gave his assessment of those units:

> I had . . . five F–100 Air National Guard squadrons. . . . Those were the five best F–100 squadrons in the field. The aircrews were a little older, but they were more experienced, and the maintenance people were also more experienced than the regular units. They had done the same work on the same weapon system for years, and they had [personnel] stability that a regular unit doesn't have.[52]

The combat performance of Air Guard flying units in South Vietnam was at least the equal of and in some cases superior to that of their active Air Force counterparts. For air guardsmen, that performance vindicated their program and seemed to promise a secure future role for them within the Air Force. They could claim, with justification, that the Air Guard had finally demonstrated the combat ready status originally planned for it in 1945.[53]

To the north, in Korea, integration of the Air Guard into Fifth Air Force operations did not go as smoothly. The previously discussed mobilization and unit integrity problems encountered by Ohio guardsmen had presaged further complications which surfaced after their early summer (1968) arrival at Kunsan Air Base. There, the 166th Tactical Fighter Squadron from Columbus combined with the 127th from Wichita, Kansas, as well as Air Force reservists and individual guardsmen from other units to form the 354th Tactical Fighter Wing.[54] The reorganization and personnel transfers involved delayed effective operations,

Guardsmen of the 136th Tactical Fighter Squadron, New York, complete processing before their deployment to Southeast Asia. The 136th and other tactical Guard units in South Vietnam compiled impressive combat records.

Loading materiel for the 136th TFS. This C-141 airlifted support equipment for the squadron's F-100 aircraft from Niagara Falls, New York to South Vietnam.

"Scramble at Phan Rang" (A National Guard Heritage Painting). The 120th Tactical Fighter Squadron, Colorado ANG, arrived at Phan Rang AB, Vietnam, during the concluding days of the second Viet Cong offensive of 1968.

F–100 aircraft belonging to the 120th TFS, Colorado ANG, in a revetment area at a base in Southeast Asia. The tactical squadron entered combat on May 5, 1968, two days after its arrival in Vietnam and completed its 1,000th mission fifty-one days later.

162

slowed the integration process, and generated complaints by disgruntled guardsmen to their congressmen and their local newspapers.[55]

Unfortunately, problems arising from poor planning were not confined to personnel. The new wing's two squadrons brought with them F–100Cs, aircraft for which the Fifth Air Force had no spare parts in stock. And, despite the knowledge that F–100Cs were slow in attaining altitude and lacked an effective all-weather air-to-air capability, the wing's original primary mission was air defense. By December, the 354th's F–100Cs were redesignated fighter-bombers to support ground force training.[56] By the same time, the wing's continual aircraft use and its lack of spare parts brought its readiness rate below the Air Force minimum. The loss of four aircraft in crashes and the death of one pilot early in the new year, 1969, aggravated the problem. Furthermore, the wing failed an operational readiness inspection. Extremely cold weather and spare parts shortages contributed to the failure, but the inspection report highlighted operational problems that implied lax training. For example, aircrews were criticized for flying nonstandard formations and achieving poor bombing scores. Air Force inspectors recommended downgrading the combat readiness ratings of the 354th's two tactical fighter squadrons to marginal.[57]

With the return of the *Pueblo's* crew, air guardsmen in South Korea were scheduled for release from active duty. Their last months overseas, April-June 1969, concluded on a positive note. The 354th Tactical Fighter Wing passed a second operational readiness inspection—both its fighter squadrons regained the fully combat ready ratings they had brought with them the previous summer. The Air Guard in Korea had not enjoyed the unalloyed success their counterparts in South Vietnam had; nevertheless, they had performed a valuable military service for the United States at a time when military resources were stretched thin. The deficiencies revealed by their service could have been minimized by better Air Force planning. F–100 spare parts should have been adequately stocked by the Fifth Air Force when those aircraft were assigned to it. But, more significantly, deployment of cohesive Air Guard units, including maintenance and other support functions, might have minimized many of the morale and operational problems that plagued the air guardsmen in South Korea.[58]

The active duty performance of the Air Guard's 123d Tactical Reconnaissance Wing was also mixed. The wing and four of its units—Louisville's 123d Tactical Reconnaissance Group, Little Rock's 189th Tactical Reconnaissance Group and 123d Reconnaissance Technical Squadron, and Reno's 152d Tactical Reconnaissance Group—were mobilized on January 25, 1968. These units were not included in the "Combat Beef" program. Due to a shortage of avionics equipment they were not rated combat ready when activated. Additional problems were created after mobilization when the Air Force directed the 123d to move to Richards-Gebaur Air Force Base, Missouri, and reorganize under Tactical Air Command's wing-augmented squadron structure. This reorganization substantially reduced the wing's unit manning document. Surplus personnel from the 123d were individually reassigned throughout the Air Force. Most of them went to units in South Korea. The lingering effects of these personnel changes contributed to the wing's unsatisfactory showing during the operational readiness inspection in October. The 123d finally passed an inspection and received an acceptable combat readiness rating in January 1969. However, it received an overall marginal rating during a no-notice inspection conducted by the 12th Air Force Inspector General at the end of February. Thus, one year after mobilization, the wing really had not fully measured up to Air Force standards.[59]

Despite its difficulties, the 123d made substantial contributions to the Air Force during its active duty service in 1968–69. Shortly after its mobilization, it became the primary working tactical reconnaissance wing in the continental U.S. Its three squadrons, flying RF–101s, conducted photo missions throughout the country. The 192d Tactical Reconnaissance Squadron and the 165th Tactical Reconnaissance Squadron also flew special missions in Alaska and the Panama Canal Zone for which they were highly commended by the commanders of those two areas. The 123d Reconnaissance Technical Squadron remained at Little Rock where its personnel processed film for Air Force, Army, and Navy reconnaissance units as well as other federal agencies. In July, each of the wing's three squadrons began rotating responsibility for temporary duty tours at Itazuke Air Base, Japan. They also operated a forward element at Osan Air Base, Korea. These units provided photo reconnaissance support for U.S. forces in Korea and Japan between July 1968 and April 1969.[60]

The 123d Tactical Fighter Wing's active duty experience in 1968–69 fell short of the rapid response capability claimed for the Air Guard. Much of this was due to the fact that it had not benefited from the manning, training, and equipment priorities established for "Beef Broth" units in 1965. Sweeping post mobilization reorganization had further delayed the 123d's achievement of operational readiness. Nevertheless, its units flew a total of 19,715 tactical hours, launched 11,561 sorties, and processed 841,601 feet of aerial film. The 192d and the 165th Tactical Reconnaissance Squadrons were each honored by the 5th Air Force with its Outstanding Unit Plaque for their service in South Korea. Underscoring this positive recognition, Lt. Gen. Thomas K. McGehee, 5th Air Force Commander, commended members of the 154th Tactical Reconnaissance Squadron for their performance. His letter of appreciation said, in part:

> I wish to take this opportunity to commend your entire squadron for its outstanding professional performance. . . . Your rapid deployment and immediate operational readiness aided immeasurably in providing a more effective combat posture. . . . Please convey to all of your people my most sincere appreciation for a job well done.[61]

Guardsmen from Arkansas' 189th Tactical Reconnaissance Group and 123d Reconnaissance Technical Squadron were demobilized in December 1968. The remainder of the 123d Tactical Reconnaisssance Wing was demobilized in June 1969.[62]

As shown by its performance in South Vietnam, the seven years following the Berlin mobilization had witnessed significant improvements in the Air Guard. Its combat readiness had substantially improved, its weapons systems had been modernized, and its operations had been more closely integrated with those of the active Air Force.

Much of the improvement was due to the acceptance by both the Air Force and the Air Guard of the gaining command concept of reserve forces' management. The major air commands required Air Guard units to meet the standards required of active force units. Air Guard leaders recognized that their program's long-term health depended upon the ability to measure up to those standards. They were extremely responsive to training supervision by the respective gaining commands.

Department of Defense policy emphasizing conventional military forces and the creation of a select force of immediately-deployable reserve units provided some of the wherewithal for the Air Guard's growing proficiency. The Vietnam War, stretching resources thin, forced the Air Force to rely on its reserve components to fulfill a variety of responsibilities which, in turn, strengthened the Guard's military capabilities.

However, the fate of the RAND report and the Selected Reserve Force program, dropped despite its success, illustrated the reluctance of the regular establishment to devote the substantial additional resources needed to maintain reserve flying units in advanced states of readiness. The Air Force feared that such a policy might weaken its own position.[63]

During the 1960s, the Air Guard had clearly emerged as a first line combat reserve force with units capable of rapid global deployment and effective employment in a broad range of contingencies. Reflecting the growing U.S. concern with conventional warfare and the availability of surplus aircraft, its force structure had been reoriented from its concentration on air defense in the 1950s to a variety of tactical aviation missions by 1969. The Air Guard's technical units continued to support active force operations with weather, communications, aircraft control and warning, and construction services. The Air Guard, by the end of the decade, had evolved into a valuable reserve component of the Air Force that could serve as a flexible instrument of national policy.

Chapter VII

Epilogue: The Air National Guard and the Total Force

Department of Defense policy has emphasized the necessity for maintaining strong reserve forces including the Air Guard. Promulgated in 1970 by Secretary of Defense Melvin R. Laird, the policy known as the "Total Force" sought to rebuild public confidence and to save money by reducing the size of the active duty establishment while strengthening the reserve components of the armed forces. Both objectives were outgrowths of American disenchantment with the stalemated Vietnam War—a disenchantment that had helped to elect Richard M. Nixon as President in 1968. After taking office, Nixon ordered a gradual deescalation of direct American involvement in that unpopular conflict. His "Vietnamization" policy returned the burden of the fighting, especially ground combat, to the South Vietnamese.\The U.S. continued to provide much aerial and logistical support, but American ground combat troops were withdrawn.[1]

In a broader context, Nixon sought to reshape U.S. national security policies in directions reminiscent of President Eisenhower's initiatives following the Korean War. The defense budget was dramatically reduced. Defense obligations for fiscal year 1971 were $78 billion, $18.1 billion below the fiscal year 1968 Vietnam era peak in U.S. military spending. American ground forces suffered substantial losses as a result of these budget cuts. Nuclear deterrent forces were maintained at approximately their current levels. Conventional air and naval forces were deemphasized. And, with the exception of treaty obligations, America's allies were told that, henceforward, they would be expected to shoulder the main burden of countering communist-inspired subversion and conventional aggression. With the exception of the NATO countries and South Korea, they could no longer automatically expect American ground force assistance in countering such conventional threats to their security. These policies were labeled the "Nixon Doctrine." Conspicuously absent from this reformulation of national security policy was any overt reference or implication that the U.S. would immediately resort to nuclear weapons to counter communist pressure on its allies.[2]

The "Total Force" policy was a corollary to the "Nixon Doctrine." Spending on reserve forces was dramatically increased. For example, the fiscal year 1972 budget for the reserves was set at $3.1 billion, an increase of nearly fifty percent above the $2.1 billion spent on them during fiscal year 1969. The weapons and equipment of reserve units were modernized. Some reserve air units began to be partially equipped with aircraft purchased directly from factory production lines. Moreover, the "Total Force" approach sought to insure that all policymaking, programming, and budgetary activities within the Defense Department considered active duty and reserve forces concurrently. Its ambitious objective was to determine the most advantageous mix of those forces in terms of their contribution to national security versus the cost to equip and maintain them. The "Total Force" policy committed the Department of Defense to using reservists as the initial and primary source of manpower to augment the active duty forces in the event of a future war or other national emergency. This provision was clearly a response to public and congressional dissatisfaction with the Johnson administration's decision to rely on the draft rather than a massive reserve mobilization during the Vietnam War.[3]

Behind the "Total Force" policy lay the Air Force's experience with its reserve programs, especially the Air Guard, and the ideas of Dr. Marrs, Deputy Secretary of Defense for Reserve Affairs, who had sponsored the previously discussed RAND study. The study's cost-effective argument for stronger reserve forces was increasingly attractive to many civilian officials and congressmen in light of the austere defense budgets of the Nixon administration. Dr. Marrs, an avid Air Guard partisan, promoted it vigorously and effectively from his position within the Department of Defense.[4]

In a larger sense, the Air Guard and the Air Force had pioneered a "Total Force" approach to reserve programs since the Korean War. Air National Guard augmentation of the Air Force's air defense runway alert program, implemented on a continuing basis in 1954, had marked the first significant attempt to integrate reserve units into the peacetime functions of the active duty military establishment. As described, this use of reserve training time, limited during the late 1950s, had been expanded in the 1960s as American military involvement escalated during the Vietnam War. As early as October 1963, Maj. Gen. Curtis R. Low, Assistant Chief of Staff for Reserve Forces, labelled this approach to utilizing the Air Force's reserve components as the "Total Force" concept.[5] Although the label did not become official until 1970, it did reflect the fact that the Air Force was beginning to use the full range of resources, including the Air Guard and the Air Force Reserve, available to it.

The "Total Force" approach included Air Force policymaking, planning, programming, and budgeting activities for its reserve components. Theoretically these responsibilities had been integrated with their active duty counterparts on a functional basis when the Air Force was established as an independent military department in 1947. However, the Air Guard's experience had been quite different. Adequate Air Force implementation of a "Total Force" approach utilizing its reserve components did not come until after the Berlin mobilization. Important in this implementation were the Air Force's gaining command concept of reserve forces management and the Department of Defense's Selected Reserve Force. The gaining command concept was probably the single most important Air Force innovation in the management of the Air Guard and Air Force Reserve. It forced them to organize and train according to the same standards as their active force counterparts. Implementation of the concept truly integrated the Air Guard and the Air Force Reserve into the "Total Force" at the operational level well before it became official Defense Department policy in 1970. The Selected Reserve Force, created by Secretary McNamara in 1965, provided the means needed by an elite group of these reserve units to achieve the high levels of operational readiness that made them immediately available to the Air Force for global deployment.

Through policy changes and crises, the Air Guard had gradually evolved into an outstanding reserve program. Despite its anomalous state-federal status, its units have achieved high degrees of operational readiness and have made substantial contributions during three mobilizations from 1950 through 1969. In the 1970s, they provided a significant percentage of the tactical fighter, reconnaissance, and transport aircraft available to the Air Force, while support units augmented the active Air Force with a host of technical services including aircraft surveillance and warning, civil engineering, weather forecasting, and communications-electronics support.[6]

Many factors have contributed to this success. Most significant has been the close integration of the Air Guard into the policymaking, planning, programming, budget, and operational processes of the active duty Air Force. Since the Korean War, the Air Guard's leadership willingly exchanged a good deal of the effective control of their organization for Air Force supervision and support. The Guard's political strength enabled them to reach the point where that concession could be made. That strength, key to their establishment, was also significant in the legislative initiatives which strengthened reserve programs in general and insured the Guard's separate legal identity. The Guard's political backing made possible intervention in the administrative processes of the Defense Department and the Air Force to protect its interests. Its political muscle had insured that the Air Guard received priority over the strictly federal Air Force Reserve in the distribution of aircraft and equipment. Consequently, Air Guard flying units have usually been equipped with more advanced and more glamorous tactical aircraft than the Air Force Reserve. This has made it easier for the Air Guard to attract the cadre of skilled personnel needed for its flying units. And, most importantly, the Guard's political strength has enabled it to defend its annual budget requests with reasonable success against crippling cuts by either the Department of Defense or the Air Force.[7]

The Air Guard has relied upon the Air Force to provide it with a large pool of experienced officers and noncommissioned officers since the end of World War II. The willingness of these trained veterans to maintain at least a part-time military affiliation once they leave active duty has been another key to the Air Guard's performance. Given adequate Air Force support and supervision, these individuals have been able to retain advanced levels of military proficiency while serving as guardsmen. For many of them, the old "weekend warrior" stereotype no longer adequately reflects the time and effort they now devote to their part-time military duties. Especially for pilots, one weekend each month and two weeks of annual training are no longer adequate. To maintain proficiency in modern military aircraft, they put in a good many extra flying and other training hours. This, plus the fact that many of them are either professional civilian pilots or operate their own private aircraft, provides a high general level of flight experience not often found in regular Air Force units.

Alongside the pilots, air technicians—maintenance, supply, administration, flight supervision specialists—have shared the personnel factor of the Air Guard's success. They account for some twenty percent of the Air Guard's total manpower and, like the pilots, most are Air Force veterans. The maintenance technicians, the largest group, have a level of experience and continuity of unit service unmatched in the active Air Force. They constitute the heart of the Air Guard's impressive capability to maintain its aircraft in an operationally-ready status and provide on-the-job training to less experienced "weekenders." Regardless of specialty, however, the technicians provide continuity and unit cohesion seldom found in regular units.

The legal and administrative arrangements governing the Air Guard's technician force are complicated. They have existed in their present form since January 1, 1969, the effective date of Public Law 90–486, The National Guard Technician Act. Prior to that date, although paid by the federal government, technicians had been considered state employees and lacked both protection under federal civil service laws and a retirement program. They were caretakers and clerks with very limited legal responsibilities for the operation of their Air Guard units prior to PL 90–486. The Technician Act specifically provided for their employment to administer and train guardsmen as well as to maintain and repair equipment and supplies. They also gained noncompetitive federal civil service status, but were still in fact employed by, and their programs administered by, the state adjutants general.[8]

In addition to policy and personnel, the availability of surplus military aircraft has been crucial in shaping the Air Guard's organization and missions. Indeed, since the establishment of aviation as an integral and permanent element of the National Guard in 1920, this factor, a mixed blessing, has largely determined what kind of flying organization it was going to be. It made possible an extensive and increasingly diverse flying program, but it also imposed substantial limitations on the operational potentials of Air Guard units. Frequently Guard units were equipped with aircraft approaching obsolescence. Several times it appeared that they were equipped with aircraft simply because they were surplus to the active force's needs—no compelling military case was evident for their continued use. This raised the issue of whether prudent reserve force planning and programming should have been so heavily influenced by the availability of surplus hardware rather than carefully developed military requirements. Although limited numbers of aircraft have been purchased for the Air Guard directly from factory production lines in recent years, continued reliance on surplus and often obsolescent aircraft remains the most crucial factor inhibiting the full development of the Air Guard's operational capabilities.

There are, however, serious limitations on the Air Guard's military utility. Advanced operational readiness is very expensive. As its tactical squadrons approach the Air Force requirement to be prepared for immediate global deployment while using increasingly sophisticated aircraft, the gap between Air Guard and regular force operating costs has narrowed. In 1967, RAND estimated that gap to be fifty percent. Recent estimates placed Air Guard unit operational costs at seventy percent of their active force counterparts.[9] Direct buys of aircraft for reserve units further narrow the cost differential. If Air Guard unit operating costs continue to approach those of their active force counterparts, they may become increasingly less attractive options to national security policymakers and planners.

International politics and management problems, both previously discussed, place further constraints on the use of the Air Guard. Because of political implications at home and abroad, Air Guard units, regardless of their operational readiness, cannot be mobilized frequently for international contingencies. In many circumstances, the political "signals" sent might be inappropriate and misleading. Furthermore, a force structure overly reliant on reserve units might also be construed as a sign of weakness or passivity by foreign governments. From a management perspective, frequent mobilizations could so disrupt the lives of guardsmen and reservists that most of them would be unlikely to maintain their military affiliation. This would rob the Air Guard of two of its most precious assets, unit cohesion and the relatively high experience levels of its personnel. In today's no draft environment, frequent mobilizations could rapidly decimate the Air Guard's ranks.

Finally, there are significant limitations on the roles and missions the Air Guard can effectively carry out. It cannot effectively operate the command and control, basic and advanced technical training, logistics, and technological research and development programs that constitute the foundations of modern air power. Nor can it take on missions such as strategic deterrence or tactical air superiority that require a constant state of extremely high readiness and frequent deployments. Rather, the reserve forces depend upon a strong active duty establishment to provide the basic infrastructure of air power and the exclusive responsibility for certain missions. As the history of the Air Guard illustrates, however, reserve units can perform extremely well when they share missions and aircraft types with their counterparts in a healthy active duty establishment. Their optimal role lies in augmenting, not replacing, a strong regular Air Force.

The lessons learned from the Air Guard's historic development cannot be mechanically applied to other reserve programs. Certain elements of the Air Guard's experience, including the technician program and the "total force" approach, obviously have had legitimate applications to other reserve programs. But, the character of the operational and training tasks facing each of the armed services is dissimilar. The Army, for example, needs large numbers of men and a great deal of empty territory to conduct realistic combat exercises. The Navy prefers to use individual reservists to augment its ships and shore installations. Consequently, the organization of reserve programs of these two services is heavily influenced by geographic considerations. The Air Force, on the other hand, has adopted a largely functional approach to reserve training. Training supervision under the gaining command concept is exercised by a functional Air Force command such as the Tactical Air Command rather than a geographic entity like an Army corps area. The nature of air operations lends itself to this approach. Air Guard units, scattered across the country at various municipal airports and Air Force bases, can fly and maintain their aircraft on a daily basis. Most of the tactical units have ready access to gunnery ranges, and the transport outfits are usually engaged in supporting Military Airlift Command operations. They can conduct realistic training programs at their home stations. Most Army and Navy reserve units or individuals cannot do this.

The Air Guard has also found it much easier to attract personnel than most other reserve programs. From the inception of National Guard aviation before World War I, flying has had a glamorous appeal that service in conventional ground or naval forces lacks. This factor, plus the relatively small size and technological orientation of the Air Guard, has enabled it to recruit the high caliber people it has needed. Many of the skills that they have developed as guardsmen are transferable to civilian life. The Air Force itself has benefited from these same circumstances while the other armed services and their reserve components have been placed at a disadvantage by them.

The nature of institutional preferences has also played a role in the history of American military reserve programs since World War II. By and large, the Air Force appears to have been much more willing than its older sister services to develop the organizational arrangements and to devote the resources necessary to build strong reserve programs. Despite the efforts of virtually every President from Truman to Nixon to limit defense spending by strengthening reserve programs, only the Air Force has managed to demonstrate a steady growth in the capabilities of its civilian components. Innovations like Air Guard participation in the air defense runway alert program and the gaining command concept attest to the Air Force's institutional commitment to building viable reserve programs.

To be sure, external political and budgetary pressures have encouraged the Air Force to strengthen these programs, but its sister services have faced these same pressures with frequently less satisfactory results. Perhaps the fact that it has been less burdened than the Army and Navy by a long history of regular-reserve animosity has made the Air Force more willing to take a pragmatic approach on this matter. Whatever the reasons, the Air Force has overcome much of its own institutional skepticism to fashion reserve programs that effectively complement the active duty establishment. The Air Guard has become a valuable reserve component of the U.S. Air Force. The integrated policymaking, planning and operational functions pioneered by the Air Guard-Air Force relationship provided the conceptual basis for the Defense Department's "Total Force" policy, and, despite its nominal state-federal status, the Air National Guard continues to set the pace for U.S. military reserve programs.

Appendices

Appendix 1

Air National Guard Observation Squadrons
Inducted into Federal Service (Air Corps)
World War II

101st Massachusetts	111th Texas	123rd Oregon
102d New York	112th Ohio	124th Iowa
103rd Pennsylvania	113th Indiana	125th Oklahoma
104th Maryland	115th California	126th Wisconsin
105th Tennessee	116th Washington	128th Georgia
106th Alabama	118th Connecticut	152nd Rhode Island
107th Michigan	119th New Jersey	153rd Mississippi
108th Illinois	120th Colorado	154th Arkansas
109th Minnesota	121st District of Columbia	
110th Missouri	122d Louisiana	

Appendix 2

Korean Mobilizations

DATE ACTIVATED	ORGANIZATION GROUP-SQUADRON	LOCATION	LOCATION MOVED	MISSION	AIRCRAFT	PERSONNEL	DATE DEACTIVATED
13 Oct 50	117 TFW	Birmingham, Ala.	Toule-Rosierses, France	Tactical Fighter		2398	10 Jul 52
26 Sep 50	159 FBS	Jacksonville, Fla.	Misawa AB, Japan	Tactical Fighter		500	8 Jul 52
10 Oct 50	116 FBG	Dobbins AFB, Ga.	George AFB, Calif.	Tactical Fighter		865	10 Jul 52
10 Oct 50	128 FBS	Georgia	Europe	Tactical Fighter	F–51	131	10 Jul 52
10 Oct 50	158 FBS	Savannah, Ga.	Misawa AB, Japan	Tactical Fighter	F–80 F–84	285	10 Jul 52
10 Oct 50	127 FBS	Kansas	Europe	Tactical Fighter			10 Jul 52
10 Oct 50	137 FBG	Oklahoma City, Okla.	France	Tactical Fighter		226	9 Jul 52
10 Oct 50	125 FS	Tulsa, Okla.	France	Tactical Fighter		416	9 Jul 52

DATE ACTIVATED	ORGANIZATION GROUP-SQUADRON	LOCATION	LOCATION MOVED	MISSION	AIRCRAFT	PERSONNEL	DATE DEACTIVATED
1 Feb 51	197 FBS	Luke AFB, Ariz.	Luke AFB, Ariz.	Tactical Fighter	F–84A	462	1 Nov 52
1 Feb 51	142 FBS	Delaware	U.S.	Tactical Fighter			11 Sep 52
1 Feb 51	113 FBW	District of Columbia	U.S.	Tactical Fighter			Feb 53
1 Feb 51	121 FBW	District of Columbia	U.S.	Tactical Fighter			1 Nov 52
10 Oct 50	165 FBS	Kentucky	Manstrom AFB, England	Fighter Bomber	B–26	539	9 Jul 52
10 Oct 50	156 FBS	North Carolina	Manstrom AFB, England	Fighter Bomber		141	9 Jul 52
10 Oct 50	112 FBS	Toledo, Ohio	Lawson Field, Ga.	Fighter Bomber	B–26	200	1 Mar 52
10 Oct 50	111 FBS	Ellington, Tex.	Korea	Fighter Bomber	F–51D	227	9 Jul 52
10 Oct 50	157 FBS	South Carolina	France	Fighter Bomber			9 Jul 52
10 Oct 50	182 FBS	San Antonio, Tex.	Taegu, Korea	Fighter Bomber	F–51 F–84		9 Jul 52

DATE ACTIVATED	ORGANIZATION GROUP-SQUADRON	LOCATION	LOCATION MOVED	MISSION	AIRCRAFT	PERSONNEL	DATE DEACTIVATED
10 Oct 50	167 FBS	Martinsburg, W.Va.	Manstrom AFB, England	Fighter Bomber	F–47		9 Jul 52
10 Oct 50	196 FBS	Ontario, Canada	Misawa AB, Japan	Fighter Bomber	F–80C		10 Jul 52
10 Oct 50	136 FBG	Dallas, Tex.	Itazuke, Japan	Fighter Bomber			9 Jul 52
1 Feb 51	123 FBW	Louisville, Ky.	Fort Knox, Ky.	Fighter Bomber	P–51D	418	1 Nov 52
1 Feb 51	127 FBW	Michigan	Luke AFB, Ariz.	Fighter Bomber	F–51 F–80 F–84		1 Nov 52 1 Sep 52
1 Feb 51	107 FBS	Michigan		Fighter Bomber			11 Sep 52
1 Feb 51	171 FBS	Michigan		Fighter Bomber			11 Sep 52
1 Feb 51	172 FBS	Battle Creek, Mich.	Selfridge AFB, Mich.	Fighter Bomber	F–51	400	11 Sep 52
1 Feb 51	188 FBS	New Mexico		Fighter Bomber			11 Sep 52
1 Feb 51	166 FBS	Columbus, Ohio	Youngstown, Ohio	Fighter Bomber	F–84C	600	1 Nov 51

DATE ACTIVATED	ORGANIZATION GROUP-SQUADRON	LOCATION	LOCATION MOVED	MISSION	AIRCRAFT	PERSONNEL	DATE DEACTIVATED
1 Feb 51	148 FBS	Pennsylvania		Fighter Bomber			11 Sep 52
1 Feb 51	122 FBW	Ft. Wayne, Ind.	Sioux City, Iowa	Fighter Bomber		510	Nov 52
1 Feb 51	113 FBS	Indiana		Fighter Bomber			11 Sep 52
1 Mar 51	192 FBS	Nevada		Fighter Bomber			15 Oct 52
1 Mar 51	103 FBW	New Jersey	Turner AFB, Ga.	Fighter Bomber	F-47		15 Nov 52
1 Mar 51	141 FBS	New Jersey	Turner AFB, Ga.	Fighter Bomber	F-47		30 Nov 52
1 Apr 51	146 FBW	Van Nuys, Calif.	Moody AFB, Ga.	Fighter Bomber	F-51D B-26A	743	31 Dec 52
1 Apr 51	115 FBS	Burbank, Calif.	Langley AFB, Va.	Fighter Bomber			Nov 52
1 Apr 51	140 FBW	Colorado	Dispersal throughout US	Fighter Bomber		1400+	
1 Apr 51	120 FBS	Buckley, Colo.	Korea	Fighter Bomber	F-51		1 Jan 53
1 Apr 51	126 FBW	Chicago, Ill.	Langley AFB, Va.	Fighter Bomber			1 Jan 53

DATE ACTIVATED	ORGANIZATION GROUP-SQUADRON	LOCATION	LOCATION MOVED	MISSION	AIRCRAFT	PERSONNEL	DATE DEACTIVATED
1 Apr 51	126 FBS	Chicago, Ill.	Langley AFB, Va.	Fighter Bomber		1376	Apr 53
1 Apr 51	168 FBS	Chicago, Ill.	Langley AFB, Va.	Fighter Bomber			15 Nov 52
1 Apr 51	108 FBS	Chicago, Ill.	Langley AFB, Va.	Fighter Bomber			15 Nov 52
1 Apr 51	132 FBW	Des Moines, Iowa	Dow AFB, Maine	Fighter Bomber	F-51		31 Dec 52 / Apr 53
1 Apr 51	124 FBS	Des Moines, Iowa	Dow AFB, Maine	Fighter Bomber	F-51		31 Dec 52 / 15 Nov 52
1 Apr 51	174 FBS	Sioux City, Iowa	Dow AFB, Maine	Fighter Bomber	F-84B	383	31 Dec 52 / 15 Nov 52
1 Apr 51	173 FBS	Lincoln, Nebr.	Bangor, Maine	Fighter Bomber	F-51	465	30 Nov 52
1 Apr 51	185 FBS	Oklahoma City, Okla.	Shaw AFB, S.C.	Fighter Bomber	F-51 / RF-80	289 +	31 Dec 52
1 Apr 51	111 FBW	Pennsylvania		Fighter Bomber			4 Jun 52
1 Apr 51	103 FBS	Pennsylvania		Fighter Bomber			15 Nov 52
1 Apr 51	117 FBS	Pennsylvania		Fighter Bomber			1 Jan 53

DATE ACTIVATED	ORGANIZATION GROUP-SQUADRON	LOCATION	LOCATION MOVED	MISSION	AIRCRAFT	PERSONNEL	DATE DEACTIVATED
1 Apr 51	191 FBS	Utah		Fighter Bomber	F–51	492	1 Jan 53
1 Apr 51	187 FBS	Wyoming		Fighter Bomber	F–51		1 Jan 53
1 Feb 51	163 FIS	Indiana	Sioux City, Iowa	Fighter Interceptor	P–51	369	1 Nov 52
1 Feb 51	103 FIS	Connecticut		Fighter Interceptor			11 Sep 52
1 Feb 51	101 FIS	Maine		Fighter Interceptor			11 Sep 52
1 Feb 51	132 FIS	Maine		Fighter Interceptor			Nov 52
1 Feb 51	133 FIS	Manchester, N.H.	Manchester, N.H.	Fighter Interceptor	P–47	391	1 Nov 52
1 Feb 51	123 FIS	Oregon		Fighter Interceptor	F–51	418	1 Nov 52
1 Feb 51	134 FIS	Vermont		Fighter Interceptor			1 Nov 52
1 Feb 51	116 FIS	Washington		Fighter Interceptor			1 Nov 52
1 Feb 51	128 FIS	Milwaukee, Wis.	Truax Field, Wis.	Fighter Interceptor	F–80A		30 Nov 52

DATE ACTIVATED	ORGANIZATION GROUP-SQUADRON	LOCATION	LOCATION MOVED	MISSION	AIRCRAFT	PERSONNEL	DATE DEACTIVATED
1 Feb 51	176 FIS	Madison, Wis.	Madison, Wis.	Fighter Interceptor	F–51	392	31 Oct 52
1 Feb 51	136 FIS	Niagara Falls, N.Y.	Niagara Falls, N.Y.	Fighter Interceptor	P–47D		30 Nov 52
1 Feb 51	175 FIS	Sioux Falls, S.D.	Ellsworth AFB, S.D.	Fighter Interceptor	P–51	430	30 Nov 52
1 Feb 51	142 FIG	Portland, Oreg.	O'Hare Field, Ill.	Fighter Interceptor		407	1 Dec 52
1 Feb 51	126 FIS	Wisconsin		Fighter Interceptor			1 Dec 52
1 Mar 51	103 FIW	Connecticut		Fighter Interceptor			15 Oct 52
1 Mar 51	133 FIW	Minnesota		Fighter Interceptor	F–51D	811	30 Nov 52
1 Mar 51	109 FIW	Minnesota		Fighter Interceptor			30 Nov 52
1 Mar 51	179 FIS	Duluth, Minn.	Duluth, Minn.	Fighter Interceptor		448	30 Nov 52
1 Apr 51	186 FIS	Great Falls, Mont.	Moody AFB, Ga.	Fighter Interceptor	F–51	384	15 Nov 52
1 Apr 51	178 FIS	Bismark, N.D.	Moody AFB, Ga.	Fighter Interceptor	F–51	400	15 Nov 52

183

DATE ACTIVATED	ORGANIZATION GROUP-SQUADRON	LOCATION	LOCATION MOVED	MISSION	AIRCRAFT	PERSONNEL	DATE DEACTIVATED
13 Oct 50	160 TRS	Birmingham, Ala.	Bremerhaven, Germany	Tactical Reconnaissance		2398	10 Jul 52
10 Oct 50	154 TRS	Arkansas	Korea	Tactical Reconnaissance			10 Jul 52
1 Mar 51	153 TFS	Meridian, Miss.	Turner AFB, Ga.	Tactical Reconnaissance	P–47N		27 Nov 52
1 Mar 51	105 TRS	Nashville, Tenn.	Knoxville, Tenn.	Tactical Reconnaissance		404	30 Nov 52
1 Apr 51	155 TRS	Memphis, Tenn.	Shaw AFB, S.C.	Tactical Reconnaissance	F–51	275	31 Dec 52
1 Apr 51	118 TRW	Nashville, Tenn.	Memphis, Tenn.	Tactical Reconnaissance	F–47 B–26 Support A/C	1237	31 Dec 52
1 Apr 51	106 TRS	Alabama	U.S.	Tactical Reconnaissance			1 Jan 53
1 Apr 51	132 AC&W	Minneapolis, Minn.	Dispersed to Radar sites	Aircraft Control & Warning		277	25 Apr 52
1 May 51	142 AC&W	Portland, Oreg.	Alaska	Aircraft Control & Warning		275	1 Nov 52
1 May 51	148 AC&W	Compton, Calif.	Tinker AFB, Okla.	Aircraft Control & Warning		200	Dec 53

DATE ACTIVATED	ORGANIZATION GROUP-SQUADRON	LOCATION	LOCATION MOVED	MISSION	AIRCRAFT	PERSONNEL	DATE DEACTIVATED
1 Oct 51	135 AC&W	New Orleans, La.	Kirtland AFB, N.M.	Aircraft Control & Warning		184	1 Oct 53
1 Nov 51	124 AC&W	Oklahoma City, Okla.	Alexandria Arpt, La.	Aircraft Control & Warning		166	31 Oct 52
1 Nov 51	125 AC&W	St Louis, Mo.	Winooski, Vt.	Aircraft Control & Warning		233	31 Oct 53
1 Nov 51	157 AC&W	St Louis, Mo.	Alexandria, La.	Aircraft Control & Warning		248	31 Oct 53

Appendix 3

Berlin Mobilizations

DATE ACTIVATED	ORGANIZATION GROUP-SQUADRON	LOCATION	LOCATION MOVED	MISSION	AIRCRAFT	PERSONNEL	DATE DEACTIVATED
1 Oct 61	131 TFS	Westfield, Mass.	Phalsbourg AB, France	Tactical Fighter	F–86H	267	20 Aug 62
1 Oct 61	138 TFS	Hancock, N.Y.	Phalsbourg AB, France	Tactical Fighter	F–86H	606	20 Aug 62
1 Oct 61	120 TFS	Buckley ANG Denver, Colo.	Denver, Colo.	Tactical Fighter	F–100C	526	24 Aug 62
1 Oct 61	136 TFS	Niagara Falls MAP, N.Y.	Niagara Falls MAP, N.Y.	Tactical Fighter	F–100C	464	
1 Oct 61	113 TFW 121 TFS	Andrews AFB, Wash., D.C.	Andrews AFB, Wash., D.C.	Tactical Fighter	F–100C	820	
1 Oct 61	170 TFS	Capitol AP, Springfield, Ill.	Capitol AP, Springfield, Ill.	Tactical Fighter	F–84F	506	
1 Oct 61	122 TFW 163 TFS	Baer Field, Ft Wayne, Ind.	Chambley, France	Tactical Fighter	F–84F	888	20 Aug 62
1 Oct 61	113 TFS	Terre Haute, Ind.	Terre Haute, Ind.	Tactical Fighter	F–84F	606	
1 Oct 61	169 TFS	Greater Peoria AP, Ill.	Greater Peoria AP, Ill.	Tactical Fighter	F–84F	488	20 Aug 62

DATE ACTIVATED	ORGANIZATION GROUP-SQUADRON	LOCATION	LOCATION MOVED	MISSION	AIRCRAFT	PERSONNEL	DATE DEACTIVATED
1 Oct 61	131 TFW 110 TFS	Lambert Field St. Louis, Mo.	Toule-Rosiere AB, France	Tactical Fighter	F-84F	827	20 Aug 62
1 Oct 61	108 TFW 141 TFS	McGuire AFB, N.J.	Chaumont AB, France	Tactical Fighter	F-84F	764	
1 Oct 61	119 TFS	Atlantic City, N.J.	Atlantic City, N.J.	Tactical Fighter	F-84F	440	
1 Oct 61	112 TFS	Toledo AP, Ohio	Toledo AP, Ohio	Tactical Fighter	F-84F	471	20 Aug 62
1 Oct 61	121 TFW 166 TFS	Lockbourne, AFB, Ohio	Etain, France	Tactical Fighter	F-84F	1185	
1 Oct 61	162 TFS	Springfield, Ohio	Springfield, Ohio	Tactical Fighter	F-84F	464	20 Aug 62
1 Oct 61	164 TFS	Mansfield MAP, Ohio	Mansfield MAP, Ohio	Tactical Fighter	F-84F	471	20 Aug 62
1 Oct 61	149 TFS	Byrd Field, Sandston, Va.	Byrd Field, Sandston, Va.	Tactical Fighter	F-84F	482	
1 Nov 61	197 TFS	Phoenix-Sky Harbor, Ariz.	Ramstein, Germany	Fighter Interceptor	F-104	48	15 Aug 62
1 Nov 61	157 TFS	Columbia, S.C.	Moran AB, Spain	Fighter Interceptor	F-104	48	
1 Nov 61	151 TFS	McGee Tyson AP, Tenn.	Ramstein, Germany	Fighter Interceptor	F-104	41	15 Aug 62

DATE ACTIVATED	ORGANIZATION GROUP-SQUADRON	LOCATION	LOCATION MOVED	MISSION	AIRCRAFT	PERSONNEL	DATE DEACTIVATED
1 Nov 61	134 FG	McGee Tyson AP, Tenn.	Ramstein, Germany	Fighter Interceptor	F–104	743	15 Aug 62
1 Nov 61	169 FG	Columbia, S.C.	Moran AB, Spain	Fighter Interceptor		747	15 Aug 62
1 Nov 61	161 FG	Phoenix Sky Harbor, Ariz.	Ramstein, Germany	Fighter Interceptor		750	15 Aug 62
1 Oct 61	102 ABG	Boston, Mass.	Phalsbourg AB, France	Fighter Interceptor		1135	20 Aug 62
1 Oct 61	101 TFS	Boston, Mass	Phalsbourg AB, France	Fighter Interceptor	F–86H	82	20 Aug 62
1 Oct 61	117 TRW 106 TRS	Birmingham MAP, Ala.	Druex AB, France	Tactical Reconnaissance	RF–84F	1003	22 Aug 62
1 Oct 61	184 TRS	Ft Smith MAP, Ariz.	Ft Smith MAP, Ark.	Tactical Reconnaissance	RF–84F	406	
1 Oct 61	153 TRS	Key Field, Meridian, Miss.	Key Field, Meridian, Miss.	Tactical Reconnaissance	RF–84F	410	9 Oct 62
1 Oct 61	160 TRS	Dannelly Field, Ala.	Dannelly Field, Ala.	Tactical Reconnaissance	RF–84F	406	20 Aug 62
1 Oct 61	146 ATW 115 ATS 195 ATS	Van Nuys, Calif.	Van Nuys, Calif.	Air Transportation	C–97	1168	31 Aug 62

DATE ACTIVATED	ORGANIZATION GROUP-SQUADRON	LOCATION	LOCATION MOVED	MISSION	AIRCRAFT	PERSONNEL	DATE DEACTIVATED
1 Oct 61	133 ATW 109 ATS	St. Paul, Minn.	St. Paul, Minn.	Air Transportation	C–97	813	31 Aug 62
1 Oct 61	133 ATS	Grenier AFB, N.H.	Grenier AFB, N.H.	Air Transportation	C–97	663	
1 Oct 61	139 ATS	Schenectady, N.Y.	Schenectady, N.Y.	Air Transportation	C–97	740	31 Aug 62
1 Oct 61	125 ATS	Tulsa, Okla.	Tulsa, Okla.	Air Transportation	C–97	702	
1 Oct 61	103 AC&W	Groton, Connecticut	Rothwestern, Germany	Aircraft Control & Warning	F–84F	220	31 Aug 62
1 Oct 61	108 AC&W	Hancock Field, N.Y.	Gutersloh, Germany	Aircraft Control & Warning		252	31 Aug 62
1 Oct 61	112 AC&W	State College, Pa.	Buchel, Germany	Aircraft Control & Warning		256	31 Aug 62
1 Oct 61	102 AC&W	Howard, R.I.	Celle, Germany	Aircraft Control & Warning		254	31 Aug 62
1 Sep 61	101 AC&W	Worchester, Mass.	Giebelstadt, Germany	Aircraft Control & Warning		315	31 Aug 62
1 Sep 61	123 AC&W	Blue Ash, Ohio	Lamdshut, Germany	Aircraft Control & Warning		228	31 Aug 62

Appendix 4

Korean and Southeast Asian Mobilizations

DATE ACTIVATED	ORGANIZATION GROUP-SQUADRON	LOCATION	LOCATION MOVED	MISSION	AIRCRAFT	PERSONNEL	DATE DEACTIVATED
Jan 68	120 TFS	Buckley Denver, Colo.	Phan Rang AB, South Vietnam	Tactical Fighter	F–100	900	30 Apr 69
Jan 68	174 TFS	Sioux City, Iowa	Phu Cat AB, South Vietnam	Tactical Fighter	F–100	853	28 May 68
Jan 68	188 TFS	Albuquerque, N.M.	Tuy Hoa AB, South Vietnam	Tactical Fighter	F–100	831	4 Jun 69
Jan 68	136 TFS	Niagara Falls, N.Y.	Tuy Hoa AB, South Vietnam	Tactical Fighter	F–100	811	11 Jun 69
Jan 68	121 TFS	Andrews AFB, Md.	Myrtle Beach AFB, S.C.	Tactical Fighter	F–100	939	18 Jun 69
Jan 68	166 TFS	Columbus, Ohio	Kusan AB, Korea	Tactical Fighter	F–100	848	18 Jun 69
Jan 68	127 TFS	Wichita, Kans.	Kusan AB, Korea	Tactical Fighter	F–100	849	18 Jun 69
Jan 68	119 TFS	Atlantic City, N.J.	Myrtle Beach, AFB, S.C.	Tactical Fighter	F–100	895	17 Jun 69

DATE ACTIVATED	ORGANIZATION GROUP-SQUADRON	LOCATION	LOCATION MOVED	MISSION	AIRCRAFT	PERSONNEL	DATE DEACTIVATED
Jan 68	154 TRS	Little Rock, Ark.	Little Rock, Ark.	Tactical Reconnaissance	F–101	757	20 Dec 68
Jan 68	165 TFS	Louisville, Ky.	Richards-Gebaur AFB, Mo.	Tactical Reconnaissance	F–101G&H	754	9 Jun 69
Jan 68	192 TRS	Reno, Nev.	Richards-Gebaur AFB, Mo.	Tactical Reconnaissance	F–101	625	7 Jun 69
May 68	175 TFG 104 TFS	Baltimore, Md.	Cannon AFB, N.M.	Tactical Fighter	F–86H	424	20 Dec 68
May 68	174 TFG 138 TFS	Syracuse, N.Y.	Cannon AFB, N.M.	Tactical Fighter	F–86H	723	20 Dec 68
May 68	147 AAS 171 AAG	Pittsburgh, Pa.	Pittsburgh, Pa.	Aeromedical Airlift	C–121	760	12 Dec 68

Appendix 5

Air National Guard Personnel
Authorized and Assigned
FY 1946–1969

Year	Military Authorized	Military Assigned	Air Technicians Authorized	Air Technicians Assigned	Total No. of Units
1946		152	131		4
1947	8,497	10,086	2,447	1,809	257
1948	25,103	29,257			393
1949	44,259	41,435	6,271	5,856	514
1950	57,287	44,982	5,642	5,554	514
1951	25,395	20,166*	5,814	7,327**	115
1952	21,419	14,888*	2,370	2,360	149
1953	66,083	35,011	6,768	6,017	544
1954	74,466	49,845	7,600	7,744	609
1955	79,604	61,306	9,254***	9,265	659
1956	82,700	63,534		10,462	614
1957	83,495	67,950		12,357	588
1958	81,000	69,995		13,655	573
1959	81,540	70,994		13,342	567
1960	85,940	70,820		13,163	546

*Does not include personnel mobilized by the federal government.
**Includes state employees supported by federal funds.
***Information on authorized air technicians not available after 1955.

1961	85,555	70,895	13,810	584
1962	64,166	50,319*	10,858	461
1963	72,000	74,325	14,821	670
1964	72,000	73,217	15,350	706
1965	75,000	76,410	15,652	728
1966	77,000	79,883	16,297	850
1967	82,742	83,758	16,483	856
1968	75,522	75,261*	14,691	756
1969	84,260	83,414	16,466	858

*Does not include personnel mobilized by the federal government.
**Includes state employees supported by federal funds.
***Information on authorized air technicians not available after 1955.

Prepared by ANG/HO, April 1983
Source: ANG Summaries 1948–1962 and CNGB Reports 1946–1969

Appendix 6

Air National Guard
Federal Funding

Fiscal Year	Congressionally Appropriated Funds to ANG	ANG Funds Obligated
1946		28,388,001*
1947	61,769,826	61,716,988*
1948	45,254,317	130,838,578*
1949	78,476,025	285,715,116*
1950	115,000,000	113,889,906
1951	103,935,000	102,098,297
1952	87,900,000	84,558,984
1953	106,000,000	95,063,172
1954	147,100,000	138,167,677
1955	160,000,000	164,435,506
1956	203,141,000	184,663,320
1957	258,700,000	249,308,536
1958	260,325,000	256,299,043
1959	252,330,800	248,572,523
1960	233,440,000	227,580,822
1961	249,331,000	258,891,459
1962	265,033,000	257,274,483
1963	261,400,000	261,989,146
1964	298,344,000	295,451,956
1965	320,900,000	306,103,312
1966	322,435,000	333,240,088
1967	346,500,000	366,015,144
1968	369,670,000	365,411,710
1969	374,100,000	382,594,115

* Entire National Guard Obligation

Prepared by ANG/HO: Jul 83
Source: Chief, NGB Reports 1946–1969

Appendix 7

Chiefs of National Guard Headquarters*
Washington, D.C.

Col. Erasmus M. Weaver	1908–1911
Brig. Gen. Robert K. Evans	1911–1912
Maj. Gen. Albert L. Mills	1912–1916
Maj. Gen. William A. Mann	1916–1917
Maj. Gen. Jessie McI. Carter	1917–1918
Brig. Gen. John W. Heavey (Acting)	1918–1919
Maj. Gen. Jessie McI. Carter	1919–1921
Maj. Gen. George C. Rickards	1921–1925
Maj. Gen. Creed C. Hammond	1925–1929
Col. Ernest R. Redmond (Acting)	1929–1929
Maj. Gen. Williams G. Everson	1929–1931
Maj. Gen. George E. Leach	1931–1935
Col. Herold J. Weiler (Acting)	1935–1936
Col. John F. Williams (Acting)	1936–1936
Maj. Gen. Albert H. Blanding	1936–1940
Maj. Gen. John F. Williams	1940–1944
Maj. Gen. John F. Williams (Acting)	1944–1946
Maj. Gen. Butler B. Miltonberger	1946–1947
Maj. Gen. Kenneth R. Cramer	1947–1950
Maj. Gen. Raymond H. Fleming (Acting)	1950–1951
Maj. Gen. Raymond H. Fleming	1951–1953
Maj. Gen. Earl T. Ricks (Acting)	1953–1953
Maj. Gen. Edgar C. Erickson	1953–1959
Maj. Gen. Winston P. Wilson (Acting)	1959–1959
Maj. Gen. Donald W. McGowan	1959–1963
Maj. Gen. Winston P. Wilson	1963–1971
Maj. Gen. Francis S. Greenlief	1971–1974
Lt. Gen. LaVern E. Weber	1974–1982
Lt. Gen. Emmett H. Walker, Jr.	1982–

---

*The National Guard headquarters was known as the Division of Militia Affairs from 1908–1916. It then became the Militia Bureau (1916–1933) and in 1933 was redesignated the National Guard Bureau.

Appendix 8

Chiefs of the Air Division
National Guard Bureau

Col. William A. R. Robertson, AAF Chief, Aviation Group	1946–1947
Col. William A. R. Robertson, USAF Chief, Air Division	1948
Maj. Gen. George Finch, ANGUS Chief, Air Force Division	1949–1950
Maj. Gen. Earl T. Ricks, ANGUS Chief, Air Force Division	1950–1952
Maj. Gen. Earl T. Ricks, ANGUS Chief, Air Force Division and Deputy Chief, National Guard Bureau	1953
Brig. Gen. Winston P. Wilson, ANGUS Chief, Air Force Division	1954
Maj. Gen. Winston P. Wilson, ANGUS Chief, Air Force Division	1955–58
Maj. Gen. Winston P. Wilson, ANGUS Assistant Chief, National Guard Bureau, Air	1959–1962
Brig. Gen. I. G. Brown, ANGUS Assistant Chief, National Guard Bureau, Air	1963–1969
Maj. Gen. I. G. Brown, ANGUS Director, Air National Guard	1970–1973

AIR NATIONAL GUARD

Maj. Gen. John J. Pesch, ANGUS   1974–1976
Director, Air National Guard

Maj. Gen. John T. Guice, ANGUS   1977–1981
Director, Air National Guard

Maj. Gen. John B. Conaway, ANGUS   1982–
Director, Air National Guard

Notes

Introduction

1. "The Air National Guard," *Air Reservist*, Feb 1966, pp 4–5; NGB "Brief History of Air National Guard Mobilizations," Fact Sheet 302–76 (Washington, 1976), p 1; Jim Dan Hill, *The Minute Man in Peace and War: A History of the National Guard* (Harrisburg, Pa., 1964), pp 519–20; Juliette A. Hennessy, *The United States Army Air Arm, April 1861 to April 1917*, USAF Historical Studies: No 98 (Maxwell AFB, Ala., USAF Historical Division, Research Studies Institute, Air University, 1958).

2. "The Air National Guard," p 2; NGB, Fact Sheet 302–76, p 1.

3. Hill, *Minute Man*, pp 521–22; NGB, Fact Sheet 302–76, p 1; Henry G. Pearson, *A Businessman in Uniform, Raynal Cawthorne Bolling* (New York, 1923), pp 247–251; Alfred Goldberg, ed, *A History of the U.S. Air Force, 1907–1957* (Princeton, N.J., reprint of 1957 publication), pp 16, 22, manuscript prepared by U.S. Air Force Historical Division.

4. NGB, Fact Sheet 302–76, p 2.

5. Hill, *Minute Man*, pp 526–28.

6. *Ibid.*, pp 534–35; NGB, Fact Sheet 302–76, p 2.

7. John Rhea, "A Vital Link," *Guardsman*, Sep 1977, p 1; intvw, author with Col Melvin E. Gourdin, Assistant to the Commander for Operations and Logistics, Air Reserve Forces, HQ Air Force Logistics Command, Wright-Patterson AFB, Ohio, Apr 16, 1980; National Guard Association of the United States, "Fiscal," *Redbook for 1980*, pp 1–2, 15–23.

8. Very little scholarly attention has been devoted to the Air Guard. Outstanding general works on American military history like Russell F. Weigley's *American Way of War: A History of United States Military Strategy and Policy* (New York, 1973), and Walter Millis' *Arms and Men: A Study in American Military History* (New York, 1958), scarcely mentioned the Air Guard. Existing published scholarly literature on the National Guard including Martha Derthick's *The National Guard in Politics* (Cambridge, Mass., 1965), and William H. Riker's *Soldiers of the States: The Role of the National Guard in American Democracy* (Washington, 1957), concentrate on its domestic political dimensions. Jim Dan Hill's *Minute Man* is defensive in tone and emphasizes the Army National Guard. Broad works on aviation like Robin Higham's *Air Power: A Concise History* (London, 1972), virtually ignore the Air Guard. Institutional histories such as Carroll Glines' *The Compact History of the United States Air Force* (New York, 1973), and Goldberg, *History of USAF to 1957* (Princeton, N.J., 1957), provide little information on the Air Guard. Martin Binkin's policy-oriented *U.S. Reserve Forces: The Problem of the Weekend Warrior* (Washington, 1974), provides a more substantial introduction to the issues generated by the costs, roles and mobilization performance of America's military reserve forces. Binkin, a retired Air Force colonel, argued that those forces could be cut by one-third thereby realizing an annual savings of $1.4 billion. His study stresses "heavy" cuts in the army reserves, "substantial" cuts in the naval reserve, and "some" cuts in the air reserves. He also urged merger of the administrative headquarters of the Army Reserve and National Guard, on the one hand, and of the Air Force Reserve and Air Guard, on the other. However, Binkin's work is flawed by exaggerated estimates of the savings to be realized through the mergers of reserve components and inaccuracies in the statistical bases of its arguments. Unpublished scholarly research on the Air Guard is difficult to identify. One example of this genre is Frank L. Howe's M.A. thesis, "A Bombsight for a Freight Train: The Air National Guard, Air Defense, and Federalization, 1946–1950" (Columbus, Ohio, Ohio State University, 1972). Howe's work is supplemented by a series of studies completed by guardsmen who were students at the Air University, Maxwell AFB, Ala.

Chapter I

Forged in Politics, 1943–1946

1. NGB, *Annual Report of the Chief, NGB for the Fiscal Year (FY) Ending 30 June 1946*, p 83; Hill, *Minute Man*, p 532; Frank Laurence Howe, "A Bombsight for a Freight Train: The Air National Guard, Air Defense and Federalization, 1946–1950," pp 12–13, 29; Thomas W. Ray, *The Air National Guard Manned Interceptor Force, 1946–1964* (Air Defense Command (ADC) Study 23, Ent AFB, Colo., 1964), pp 7–11; ADC, *History, March 1946 to June 1946* Mitchel AFB, N.Y., 1948), p 36.

2. Michael S. Sherry, *Preparing for the Next War: America Plans for Postwar Defense, 1941–1945* New Haven, Conn., Yale University, 1977), p 54.

3. Charles J. Gross, "Universal Military Training: A Study in American Ideology" (Thesis, Utah State University, 1973), p 23, Note 12.

4. *Ibid.*, p 14, Note 5, p 18, Notes 20, 22.

5. Sherry, *Next War*, p 36; Russell F. Weigley, *Towards an American Army: Military Thought from Washington to Marshall* New York, 1962), pp 242–43.

6. Sherry, *Next War*, pp 8–9; John McAuley Palmer, "Selected Documents from the Records of the President's Advisory Commission on UMT" (unpublished volume, Harry S. Truman Library), pp 1124–25; Perry McCoy Smith, *The Air Force Plans for Peace, 1943–45* Baltimore, 1970); Sherry *Next War*, pp 15, 17, 21.

7. Smith, *Air Force Plans*, pp 2, 5, 25.

8. *Ibid.*, p 2.

9. *Ibid.*, pp 56–61, 64, 71, 73; Sherry, *Next War*, p 41.

10. Hill, *Minute Man*, pp 430, 433–34, 446–47. (Discusses mobilization and preparation of the National Guard for World War II. Extremely partisan pro-guard view. Bitter attack on the regular Army.)

11. *Ibid.*, pp 490–91; NGB, *Report for FY 46*, p 62.

12. NGAUS, *Official Proceedings at the NGAUS Sixty-Sixth General Conference* (Baltimore, 1944), p 25; Hill, *Minute Man*, p 343.

13. Hill, *Minute Man*, p 343.

14. Martha Derthick, *The National Guard in Politics* (Cambridge, Mass., 1965), pp 1–3; William H. Riker, *Soldiers of the States: The Role of the National Guard in American Democracy* (Washington, 1957), pp 67, 102–3.

15. Derthick, *The National Guard in Politics*, pp 132–35.

16. *Ibid.*, pp 132–35.

17. *Ibid.*, pp 85–86.

18. NGAUS, *1944 Proceedings*, p 138; Adjutants General Association of the United States (AGAUS), *1944 Conference of the AGAUS Proceedings* (Baltimore, 1944), p 35. (Joint meeting held with NGAUS. 1944 AGAUS Proceedings printed in NGAUS, *1944 Proceedings.*)

19. AGAUS, *1944 Conference*, p 36.

20. Hill, *Minute Man*, pp 311, 499.

21. *Ibid.*, p 495; Sherry, *Next War*, p 58 (notes).

22. NGAUS, *1944 Proceedings*, pp 25–140.

23. U.S. Congress, House, Select Committee on Post War Military Policy, *Hearings before the Select Committee on Post War Military Policy to Establish a Single Department of the Armed Forces*, 78th Cong, 2d sess (Washington, 1944), p 291.

24. *Ibid.*, pp 292–93.

25. NGB, *Report for FY 46*, pp 5, 61; Hill, *Minute Man*, p 368.

26. Sherry, *Next War*, pp 95–96.

27. *Ibid.*, pp 102–14.

28. Memo, Director, Special Planning Division, War Department Special Staff, to Commanding General (CG), Army Air Forces (AAF), subj: "Post-war Air Force National Guard," Aug 30, 1944; DC/AS, HQ AAF, Study of the Air Component for the Post-War National Guard, Oct 21, 1944, Army Adjutant General File, Postwar Vol 2, Records Group (RG) 18, File 381, Box 189, NARS.

29. Memo, Col L. W. Sweetser, Jr., Chief, Reserve and National Guard Division to the ACAS–1, Aug 13, 1945, in Howe, "Bombsight," p 12.

30. U.S. Congress, House, Select Committee on Postwar Military Policy, *Hearings on Universal Military Training*, 79th Cong, 1st sess (Washington, 1945), p 501.

31. *Ibid.*, pp 52, 501.

32. R&R Sheet, Col J. J. Ladd, ACAS–3 to ACAS–1, subj: AAF Troop Program for 1 July 1946, Nov 21, 1945, RG 18, AG 320.2, AAF Program/91; R&R Sheet, Col John S. Hardy, ACAS–1 to ACAS–3, subj: AAF Troop Program

for 1 July 1946, Nov 26, 1945, RG 18, AAG 320.2, AAF Program/91, NARS.

33. Vincent Davis, *Postwar Defense Policy and the U.S. Navy, 1943–1946* (Chapel Hill, N.C., 1962, 1666). This is an excellent treatment of the role of the Navy Forrestal and senior Naval officers in U.S. national security policymaking during the 1943–46 period. Navy postwar planning, like that of the Army and AAF, was largely a parochial matter conducted without benefit of nationally-oriented guidance. It called for a large peacetime fleet dominated by carrier task forces. The author concludes that the Navy's postwar planning was stimulated more by a fear of inadequate budgets and Army domination under military unification schemes than by any potential enemy including the Russians. An independent Air Force, allied with the Army, was seen as a great threat to postwar Naval budgets and continued Navy control of carrier aviation.

34. U.S. Congress, House, Committee on Military Affairs, *Hearings on Universal Military Training,* 79th Cong, 1st sess (Washington, 1945), p 812; Hill, *Minute Man,* p 341.

35. House, *UMT Hearings, Dec 45,* p 812.

36. NGB, *Report for FY 46,* p 64.

37. House, *UMT Hearings, Dec 45,* p 812.

38. NGB, *Report for FY 46,* p 64; House, *UMT Hearings, Dec 45,* p 812; Russell F. Weigley, *History of the United States Army* (New York, 1967), p 487.

39. NGB, *Report for FY 46,* p 80; AAF Plan for ANG, Air Reserve, Air ROTC, First Revision, Nov 1, 1945, RG 18, AAG File 381, Box 454, NARS; ltr, HQ Continental Air Force to CG AAF, subj: National Guard for Post War AAF, Oct 25, 1945, DRB 325, National Guard 1945, CVAH(S).

40. Memo, R&R ACAS–3, Assistant for P&O to ACAS–3, Fighter and Air Defense Branch, subj: National Guard for Air Defense, Nov 6, 1945, CHAV(S); Howe, "Bombsight," p 12.

41. NGB, *Report for FY 46,* p 80.

42. *Ibid.,* p 80; NGB, *Report for FY 46,* p 80; Ray, ADC Study 23, pp 7–11; Howe, "Bombsight," p 28.

43. Ray, ADC Study 23, pp 7–11.

44. Howe, "Bombsight," pp 14–16; memo attached to AAF Plan for ANG, Air Reserve, Air ROTC First Revision, Nov 1, 1945, Spaatz Papers, Box 255, MD, LC.

Chapter II

Struggle for Control, 1946–1950

1. NGB, *Report for FY 46,* p 83; U.S. Congress, House, Committee on Appropriations, *Hearings on the Department of Defense Appropriations for Fiscal Year 1951. Part Three. Department of the Air Force,* 81st Cong, 2d sess (Washington, 1950), p 1672 [hereafter cited as House, *Air Force Appropriations, FY 51;* Col William M. Reid, "The Air National Guard" (Paper, Air War College, Maxwell AFB, Ala., 1949), p 5; NGB, *Annual Report of the Chief, NGB for the Fiscal Year Ending 30 June 1949* (Washington, 1949), p 3; House, *Air Force Appropriations, FY 51,* pp 1672–74; CONAC, *History for Jul-Dec 1950* (Mitchel AFB, N.Y., 1951), p 205; NGB, *Annual Report of the Chief, NGB for the Fiscal Year Ending 30 June 1950* (Washington, 1950), pp 22–23.

2. Howe, "Bombsight," p 75; intvw, author with Maj Gen Winston P. Wilson, Forrest City, Ark., Dec 17–18, 1978; intvw, author with Brig Gen Paul E. Hoover, Ohio Assistant Adjutant General for Air, Worthington, Ohio, May 30, 1978; Lt Col Thomas G. Lanphier, "Forty-Eight Air Forces Too Many," *Air Force,* Jan 1949, pp 11–12.

3. Memo, Lt Gen Ennis C. Whitehead, CG CONAC to Maj Gen Charles T. Meyers, Nov 12, 1949, in Richard F. McMullen's *The Air National Guard in Air Defense, 1946–1971* (Air Defense Command (ADC) Study 38, Ent AFB, Colo., n.d.), p 11.

4. Memo, Brig Gen J. P. McConnell, Deputy Special Assistant to the Chief of Staff for Reserve Forces (SARF), subj: Mission of the ANG, Vandenberg Papers, Jan 5, 1950, File 1950, Box 33, MD, LC.

5. Howe, "Bombsight," pp 22–23; Lt Gen Stratemeyer, "Air National Guard," *Commanding General's Address to the Air War College,* Oct 15, 1966, ADC Doc 419, pp 101–25, CVAH(S).

6. Howe, "Bombsight," p 25; McMullen, ADC Study 38, pp 1–2.

7. Ltr, HQ ADC to Maj Gen Earle E. Partridge, Assistant Chief of Staff for Operations, HQ AAF, Aug 11, 1947, CONAC, *Hist, Jul–Dec 50,* p 208.

8. Howe, "Bombsight," p 22.

9. Ltr, Lt Gen George Stratemeyer to Maj Gen Butler B. Miltonberger, Chief, NGB, Apr 15, 1946, in McMullen ADC Study 38, pp 1–5.

10. *Ibid.,* pp 1–5.

11. *Ibid.,* pp 1–5.

12. Ray, ADC Study 23, p 11; U.S. Congress, Senate, Committee on Armed Services, *The National Defense Establishment (Unification of the Armed Services), Hearings on S. 758,* 80th Cong, 1st sess (Washington, 1947), p 705 [hereafter cited as Senate, *Unification Hearings, 1947];* hist, ADC, Jul 47–Nov 48, in ltr, Gen Carl Spaatz to all major AAF commanders, subj: Air Reserve Training, Jul 13, 1946, p 2 (Mitchel AFB, N.Y., 1948).

13. Ltr, HQ AAF to CG ADC, CVAH(S), subj: Special Directive on Method and Procedure, May 10, 1946, ADC Historical Documents, (letter also cited in McMullen's ADC Study 38, pp 1–5). [Hereafter cited as AAF ltr on Method and Procedure, May 1946].

14. Ltr, Col Gerald C. Ward to author, Mar 17, 1948, pp 1–2. (Col Ward, a regular Air Force officer, was assigned to the National Guard Bureau during the 1945–48 period. His job was to help Air Guard units obtain flying facilities in each of the states.)

15. Ibid., pp 1–2; ltr, Maj Gen C. D. O'Sullivan, Calif. Adjutant General, to Gen H. H. Arnold, Sep 8, 1947, Arnold Papers, National Guard File, Box 220, MD, LC.

16. Ward, ltr to author, pp 1–2.

17. Memo, Assistant Secretary of War for Air to the Secretary of War, subj: National Guard Airport Facilities, Jun 15, 1946, Spaatz Papers, File Asst Secy of War for Air, Box 256, MD, LC.

18. Hist, ADC, Mar 46–Jun 47, in ltr, HQ ADC to CG AAF, Apr 16, 1945 (Mitchel AFB, N.Y., 1947).

19. *Ibid.*

20. McMullen, ADC Study 38, p 17.

21. AAF ltr on Method and Procedure, May 1946.

22. First Air Force, *History, 1st Air Force, Mar 21 to Dec 31, 1946* (Mitchel AFB, N.Y., 1947), pp 16–17.

23. McMullen, ADC Study 38, pp 1–5.

24. Memo, U.S. War Department, subj: Clarification of War Department Policies Pertaining to the National Guard and Organized Reserve Corps, Dec 20, 1946, Printed in U.S. Congress, House, Committee on Appropriations *Hearings on the Military Establishment's Appropriations Bill for (FY) 1948,* 80th Cong, 1st sess (Wash-

ington, 1947), pp 1130–31 (same memo also cited in ADC, *Hist, Mar 46 to Jun 47,* p 45).

25. ADC, *Hist, Mar 46 to Jun 47,* p 46; McMullen, ADC Study 38, p 5. See also NGB, *Report for FY 46,* p 79.

26. U.S. Congress, House, Committee on Appropriations, *Hearings on the Military Establishment's Appropriations Bill for (FY) 1948,* 80th Cong, 1st session (Washington, 1947), pp 1110, 1523, 1171, 1532 !hereafter cited as House, *Military Appropriations for FY 48];* subsection D of report, The Civilian Components of the U.S. Air Force, submitted by the Air Force Chief of Staff (AFCC) to the Secretary of Defense's Committee on Civilian Components (the Gray Committee), Mar 26, 1948, Records of Secretary of the Air Force, Office of the Administrative Assistant, Correspondence, RG 340, Special Interest File 1948–49, Items 6–7, NARS.

27. Ltr. CG AAF to CG ADC, subj: Interim Ceiling on National Guard Organization, Mar 14, 1947 in ADC, *Hist, Mar 46 to Jun 47,* p. 48.

28. Ltr, Gen Hoyt Vandenberg to Rep Albert Thomas (Texas), Jul 30, 1947, Vandenberg Papers, Box 8, LC; hist, CONAC, Jul–Dec 50, Vol II, in ltr, HQ ADC to Maj Gen E. E. Partridge, AAF Assistant Chief of Staff for Operations, Aug 11, 1947 (Mitchel AFB, N.Y., 1951); hist, ADC, Jul 47–Nov 48, Doc 179, in memo, Col William A. Robertson, NGB, to CG ADC, May 1, 1947 (Mitchel AFB, N.Y., 1948).

29. NGB, *Annual Report of the Chief, NGB for the Fiscal Year Ending 30 June 1947* (Washington, 1947), pp 103–4.

30. Plan, HQ AAF, Jun 1947, AAF Plan for the National Guard, Appendix B, in ADC, *Hist, Mar 46 to Jun 47,* p 51.

31. Goldberg, *History of USAF through 1957,* pp 105–6.

32. Ltr, USAF to ADC, subj: Air Defense, Dec 17, 1947, in McMullen's ADC Study 38, p 8.

33. *Ibid.*

34. Ltr, HQ USAF to Chief, NGB, subj: Release of Regular Air Force Officers as Commanders of National Guard Air Units, Jul 30, 1948; Records of the NGB, RG 168, File 210.1 (Air), 1946–1948, Box 791, WNRC; Col C. E. Hughes, "The Air National Guard" (Thesis, Air War College, Maxwell AFB, Ala., 1949), pp 6–8 (Col Hughes bases his thesis on his mid–1940s experiences as head of a Federal Recognition Board appointed by the CG, Second Air Force); ltr, Chief, NGB to CG AAF, Jun 6, 1946, Records of the NGB, RG 168, File 210.1, 1946–1948, Box 791, WNRC; NGB, *Annual Report of the*

Chief, NGB for the Fiscal Year Ending 30 June 1948 (Washington, 1948), p 13.

35. Hist, ADC, Jul 47–Nov 48, Doc 237, in ltr, Brig Gen J. P. McConnell, Chief, National Guard and Reserve Affairs Div, Directorate of Training and Requirements, HQ USAF, to CG ADC, subj: Air National Guard Caretaker Personnel, Mar 18, 1948 (Mitchel AFB, N.Y., 1948).

36. Howe, "Bombsight," p 41; NGB, *Report for FY 48*, p 13.

37. Howe, "Bombsight," p 41.

38. Presentation (untitled), Lt Gen George Stratemeyer, ADC Commanders' Conference, Oklahoma City, Okla., Nov 15, 1947, ADC Historical Documents, CVAH(S).

39. *Ibid.*

40. Howe, "Bombsight," pp 40–42.

41. *Ibid.*, p 42.

42. NGAUS, *Official Proceedings at the NGAUS Seventieth General Conference* (St. Louis, Mo., 1948), p 41.

43. U.S. Department of Defense, *Report of the Committee on Civilian Components* (Washington, 1948), p 14.

44. *Ibid.*, p 9.

45. *Ibid.*, p 10.

46. Memo, Col Bruce K. Holloway, HQ USAF to Lt Gen Stratemeyer, CG ADC, subj: Training of Reserve and National Guard Personnel, Jan 26, 1948, Records of the AFCC, Office of the SARF, RG 341, File 210.3 to 300.0, 1946–1949, Box 3, NARS.

47. Memo, Gen Spaatz for Secretary of the Air Force Symington, subj: Letter, 15 December 1947, From Director Montana Aeronautical Commission to Mr.C. C. Mosely, 9 President, California Aeronautical Technical Institute, Jan 8, 1948, Records of the SAF, Mail and Records Branch, RG 340, File 325 to 334, Nov 1947 to Jun 1948, Box 40, NARS.

48. *Ibid.*

49. Lanphier, "Forty-Eight Air Forces"; Col Carroll V. Glines, *The Compact History of the United States Air Force* (New York, 1973), p 194.

50. Lanphier, "Forty-Eight Air Forces," p 11.

51. *Ibid.*, p 12.

52. *Ibid.*, pp 13, 15.

53. U.S. Department of Defense, *First Annual Report of the Secretary of Defense to the President* (Washington, 1948), App E, p 161.

54. Memo, Secretary of Defense Forrestal to President Truman, subj: Federalization of the Air National Guard, Dec 7, 1948, Records of the AFCC, Office of the Secretary of the Air Staff,

RG 341, Special File 34A, Legislative Program, 81st Cong (Staff Actions), NARS.

55. *Ibid.*

56. *Ibid.*

57. CONAC, *History, Dec 1948 to Dec 1949* (Mitchel AFB, N.Y., 1950), pp 1–2.

58. Ltr, Col Jacob E. Smart, HQ ADC to Brig Gen J. P. 0 McConnell, National Guard and Reserve Affairs Div, HQ USAF, subj: Revising the Air Reserve Program, Feb 27, 1948, Historical Archives, HQ AFR; memo, Symington for Forrestal, subj: Report to the President re Progress in (Reserve) Effectiveness Under Executive Order 10,007, Dec 8, 1948, Records of the AFCC, Office of the AFCRF, RG 341, File 315 to 322, Box 5, NARS [hereafter cited as Symington, Progress under EO 10,007, Dec 8, 1948]; CONAC, *Hist, Dec 48 to Dec 49*, pp 1–19; Information Division, SARF, "Air Force's Baby: The Continental Air Command," *Air Reserve Forces Review*, Jun 1949, pp 4–5.

59. CONAC, *Hist, Dec 48 to Dec 49*, p 16; Howe, "Bombsight," pp 63–64.

60. NGB, The Air National Guard Summary, report prepared by the Air Plans Group, Air Force Div, NGB, Mar 31, 1949, p 2, Doc 160.801197, AFSHRC [hereafter cited as NGB, ANG Summary, Mar 31, 1949]; Howe, "Bombsight," pp 63–64.

61. Memo, President Truman to Secretary of Defense Forrestal, Aug 12, 1948, in Howe, "Bombsight," p 47.

62. Memo, Gen Vandenberg to Lt Gen Quesada, subj: Terms of Reference for Study of Matters Pertaining to the Merger of the Reserve Forces of the Air Force, Jan 19, 1949, Records of the SAF, Office of the Administrative Assistant, RG 340, Special Interest File 1950, Box 55, NARS [hereafter cited as Vandenberg, Quesada's Terms of Reference, Jan 19, 1949].

63. CONAC, *Hist, Dec 48 to Dec 49*, pp 2–4; Brig Gen J. P. McConnell, "The Air Reserve and National Guard," Air War College lecture, Nov 29, 1948, pp 14–15, CVAH(S); memos, Brig Gen McConnell to Air Staff, subj: Staff Functional Support of USAF Civilian Component Programs, Jul 30, 1948, Secretary, Air Staff to the Air Staff, subj: Amendments to Headquarters, USAF Organization and Functions Chartbook Pertaining to Civilian Components, n.d., both memos in Records of the AFCC, Office of the SARF, RG 341, File 324, Box 6, NARS.

64. "Forrestal Has Plan to Invigorate Reserve Forces," *Air Force*, Jan 1949, pp 32–33.

65. *Ibid.*, p 33.

66. Howe, "Bombsight," p 30; memo, Maj Gen S. E. Anderson, Director, Plans and Operations, HQ USAF to Whitney, Assistant SAF, Apr 13, 1948 Records of the SAF, Correspondence Control Div, RG 340, File 325 to 334 Misc, Nov 1947 to Jun 1948, Box 40, NARS.

67. Memo, SAF Symington to SECDEF Forrestal, subj: Federalization of the Air National Guard, Feb 10, 1949, Records of the SAF, Office of the Administrative Assistant, RG 340, Special Interest File 1949, Box 36, NARS [hereafter cited as Memo, Symington to Forrestal, ANG Federalization, Feb 10, 1949].

68. Vandenberg, Quesada's Terms of Reference, Jan 19, 1949.

69. NGAUS, "A Situation Report: The Battle of Washington," *The National Guardsman,* Mar 1949, pp 18–21.

70. U.S.Congress, House, Committee on Armed Services, *Hearings on the Bill to Authorize the Composition of the Army of the United States and the Air Force of the United States and for Other Purposes,* H.R. 1437, 81st Cong, 1st sess (Washington, 1949), pp 201, 216–17 [hereafter cited as House, *Hearings on Army and Air Force Composition, 1949*].

71. *Ibid.,* pp 24–45; NGB, *Report for FY 48,* p 6.

72. House, *Hearings on Army and Air Force Composition, 1949,* p 273.

73. *Ibid.,* p 273.

74. *Ibid.,* pp 273–74.

75. *Ibid.,* p 274.

76. *Ibid.,* p 278.

77. *Ibid.,* p 276.

78. *Ibid.,* p 277.

79. *Ibid.,* pp 289, 297, 308.

80. Press Release, Department of the Air Force, Feb 18, 1949, Records of the SAF, Office of the Administrative Assistant, RG 340, Special Interest File 1950, Box 55, NARS.

81. NGAUS, "Air Guard Training Agreement O'Kayed," *The National Guardsman,* Feb 1949, p 14.

82. *Ibid.*

83. *Ibid.*

84. Lee E. Sharff, "The National Guard Bureau," *1977 National Guard Almanac* (Washington, 1977), p 90; House, *Hearings on Army and Air Force Composition, 1949,* pp 273–74.

85. Adjutants General Association of the United States, AGAUS Annual Meeting, May 2–4, 1946, Washington, D.C. (unpublished stenographic transcript, Edwin L. Martin Memorial Library, NGAUS, Washington), p 320.

86. Senate, *Unification Hearings, 1947,* p 701.

87. *Ibid.,* p 705.

88. *Ibid.,* pp 701–702.

89. NGB, *Report for FY 48,* p 5; memo, Civilian Component Group, Directorate of Operations, HQ USAF to Directorate of Training and Requirements, subj: Reorganization of the National Guard Bureau, May 6, 1948, Records of the AFCC, Office of the SARF, RG 341, File 210.3 to 300, 1946–49, Box 3, NARS.

90. NGAUS, untilted news item, *The National Guardsman,* Nov 1945, p 5.

91. Memos, SARF to Chief, NGB, subj: Reclama to the Proposed FY 51 Budget Estimate Reduction, Dec 6, 1949, SARF to Chief, NGB, subj: Air National Guard Budget Activity, Dec 8, 1949, both memos in Records of the AFCC, Office of the SARF, Mail and Records Div, RG 341, File 032 to 200, 1946–49, Box 1, NARS; intvw, author with Curtis E. Metcalf, Deputy Chief, Plans and Operations, Air Force Div, NGB, Washington, D.C., Oct 18, 1977. (Metcalf served as an Air Force officer with the NGB from July 1957 through June 1962 and again from 1965 to his retirement in February 1970. He has been employed there as a civilian since mid–1970).

92. NGB, ANG Summary, Mar 31, 1949, p 2; Maj Gen Earle E. Partridge, HQ USAF, "Address to the National Convention of the Air National Guard Association," Columbus, Ohio, Sep 19, 1947, Doc 410.161–10, p 1, AFSHRC.

93. U.S. Congress, House, Committee on Appropriations, *Hearings on the National Military Establishment Appropriations Bill for (FY) 1949,* 80th Cong, 2d sess (Washington, 1948), p 410.

94. *Ibid.*

95. Memo, Brig Gen C. P. Kane to Inspector General, subj: The Air National Guard, Apr 1, 1949, pp 2–5, Records of the AFCC, Office of the SARF, RG 341, File 032 to 200, 1946–49, Box 1, NARS; memo, SARF to Chief, NGB, subj: Reclama to the Proposed FY 51 Budget Estimate Reduction, Dec 6, 1949, Records of the AFCC, Office of the SARF, RG 341, File 032 to 200, 1946–49, Box 1, NARS.

96. 10th Air Force, *Historical Data, 10th Air Force, 1 July 1949 to 31 Dec 1949* (Selfridge AFB, Mich., 1950), IV, 206, Doc 830.01, AFSHRC.

97. *Ibid.*

98. Memo, Maj Gen Earl S. Hoag, SARF to USAF Inspector General, subj: Joint Inquiry Concerning NGB, Dec 19, 1949, Records of the AFCC, Office of the SARF, RG 341, File 324,

Box 6, NARS; Symington, Progress Under EO 10,007, Dec 8, 1948; NGAUS, untitled news item, *The National Guardsman*, Nov 1948, p 5; memo, USAF Inspector General to SARF, Dec 13, 1949, Records of AFCC, Office of SARF, RG 341, File 324, Box 6, NARS.

99. Memo, Gen Vandenberg to Secretary of the Air Force, subj: National Guard Bureau, Nov 16, 1949, Records of the SAF, Correspondence, RG 340, File 325, Sep 24, 1948 to Dec 29, 1949, NARS.

100. *Ibid.*

101. *Ibid.*

102. *Ibid.*

103. *Ibid.*

104. Memo, Brig Gen McConnell, Deputy SARF to Stuart, Assistant SAF, subj: National Guard Bureau, May 5, 1950, pp 2–4, Records of SAF, Office of the Administrative Assistant, RG 340, File by Organization and Subject, 1947–Jan 1953 (Assistant SAF (Mgt) Frank T. McCoy), Box 208, NARS [hereafter cited as McConnell, NGB, May 5, 1950].

105. *Ibid,* p 5.

106. *Ibid,* pp 6–7.

107. *Ibid,* p 7.

108. Maj Gen Kenneth F. Cramer, Chief, NGB, "The State of the National Guard," AGAUS Annual Meeting, Feb 23–26, 1950, Washington, D.C., Feb 23, 1950, pp 121–22 (stenographic transcript, Edwin L. Martin Memorial Library, NGAUS, Washington).

109. McConnell, NGB, May 5, 1950, p 9.

110. *Ibid.*

111. Memo, Harold Stuart to McCone, Sep 18, 1950, Records of the SAF, Correspondence, RG 340, File 324.5 to 325, Box 880, NARS.

112. House, *Air Force Appropriations, FY 51,* pp 1673, 1678–79, 1688; CONAC, *Hist, Jul–Dec 50,* Vol II, in ltr, Lt Gen Whitehead, HQ CONAC to Maj Gen Willis H. Hale, CG Ninth Air Force, Jan 6, 1950 (Mitchel AFB, N.Y., 1951) [hereafter cited as Whitehead ltr to Hale, Jan 6, 1950]; memo, Gen Muir Fairchild to Air Staff, subj: Mission of the Air National Guard,

Nov 16, 1949, Fairchild Papers, File ANG, Box 2, MD, LC.

113. Memo, Gen Vandenberg for Symington, subj: Mission of the Air National Guard, Feb 13, 1950, Vandenberg Papers, File 1950, Box 33, MD, LC; memo, Maj Gen Earl S. Hoag, Feb 20, 1950, Vandenberg Papers, Box 53, MD, LC.

114. Hoag, ANG, Feb 20, 1950; Vandenberg, Mission of ANG, Feb 13, 1950.

115. Ltr, Lt Gen Ennis C. Whitehead to Gen Vandenberg, Jan 11, 1950, Vandenberg Papers, Box 52, MD, LC; Hoag, ANG, Feb 20, 1950; Whitehead ltr to Hale, Jan 6, 1950.

116. Vandenberg, Mission of ANG, Feb 13, 1950; memo, Maj Gen W. E. McKee, Assistant Vice Chief of Staff to Gen Vandenberg, Jan 11, 1950, subj: Mission of the Air National Guard, Vandenberg Papers, Box 36, MD, LC.

117. Vandenberg, Mission of ANG, Feb 13, 1950.

118. *Ibid.*

119. Memo, SAF Symington to SECDEF Johnson, subj: Mission to the Air National Guard, Apr 20, 1950, with attached memo from Gen Vandenberg, subj: Mission of the Air National Guard, Feb 13, 1950, Records of the SAF, Correspondence, RG 340, File 325–326, Box 543, NARS.

120. Goldberg, *History of USAF through 1957,* p 164; memo, NGB for Gen David C. Jones, AFCC, subj: Mobilizations of the National Guard, 1915–1970, Jul 26, 1974, p 2, Doc K160.801–1, AFCHO.

121. Memo, Col C. W. Schott, Deputy SARF to Gen Nugent, subj: Federalization of the Air National Guard, Jun 22, 1949, Records of the AFCC, Office of the SARF, Correspondence, RG 341, File 324, Box 6, NARS.

122. Ltr, Lt Gen Whitehead to AFCC, subj: The USAF Reserve Forces, Dec 13, 1950, p 1, Records of the AFCC, Office of the SARF, RG 341, Classified File, Jan–Jun 1951, NARS.

123. *Ibid.,* pp 2–3.

124. *Ibid.,* p 4.

125. *Ibid.,* p 10.

126. *Ibid.,* p 11.

127. *Ibid.,* pp 11–12.

Chapter III

Rejuvenation, 1950–1953

1. Russell F. Weigley, *American Way of War: A History of United States Military Strategy and Policy* (New York, 1973), p 383 [hereafter cited as Weigley, Way of War].

2. *Ibid.*, pp 383–84; Weigley, *U.S. Army,* p 507.

3. Weigley, *U.S. Army,* p 508.

4. Goldberg, *History of USAF through 1957,* pp 162, 164; Hoover intvw, May 30, 1978; U.S. Congress, House, Committee on Armed Services, *Reserve Components, Hearings,* 82d Cong, 1st sess (Washington, 1951), pp 226, 256–57 [hereafter cited as House, *Reserve Hearings 1951*].

5. Memo, NGB to the Air Force Chief of Staff (AFCC), subj: Mobilizations of the ANG, Jul 26, 1974, p 1, Doc K160.801–1, CVAH(S); NGB, Fact Sheet 102–76, Apr 1976, "Compact History of the National Guard," p 4; NGB, Fact Sheet 302–76, p 2; U.S. Congress, Senate, Committee on Appropriations, *Hearings on the Department of Defense (DOD) Appropriations for Fiscal Year (FY) 1954,* 83rd Cong, 1st sess (Washington, 1953), p 1466 [hereafter cited as Senate, *DOD Appropriations FY 54*]; Lt Col Duane M. Benton (ANG), "ANG Weather Flights in the Total Force Concept" (Study 4849, Air War College, Maxwell AFB, Ala., Apr 1973), p 37.

6. NGB, *Report for FY 50,* p 22; Maj Gen Earl J. Ricks, Chief, NGB, "The Post Korea Air National Guard," *National Guardsman,* Dec 1951, pp 12–13; "Finletter Approves Long Range Program for Air Reserve Forces," *Air Reserve Forces Review,* Oct 1951, pp 3–6.

7. Hill, *Minute Man,* p 535; Hoover intvw, May 30, 1978. (Brig Gen Hoover is a career Air Guardsman who entered the program in 1946. He was mobilized during the Korean War and saw combat in that conflict. Both Hill and Hoover argue that the Air Guard's fine performance during the Korean War led to a better relationship with the active duty Air Force following the war. This argument is quite common among veteran Air Guardsmen and their supporters.)

8. Goldberg, *History of USAF through 1957,* pp 164–66; House, *Reserve Hearings 1951.* (These hearings were a result of DOD's lack of preparedness in the 1950–51 reserve mobilizations.)

9. Alfred Goldberg, *History, Headquarters U.S. Air Force, 1 Jul 1950 to 30 Jun 1951* (Air University Historical Office, Maxwell AFB, Ala., 1955), pp 9–10.

10. NGAUS, *Official Proceedings at the NGAUS Seventy-Third General Conference* (Washington, D.C., Oct 22–24, 1951), p 117; U.S. Congress, Senate, Armed Services Committee, *Hearings on the Armed Forces Reserve Act (of 1952),* 82d Cong, 2d sess (Washington, 1952), p 120 [hereafter cited as Senate, *Reserve Hearings 1952*]; Goldberg, *Hist, HQ USAF, Jul 50–Jun 51,* p 100; memo, Harold Stuart, Asst SAF, to Gen Earl S. Hoag, SARF, subj: Harmony with ANG, Jul 11, 1950, Records of the SAF, Correspondence, RG 340, File 325 to 326, Box 543, NARS.

11. USAF Historical Div, Research Studies Institute, subj: Air Reserve Unit Participation in the Korean War (Maxwell AFB, Ala., 1954), pp 1–5; Robert F. Futrell, *The United States Air Force in Korea, 1950–1953* (New York, 1961), pp 71–72; Directorate of Historical Services, HQ AFR, The Air Force Reserve T/O&E Wings and the Korean War, Jun 1973, pp 2, 16, 17, Air Force Reserve, Historical Archives, Robins AFB, Ga.

12. NGAUS, *1951 Proceedings,* p 117; NGB, *Annual Report of the Chief, NGB for the Fiscal Year Ending 30 June 1951* (Washington, 1951), p 32; memo, Gen Nathan F. Twining, Air Force Vice Chief of Staff (AFCVS) to Thomas K. Finletter, SAF, subj: ANG Phase-Out, Oct 27, 1950, Twining Papers, Air Force Council, AFCVS Reading File, Dec 1950, Box 54, MD, LC.

13. Goldberg, *Hist, HQ USAF, Jul 50–Jun 51,* p 100.

14. NGAUS, *1951 Proceedings,* p 118; Goldberg, *Hist, HQ USAF, Jul 50–Jun 51,* pp 100, 118.

15. ADC, *The Air Defense of the U.S.: A Study of the Work of ADC and its Predecessors through June 1951* (Mitchel AFB, N.Y., 1952), pp 126–29 [hereafter cited as ADC, *Air Defense of U.S. through Jun 51*]; memo, Col Philip H. Creasley to Finletter, subj: Augmentation of USAF by ANG for use in Air Defense, Dec 18, 1950, Records of the SAF, WNRC; buckslip, Maj Gen Truman H. Landon, USAF Director of Plans, to Assistant VCOS/USAF, subj: Use of

ANG Units for Air Defense, Dec 27, 1950, Records of the SAF, WNRC; MR, Col Floyd E. Evans, Chief, National Guard Div, SARF, subj: The ANG, Feb 8, 1951, Records of the AFCC, AFCRF, RG 341, File 300.61, NARS; McMullen, ADC Study 38, pp 15–16; memo, Finletter, SAF, to SECDEF Marshall, subj: Activation of ANG Units for Air Defense, Dec 29, 1950, Records of the SAF, WNRC.

16. ADC, *Air Defense of U.S. through June 1951*, p 129.

17. "Sound the Rally Call," *Air Reserve Forces Review*, Mar 1951, pp 4–5; MR, Col Floyd E. Evans, C/NGD, subj: Mobilization of the ANG, Apr 3, 1951, pp 4–7, Records of the AFCC, AFCRF, RG 341, File 300.61, NARS; untitled news item, *Air Reserve Forces Review*, Jan 1952, p 12.

18. NGB, *Annual Report of the Chief, NGB for the Fiscal Year Ending 30 June 1952* (Washington, 1952), p 26; Eileen Galloway, *History of U.S. Military Policy on Reserve Forces, 1775–1957* (Washington, 1957), p 469; Senate, *DOD Appropriations FY 54*, p 1463.

19. Memo, Maj Gen R. M. Ramey, Director of Operations, DCS Operations, HQ USAF, to Col Frank T. McCoy, Jr., Deputy For Civilian Components, Office of the SAF, subj: ANG Post Mobilization Training, Jun 25, 1951, Records of the SAF, Correspondence, RG 340, File 324.5 to 325, Box 880, NARS; MR, Col Evans, Apr 3, 1951; CONAC, *History, 1 Jan to 30 Jun 1951* (Mitchel AFB, N.Y., 1951), p 25.

20. "Another ANG Wing Flying F–84 Jets Joins NATO Forces," *Air Reserve Forces Review*, Jun 1952, p 13. (The 137th Fighter Bomber Wing (FBW) was redesignated the 48th Fighter Wing in December 1952. Its personnel and equipment remained with the Air Force while its previous unit designation was returned to the states.) NGB, *Annual Report of the Chief, NGB for the Fiscal Year Ending 30 June 1953* (Washington, 1953), p 26; Hoover intvw, May 30, 1978.

21. Wilson intvw, Dec 17–18, 1978.

22. House, *Reserve Hearings 1951*, p 127; NGAUS, *1950 Proceedings*, pp 84, 217–18.

23. NGAUS, *1951 Proceedings*, pp. 117–18.

24. Memo for AFCC, subj: Report of the Department of the Air Force Air Staff Committee on ANG Policy, Oct 8, 1948, p 3, ANG File L2, Air Force Museum, Wright-Patterson AFB, Ohio; SARF, *Historical Summary of SARF, 1 Jul to 31 Dec 1950* (Washington, 1951), p 9; memo, Col Daniel S. Campbell to AFCC, subj: Conversion of the ANG to Wing Base Type Organization, Aug 9, 1950, Vandenberg Papers, Subject File (Air Reserve and National Guard), Box 36, MD, LC; First Air Force, *History of the 1st Air Force, 1 Jul–31 Dec 1950* (Mitchel AFB, N.Y., 1951), p 100.

25. SARF, *Hist, Jul–Dec 50*, p 9; Ricks, "Post Korea ANG," p 13.

26. Memo, SARF to Chief, NGB, subj: ANG on Active Military Duty, Sep 27, 1951, Records of the AFCC, Office of the SARF, RG 341, File 600, Box 26, NARS: U.S. Congress, House, Committee on Appropriations, *Hearings on DOD Appropriations for (FY) 1952, Part Four. Department of the Air Force*, 82d Cong. 1st sess (Washington, 1951), p 667.

27. Memo, SARF, Sep 27, 1951; 136th FBW, *History of the 136th FBW, 26 Oct–31 Dec 1950* (Langley AFB, Va., n.d.), pp 1–7; 116th FBW, *History of the 116th FBW, 1 Nov–31 Dec 1950* (George AFB, Calif., n.d.), pp 1–2; TAC, *History of TAC, 1 Jul–30 Nov 1950* (Langley AFB, Va., 1951), pp 82–94; 116th FBW, *History of the 116th FBW, 1 Jan–31 Mar 1951* (George AFB, Calif., n.d.), p 2.

28. Memo, SARF, Sep 27, 1951; CONAC, *Hist, Jul–Dec 50* (Mitchel AFB, N.Y., 1951), pp 260–61; 136th FBW, *Hist, Oct–Dec 50*, p 21; 1st AF, *Hist, Jul–Dec 50*.

29. Memo, Col Floyd E. Evans to Gen Hoag, subj: TAC's Impression of Mobilized ANG Units, Dec 15, 1950, Records of the AFCC, Office of SARF, RG 341, File 400 to 680.2, Box 20, NARS; 136th FBW, *History of the 136th FBW, 1 Jan–31 Mar 1951* (Langley AFB, Va., n.d.), and *History of the 136th FBW, 1 Apr–30 Jun 1951* (Langley AFB, Va., and Itazuke AB, Japan, n.d.).

30. Robert F. Futrell, *U.S. Air Force Operations in Korea, 1 Nov 1950–30 Jun 1952* (USAF Historical Study 72, Maxwell AFB, Ala., 1953), pp 87–89; Hoover intvw, May 30, 1978. Also, see unit histories of the 116th and 136th FBW's for accounts of their combat activities.

31. Hoover intvw, May 30, 1978.

32. Futrell, *USAF in Korea*, pp 22, 87–88, 99, 114; Senate, *DOD Appropriations FY 54*, p 1466; NGAUS, *1951 Proceedings*, p 120; Hoover intvw, May 30, 1978.

33. ADC, *Air Defense of U.S. through Jun 51*, pp 132–33.

34. MR, Col Evans, Apr 3, 1951; address before Department of the Air Force Section V Committee, Lt Gen Ennis C. Whitehead, May 15, 1951, Doc 168.6008–14, Whitehead Papers, AFSHRC.

35. Fifteenth Air Force, *History of the 15th Air Force (SAC), Jan–Jun 1951* (March AFB, Calif., 1951), pp 10–98; Fifteenth Air Force, *History of 15th Air Force (SAC), Jul–Dec 1952* (March AFB, Calif., 1952), p 110.

36. Fifteenth Air Force, *History of the 15th Air Force (SAC), Jul–Dec 1951* (March AFB, Calif., 1952), pp 35–38; Fifteenth Air Force, *History of the 15th Air Force (SAC), Jan–Jun 1952* (March AFB, Calif., 1952), pp 56–59; Fifteenth Air Force, *History of the 15th Air Force (SAC), Jul–Dec 1952* (March AFB, Calif., 1953), p 110. Unit histories of the 106th and 111th Bomb Wings during 1951–1952 also confirm much of the information in the Fifteenth Air Force histories for that same period.

37. CONAC, *Hist, Jul–Dec 50*, pp 220–234; TAC, *Hist, Jul–Nov 50*, pp 82–96; memo, SARF, Sep 27, 1951.

38. DOD, "Secretary of Defense Appoints Committee to Study Long Range Reserve Plans and Policies," DOD Press Release 1334–50, Oct 27, 1950, Records of the SAF, Office of the Administrative Assistant, RG 340, General File by Organization and Subject, 1947–Jan 1953, Assistant SAF, Frank T. McCoy's Ad Hoc Committee CCPB to Agenda and Minutes of the Civilian Components Committee, Box 208, NARS; "Marshall Names Eight on Reserve Policy," *New York Times*, Oct 28, 1950, p 6; "Reservists Freed From Forced Duty," *New York Times*, Oct 24, 1950, p 20.

39. House, *Reserve Hearings 1951*, p 213; "A Look into the Future. Long-Range Policies for Reserve Forces Announced," *Air Reserve Forces Review*, Jan 1951, pp 2–5.

40. "A Look into the Future," pp 2–5.

41. USAF Air Reserve Planning Board, "Outline of Long Range Plan for Air Reserve Forces," Apr 9, 1951, p iii, Records of the SAF, Office of the Administrative Assistant, RG 340, General File by Organization and Subject, 1947–Jan 1953, Assistant SAF (Mgt) 1947–1951, Box 208, NARS.

42. Ltr, Maj Gen Hoag, SARF, to USAF Major Air Commands, subj: Long Range Plan for Air Reserve Forces, Apr 18, 1951, Records of the AFCC, Office of SARF, RG 341, General Decimal File, 1951, Box 26, NARS [hereafter cited as Hoag to MAJCOMS, Reserve Plan 1951].

43. Eugene M. Zuckert, Remarks by the Hon E. M. Zuckert, Assistant SAF, before the Fifth Annual National Convention and Reunion of the Air Force Association, Aug 24, 1951, pp 1–15, Records of the AFCC, Office of the SARF, Reserve Program Review Boards Records, 1950–1953, RG 341, Box 28, NARS [hereafter cited as Zuckert, Presentation to AFA 1951]; Hoag to MAJCOMS, Reserve Plan 1951; "Finletter Approves Long Range Plan for Air Force Reserve Forces," *Air Reserve Forces Review*, Oct 1951, p 2.

44. Finletter, "Approves Reserve Plan," pp 2–5.

45. Maj Gen Earl T. Ricks, "Post Korea ANG," pp 12–13, 39; Zuckert, Presentation to AFA 1951, pp 1–15; Finletter, "Approves Reserve Plan," pp 2–5; NGB, *Report for FY 52*, p 27.

46. Memo, Zuckert, Assistant SAF, to George Moore, subj: Need to Prevent Reductions in Air Reserve Forces' Programs, Dec 21, 1951, p 1, Records of SAF, Correspondence, RG 340, File 326–330.13, Box 885, NARS.

47. "Hal Stuart Proffers Friendly Hand to Air Guard," *Air Force*, Apr 1951, p 40; intvw, author with Harold Stuart, Tulsa, Okla., Aug 28, 1978. (Stuart was Assistant Secretary of the Air Force, 1949–1951.)

48. Ltr, Harold Stuart to Maj Gen John W. Huston, AFCHO, subj: Oral History Interview with Author, May 15, 1978; memo, Brig Gen Copsey to Maj Gen Hoag, subj: Conference Luncheon, Office of (Assistant) Secretary Stuart, May 9, 1951, Records of SAF, Office of SARF, General Decimal File, 1951, Box 22, NARS; Stuart intvw, Aug 28, 1978; Wilson intvw, Dec 17–18, 1978.

49. *National Guardsman*, May 1948, p 31; Department of the Air Force (DAF) Order, AFCAG–13 334, subj: DAF Air Staff Committee on National Guard and Reserve Policy, Mar 31, 1948, NGB Records, RG 168, File 008, 1946–1948, Box 767, WNRC; memo, Col C. A. Burrows, Secretary of Air Staff Committee on National Guard Policy to Brig Gen Copsey, subj: Reserve Forces Planning, Jun 18, 1951, Records of the AFCC, Office of SARF, General Decimal File, 1951; memo, Col C. A. Burrows to Brig Gen Copsey, subj: Joint Meetings of Air Staff Committee on National Guard and Reserve Policy, Jun 5, 1951, Records of AFCC, Office of SARF, RG 341, General Decimal File, 1951, Box 22, NARS.

50. NGAUS, *Official Proceedings at the NGAUS Seventy-Fourth General Conference*

(Denver, Colo., Oct 6–9, 1952), p 296; NGAUS, *1951 Proceedings,* p 120.

51. Memo, Gen Copsey, May 9, 1951, p 1.

52. *Ibid.,* p 1; C. William Evans, "War Roles Written for the ANG," *National Guardsman,* Nov 1952, pp 10–11.

53. SARF, *Historical Summary, Office of the SARF, 1 Jan–30 Jun 1951* (Washington, n.d.), p 1, Records of AFCC, Office of the SARF, Reserve Review Board Records, 1950–1953, RG 341, Box 29, NARS; SARF, *Historical Summary, Office of the SARF, 1 Jul–31 Dec 1951* (Washington, 1952), p 1, Doc K132.3, AFCHO; memo, Stuart to Maj Gen William F. McKee, subj: Strong Action Needed to Insure Air Staff Responsibility for Reserve Matters, Mar 23, 1951, Records of the AFCC, Office of the SARF, RG 341, File 210.455 to 311.2, Box 22, NARS; memo, Gen Twining, AFCVC, to Gen Vandenberg, AFCC, subj: Reorganization of the Office, SARF, Sep 7, 1951, Twining Papers, AFCVC Read File, Sep 1951, Box 55, MD, LC.

54. MR, Col William F. Harrison, Board Recorder, subj: Establishment of Reserve Program Review Board (RPRB) and Working Staff, n.d., Records of the AFCC, Office of the Assistant Chief of Staff for Reserve Forces (AFCRF), RPRB Records 1950–1953, RG 341, Historical File, Parts 1–3, Box 27, NARS; CONAC, *History, 1 Jul–31 Dec 1953* (Mitchel AFB, N.Y., 1954), p 13.

55. CONAC, *Hist, Jul–Dec 53,* p 15.

56. *Ibid.,* p 15; Galloway, *U.S. Reserve Policy,* p 474.

57. Record of Proceedings, RPRB, subj: Statement of Gen White, AFCVC, Jul 14, 1953, pp 1–2, Records of AFCC, Office of AFCRF, RPRB Records 1950–1953, RG 341, Historical File, Parts 1–3, Box 27, NARS.

58. Deliberations of RPRB, subj: Discussion with Col Mark H. Galusha, NGAUS, Jul 29, 1953, pp 90–98, Records of the AFCC, Office of AFCRF, RPRB Records 1950–1953, RG 341, Historical File, Parts 1–3, Box 27, NARS; report, Lt Gen Leon W. Johnson to AFCC, subj: Final Report of the RPRB, Aug 24, 1953, p 1, Records of the AFCC, Office of the AFCRF, RPRB Records, AFCRF Actions Re Implementation of Recommendation of the Johnson Report, RG 341, Box 28, NARS [hereafter cited as Johnson Board, Final Report].

59. Johnson Board, Final Report, p 2.

60. *Ibid.,* p 1.

61. Wilson intvw, Dec 17–18, 1978.

62. Johnson Board, Final Report, p 1.

63. *Ibid.*

64. *Ibid.,* pp 3–6; CONAC, *History, Jan–Jun 1954* (Mitchel AFB, N.Y., 1954), p 2.

65. Memo, Maj Gen William E. Hall, AFCRF to AFCCR, subj: Air Staff Comments on Report of the RPRB, Sep 15, 1953, AFCC, Office of the AFCRF, RPRB Records 1950–1953, RG 341, Historical File, Part 8, Box 29, NARS.

66. NGAUS, *Official Proceedings at the NGAUS Seventy-Second General Conference* (Washington, Oct 23–25, 1950), pp 213–17; House, *Reserve Hearings 1951,* pp 6–12, 52–56, 82–85.

67. NGAUS, *1951 Proceedings,* pp 295–97.

68. *Ibid.,* p 297.

69. House, *Reserve Hearings 1951,* p 112.

70. *Ibid.,* p 127.

71. Senate, *Reserve Hearings 1952,* pp 105–106; Galloway, *U.S. Reserve Policy,* pp 473–74.

72. U.S. Congress, Senate, *Armed Services Committee Report 117,* 82d Cong, 2d sess (Washington, 1952), p 1.

73. Galloway, *U.S. Reserve Policy,* pp 471, 473.

74. *Ibid.,* pp 472–73.

75. Section 252, *Armed Forces Reserve Act of 1952,* Twining Papers, AFCVC Read File, Box 54, MD, LC; NGAUS, *1952 Proceedings,* p 86; DOD, *Semiannual Report of the Secretary of Defense, Jan 1 to Jun 30, 1953* (Washington, 1953), p 259.

76. Senate, *Reserve Hearings 1952,* pp 106–121, (NGAUS representatives, Generals Walsh and Reckford, reviewed postwar concerning Congressional intent that the National Guard and organized reserve should be called upon first if the armed services had to be augmented.) William F. Levantrosser, *Congress and the Citizen Soldier: Legislative Policy-Making for the Federal Armed Forces Reserve* (Columbus, Ohio, 1967), pp 54–60 [hereafter cited as Levantrosser, *Congress and the Citizen Soldier*].

Chapter IV

Integrating with the Active Force, 1953–1960

1. Hoover intvw, May 30, 1978; intvw, author with Maj Gen John J. Pesch (ANGUS, Ret), Arlington, Va., Jun 25, 1978. (General Pesch was director of the ANG from 1974 to 1977.)

2. NGB, *Report for FY 51,* p 22; NGB, *Annual Report of the Chief, NGB for the Fiscal Year Ending 30 June 1960* (Washington, 1960), pp 6, 8; NGB, "Congressional Budget Appropriations, FY 1948–1976," Fact Sheet 114–77, May 1977, p 1; McMullen, ADC Study 38, pp 57–58.

3. Hoover intvw, May 30, 1978; Pesch intvw, Jun 25, 1978; Lt Col Robert R. Fredette, "Training and Operational Control of ANG Organizations" (Thesis 1749, Air War College, Maxwell AFB, Ala., Apr 1960), p 14; NGB, *Report for FY 60,* pp 52–53, 57; "Air Guard Gets Transports, Starfighters," *Air Force Times,* Jan 23, 1960, p 1; DOD *Annual Report of the Secretary of Defense, Jul 1, 1959 to Jun 30, 1960* (Washington, 1961), p 63.

4. Hoover intvw, May 30, 1978; Johnson Board, *Final Report,* p 3; CONAC, *History, January–June 1960* (Mitchel AFB, N.Y., n.d.), p 2; intvw, author with Gen Leon W. Johnson (USAF, Ret), McLean, Va., Jun 25, 1978 (General Johnson commanded CONAC from Feb 1952 through Dec 1955.)

5. NGAUS, *1953 Proceedings,* pp 88, 298–99.

6. *Ibid.,* p 87.

7. *Ibid.,* p 127; Benton, "ANG Weather Flights," p 41.

8. Goldberg, *History of USAF through 1957,* p 169; Secretary of the Air Force, *History of the Office of the Secretary of the Air Force, 1 January 1952–30 June 1952* (Washington, 1952), I, 555.

9. NGB, *Annual Report of the Chief, NGB for the Fiscal Year Ending 30 June 1957* (Washington, 1957), p 48; CONAC, *History, January–June 1955* (Mitchel AFB, N.Y., 1956), p 175; Wilson intvw, Dec 17–18, 1978.

10. Hoover intvw, May 30, 1978.

11. NGAUS, *1953 Proceedings,* pp 87–88; Johnson Board, *Final Report,* p 4.

12. NGAUS, *1954 Proceedings,* p 139; NGAUS, *1952 Proceedings,* p 80; Stuart intvw, Aug 28, 1978.

13. Ricks, "Post Korea ANG," p 12; Wilson intvw, Dec 17–18, 1978; memo, NGB to Air Instructors and Air Advisors, subj: Outline Orientation of Air Instructors and Air Advisors Assigned to Duty with the ANG, n.d., pp 22–23, Records of the Army Staff, NGB, RG 319, File 210.65, 1951–1952, Box 1212, WNRC.

14. Reserve Program Review Board (Johnson Board) Proceedings, Jul 14, 1953, pp 1–3; Reserve Program Review Board Records 1950–1953, Parts 1–3, Records of the AFCC, RG 341, Office of the AFCRF, Historical File 1951, Box 27, NARS; memo, H. Lee White, Asst SECDEF, subj: Mobilization Requirements for Reserve Components, Feb 3, 1954, RG 340, File 324.5 to 326, 1954, Box 1491, NARS; DOD *Semi Annual Report of the Secretary of Defense, January 1 to June 30, 1954* (Washington, 1955), p 272; U.S. Congress, House, Armed Services Committee, *Hearings on The Air Force Reserve Program,* 83rd Cong, 2d sess (Washington, 1954), p 3856.

15. Memo, Maj Gen Finch to Lt Gen Johnson, subj: Air National Guard, May 20, 1952, quoted in McMullen, ADC Study 38, pp 24–25; Johnson intvw, Jun 25, 1978, Wilson intvw, Dec 17–18, 1978.

16. Johnson intvw, Jun 25, 1978.

17. *Ibid.*

18. Ltr, Col Clayton E. Hughes (USAF, Ret) to author, Mar 20, 1978. (Col Hughes was Chief of the Operations Div, Air Force Div of the NGB from Dec 1952 until Jul 1956. During this period, the Air Guard's participation in the air defense alert program was planned and implemented.) McMullen, ADC Study 38, p 24; Johnson intvw, Jun 25, 1978; HQ ADC, *Semi-Annual Historical Report, 1 Jan–30 Jun 1953* (Ent AFB, Colo., 1954), p 6.

19. ADC, *Historical Report, Jan–Jun 1953,* p 6; McMullen, ADC Study 38, p 25.

20. McMullen, ADC Study 38, pp 25–27.

21. McMu,len, ADC Study 38, pp 27–28; ADC, *Historical Report, Jan–Jun 1953,* p 109; NGAUS, *1953 Proceedings,* pp 88, 110, 112; memo, Maj Gen George W. Mundy to Asst SAF (Material), subj: Logistical Problems of the ANG, Mar 26, 1954, Records of the SAF, Correspondence, RG 340, Unclassified File 324.5 to 326, 1954, Box 1491, NARS.

22. Weigley, *Way of War,* p 400; Douglas Kinnard, *President Eisenhower and Strategy*

Movement: A Study in Defense Politics (Lexington, Ky., 1977), pp 2, 8–10.

23. Kinnard, *Eisenhower and Strategy,* pp 10, 18–19, 23, 136; Dwight David Eisenhower, *Mandate for Change: The White House Years, 1953–1956* (Garden City, N.J., 1963), pp 446, 451.

24. Weigley, *Way of War,* pp 401–02; Kinnard, *Eisenhower and Strategy,* pp 22–23.

25. Weigley, *Way of War,* pp 402–03.

26. *Ibid.,* p 403; Goldberg, *History of USAF through 1957,* p 165.

27. SAF, Harold Talbott, testimony before the Senate Armed Forces subcommittee, Jun 8, 1953, quoted in CONAC, *History, July 1953–December 1953* (Mitchel AFB, N.Y., 1954), pp 14–15.

28. U.S. Congress, Senate, Committee on Appropriations, *Hearings on DOD Appropriations for Fiscal Year 1954,* 83rd Cong, 1st sess (Washington, 1953), p 177.

29. Galloway, *U.S. Reserve Policy,* p 474; U.S. Congress, Senate, Interim Subcommittee on Preparedness of the Senate Armed Services Committee, *Status of Reserve and National Guard Forces,* Committee Print, 83rd Cong, 2d sess (Washington, 1954), pp 15–16; U.S. National Security Training Commission, *Twentieth Century Minutemen: A Report to the President of the Reserve Forces Training Program, December 1, 1953* (Washington, 1953), pp 123–130; Office of Defense Mobilization, *Manpower Resources for National Security: A Report to the President by the Director of the Office of Defense Mobilization, January 6, 1954* (Washington, 1954), pp iii–v; U.S. Congress, Senate, Armed Services Committee, *Hearings on a National Reserve Plan,* 84th Cong, 1st sess (Washington, 1955), p 81 [hereafter cited as Senate, *Hearings on NRP];* DOD, *Semi Annual Report of the Secretary of Defense, January 1 to June 30, 1954* (Washington, 1955), p 25.

30. Galloway, *U.S. Reserve Policy,* pp 476–77; ltr, President Eisenhower to Senator Leverett Saltonstall, Jul 27, 1954, Official File/File 3–4, Box 109, Eisenhower Library, Abilene, Kans.; ltr, Sherman Adams to Gen Ray McClain, Jun 18, 1954, Official File/File 3–4, Box 109, Eisenhower Library. (Adams noted that the NSC had discussed military reserve components' problems thoroughly on Jun 17, 1954); NSC 5420/2, "Reserve Mobilization Requirements," (Washington, D.C., Jun 17, 1954). (Copy provided to author by NSC in Aug 1978.)

31. Galloway, *U.S. Reserve Policy,* pp 477–79; "National Reserve Plan," Apr 22, 1955,

Ann Whitman File/Papers of Dwight David Eisenhower, Cabinet Series, Box 5, Eisenhower Library; Hanson W. Baldwin, "The Military Reserve Bill: An Analysis of Present Objections to Defense Measure Before House," *New York Times,* Jun 9, 1955, p 1; Carter L. Burgess, Asst SECDEF (Manpower and Personnel), Report for Gen Nathan F. Twining, subj: National Reserve Plan, Jan 13, 1955, Air Force Council/ Chief of Staff Papers 1953–1957, 1955 National Reserve Plan File, Box 79, Papers of Nathan F. Twining, MD, LC; Asst SAF, Staff Summary Sheet, Staff Study Evaluation of Effectiveness of Current Legislation and Policies and Recommended Changes Toward the Development of More Effective Reserve Programs, Feb 5, 1954, Office of Plans and Program/Directorate of Personnel Planning, DCS Personnel; Staff Summary Sheet attached to memo, AFCRF to the AFCC and Asst SAF (Manpower and Personnel), Reserve Forces Training Program, Nov 23, 1954, RG 340, Records of the Office of the SAF, Correspondence Control Div, File 324.5 to 326, Box 1491, NARS.

32. U.S. Senate, *Hearings on NRP,* pp 81–95; Galloway, *U.S. Reserve Policy,* p 485.

33. Galloway, *U.S. Reserve Policy,* pp 479–81; President Eisenhower, Statement by the President, Aug 9, 1955, pp 1–2, Official File/File 3–4, Box 109, Eisenhower Library; ltr, SECDEF to the President, Re: Reserve Forces Act of 1955, Aug 1, 1955, Reports to the President on Pending Legislation, Bill File, Box 62, Eisenhower Library.

34. AFCRF, Semi-Annual Report: The Air Reserve Forces Plans and Programs, 1 January to 30 June 1955, pp 1, 29, Records of the AFCC, Office of the AFCRF, Liaison Div, Subject Correspondent File, RG 341, 1955, Box 49, NARS.

35. U.S. Congress, House, Committee on Armed Services, *Review of Reserve Program, Hearings Before Subcommittee No One* 85th Cong, 1st sess (Washington, 1957), pp 885–86; memo, Maj Gen George Mundy to the Asst SAF, Logistical Problems of the ANG, Mar 26, 1954, Records of the SAF, Correspondence, RG 340, File 324.5 to 326, 1954, Box 1491, NARS; HQ USAF, Analysis of Status and Development ANG Program, Jun 20, 1954, pp 2–4, 18–19, Directorate of Management Analysis, DCS/Comptroller, Papers of Nathan F. Twining, AFCC File 1953–1957, Air Reserve and ANG, Box 65, MD, LC; report, HQ USAF, Analysis of Status and Development of ANG Program, Jan 20, 1954, Records of the SAF, Correspondence, RG 340, File 324.5 to 326, 1954, Box 1491, NARS.

36. CONAC, *Hist, Jul–Dec 53* (Mitchel AFB, N.Y., 1954), p 16; McMullen, ADC Study 38, pp 29–31.

37. McMullen, ADC Study 38, pp 31, 35–36, 46; "60 Day Consent Tours Begin for 9 ANG Units," *Air Force Times*, Aug 10, 1954, p 1; report, Maj Gen Winston P. Wilson, Report of the Accomplishments and Plans of the ANG, in CONAC, *Hist, Jan–Jun 55* (Mitchel AFB, N.Y., 1956), Doc 39, V, 4.

38. McMullen, ADC Study 38, p 47; NGAUS, *Official Proceedings at the NGAUS Seventy-Eighth General Conference* (Spokane, Wash., Oct 8–11, 1956), p 72; ltr, CONAC to p O/ USAF, Attn: AFOOP–CP, subj: Supervision of Training of the ANG, Jan 3, 1955, in CONAC, *Hist, Jan-Jun 55* (Mitchel AFB, N.Y., 1956), Doc 23–2, VI, 2.

39. ADC, *History, July–December 1957* (Ent AFB, Colorado Springs, Colo., n.d.), p 123; memo, Gen Twining to SECDEF, subj: Employment of National Guard Units, Nov 16, 1959, JCSM–449–59, Twining Papers, MD, LC; ltr, Maj Gen Berquist, DCS/Operations, ADC to Maj Gen Garney, Director/Operations, DCS/Operations, HQ USAF, Dec 9, 1954, in McMullen, ADC Study 38; ltr, ADC to HQ USAF, subj: ADC Policy on Reserve Components in Air Defense, Nov 14, 1956, in McMullen, ADC Study 38, p 45.

40. NGAUS, *Official Proceedings at the NGAUS Eightieth General Conference* (Atlantic City, N.J., Sep 29–30, and Oct 1–2, 1958), p 260; ltr, Lt Gen Atkinson, Commander, ADC to General White, AFCC, subj: Policy on Reserve Forces, May 25, 1959, in McMullen, ADC Study 38, pp 53–54.

41. Ltr, Gen White to Lt Gen Atkinson, Jun 25, 1959, in McMullen, ADC Study 38, p 55.

42. "LeMay Asks Full Merger of Reserves," *Air Force Times*, Oct 3, 1959, pp 1, 39; "Official Text Concerning General LeMay's Reserve Forces Statement Released," *Army, Navy, Air Force Journal*, Oct 10, 1959, p 8.

43. "Guard Association Demands Reevaluation of General LeMay's Qualifications, Usefulness," *Army, Navy, Air Force Journal*, Oct 10, 1959, p 1; telegram, James G. Douglass, Jr., SAF to Maj Gen William H. Harrison, President, NGAUS, Re: General LeMay's Remarks on ANG/Air Force Reserve Merger, Oct 6, 1959, files of *Guardsman* magazine, Reserve Forces File, NGAUS Headquarters, Washington, D.C. [hereafter cited as SAF, telegram to NGAUS Pres, Oct 1959].

44. SAF, telegram to NGAUS Pres, Oct 1959.

45. NGAUS, *Official Proceedings at the NGAUS* Eighty-First General Conference (San Antonio, Tex., Oct 5–8, 1959), p 90.

46. NGAUS, *1959 Proceedings*, pp 96, 98.

47. MR, Gen White, subj: Chief of Staff Meeting with the Deputies, 21 October 1958, Oct 21, 1958, Papers of Gen Thomas D. White, Box 15, Chief of Staff Meetings, MD, LC.

48. CONAC, *Hist, Jan–Jun 55*, pp 109–111.

49. Ltr, Gen White to Lt Gen Stone, Re: Lt Gen Stone's Suggestion That an Ad Hoc Committee be Established to Provide Recommendations for the Optimum Use of Reserve Components, Aug 27, 1956, Papers of Gen Nathan F. Twining, Box 84, 1956 CONAC File, MD, LC; CONAC, *History, January–June 1957* (Mitchel AFB, N.Y., 1958), pp 111–13.

50. CONAC, Hist, Jan–Jun 57, pp 113–15.

51. *Ibid.*, p 115.

52. CONAC, *History, July–December 1957* (Mitchel AFB, N.Y., n.d.), pp 107–9; SAF James H. Douglass, Jr., Special Report on the Reserve Forces of the U.S. Air Force, Dec 25, 1957, Doc K168.041–8, AFSHRC, Maxwell AFB, Ala.

53. CONAC, *Hist, Jul–Dec 57*, pp 30–34.

54. Memo, Gen White, AFCC to Deputy CCF, Plans and Programs, subj: Air Reserve Forces, Aug 9, 1957, Papers of Gen Thomas D. White, Box 4, AFCC File, MD, LC; CONAC, *Hist, Jul–Dec 47*, pp 22, 42, 110; Edmund F. Hogan, "Reserve and Guard Wings Axed to 39," *Air Force*, Nov 1957, pp 67, 69; CONAC, *History, January–June 1958* (Mitchel AFB, N.Y., 1959), pp 85–86; DOD, *Semi-Annual Report of the Secretary of Defense, January to June 1958* (Washington, 1959), pp 41–42; DOD, *Annual Report of the Secretary of Defense on Reserve Forces, January 1958*, p 19; Harlow Papers, Box 20, Reserves File 1958, 1959, Eisenhower Library.

55. NGAUS, *Official Proceedings at the NGAUS Seventy-Ninth General Conference* (Lousiville, Ky., Oct 7–10, 1957), pp 77–80.

56. CONAC, *Hist, Jan–Jun 58*, pp 87–88; "New Type Bombing Mission Given to Eleven F–84F Equipped Guard Units," *Air Force Times*, Jun 21, 1958, p 5; NGB, *Annual Report of the Chief, NGB for the Fiscal Year Ending 30 June 1958* (Washington, 1958), p 50; DOD, *SECDEF Report Jan–Jun 58*, p 90.

57. NGAUS, *1957 Proceedings*, pp 132–33.

58. *Ibid.*

59. Weigley, *Way of War*, pp 427–28; DOD, *SECDEF Report Jan–Jun 58*, p 357; DOD, *Semi-*

Annual Report of the Secretary of Defense, January–June 1957 (Washington, 1958), pp 370–71.

60. Memo, Under Secretary of the Air Force to AFCC, subj: Air Force Manpower Ceiling, Jun 1, 1959, in CONAC, *Hist, Jul–Dec 59* (Mitchel AFB, N.Y., 1960), p 5.

61. Ltr, USAF to CONAC, subj: Air Force Policy Re the Air Reserve Forces, Sep 21, 1959, Headquarters CONAC Commander's Policy File, in CONAC, *History, July–December 1959* (Mitchel AFB, N.Y., n.d.), II, Doc 45–22; DOD, *SECDEF Report Jan–Jun 58*, p 356; DOD, *Annual Report of the Secretary of Defense, July 1, 1958 to June 30, 1959* (Washington, 1960), p 367; DOD, *SECDEF Report for FY 60*, p 397.

62. CONAC, *Hist, Jul–Dec 59*, pp 11–12.

63. *Ibid.*

64. Report of the Reserve Forces Review Group, in CONAC, *Hist, Jul–Dec 59*, p 21.

65. *Ibid.*, pp 22–23.

66. McMullen, ADC Study 38, p 33; CONAC, *Hist, Jan–Jun 57*, pp 6–8; Wilson intvw, Dec 17–18, 1978.

67. U.S. Congress, House, Armed Services Committee, *Review of the Reserve Program, Hearings Before Subcommittee Number Three*, 86th Cong, 2d sess (Washington, 1960), pp 6666–67 [hereafter cited as House, *Review of Reserve Program, 1960*]; Levantrosser, *Congress and the Citizen Soldier*, pp 51–69; Gen White, AFCC to Brig Gen Howard T. Markey, USAF Reserve, Re: Continued Air Staff Study of Recommendations of Reserve Forces Review Group, Dec 28, 1959, Papers of Gen Thomas D. White, Box 25, MD, LC; CONAC, *History, January–June 1960* (Mitchel AFB, N.Y., n.d.), pp 2–7; Office of the Secretary of the Air Force/ Assistant for Manpower, Personnel and Reserve Forces, *History of the Office of the Special Assistant for Manpower, Personnel, and Reserve Forces, 1 January–30 June 1960* (Washington, n.d.), p 17.

68. CONAC, *Hist, Jul–Dec 59*, p 25; CONAC, *Hist, Jan–Jun 60*, pp 17–19.

69. CONAC, *Hist, Jan–Jun 60*, pp 10, 39–40; House, *Review of Reserve Program, 1960*, p 6545; "Air Force Rapped for Policy on Air Guard Planes," *Air Force Times*, May 2, 1959, p 1; NGB, *Report for FY 60*, p 53; "Air Guard Gets Transports, Starfighters," *Air Force Times*, Jan 23, 1960, p 39; DOD, *SECDEF Report for FY 60*, p 108; NGB, *Annual Report of the Chief, NGB for the Fiscal Year Ending 30 June 1959* (Washington, 1960), p 50; DOD, *SECDEF Report for FY 59*, p 295.

70. Wilson intvw, Dec 17–18, 1978.

71. *Ibid.*

72. NGAUS, *Official Proceedings at the NGAUS Eighty-Second General Conference* (Honolulu, Hawaii, Oct 10–14, 1960), pp 75, 127, 265.

73. Twelfth Air Force, *History, 12th Air Force (TAC), 1 July–31 December 1960* (Waco, Tex., n.d.), Pt I, p 15; McMullen, ADC Study 38, pp 52, 61–63; TAC, *History, 1 July–31 December 1960* (Langley AFB, Va., n.d.), pp 84–85.

Chapter V

The Cold Warriors, 1961–1962

1. Maxwell P. Taylor, *The Uncertain Trumpet* (New York, 1960); Henry A. Kissinger, *The Necessity for Choice: Prospects of American Foreign Policy* (New York, 1961).

2. DOD, *SECDEF Report for FY 60*, p 397; DOD, *Annual Report of the Secretary of Defense, July 1, 1961 to June 30, 1962* (Washington, 1962), p 368.

3. Weigley, *Way of War*, pp 443–44.

4. *Public Papers of the Presidents of the United States: John F. Kennedy, 1961* (Washington, 1962), p 232.

5. Weigley, *Way of War*, p 445.

6. CONAC, *History, 1 July 1960 through 30 June 1961* (Mitchel AFB, N.Y., n.d.), pp 52–54.

7. NGB, *Annual Report of the Chief, NGB for the Fiscal Year Ending 30 June 1961* (Washington, 1961), pp 57, 64, 68.

8. TAC, *History, 1 January–30 June 1961* (Langley AFB, Va., n.d.), p 136.

9. DOD, *Annual Report of the Secretary of Defense, July 1, 1960 through June 30, 1961* (Washington, 1961), p 53.

10. Arthur M. Schlesinger, Jr., *A Thousand Days: John F. Kennedy in the White House* (Boston, 1965), pp 370–374; Thomas W. Wolfe, *Soviet Power and Europe, 1945–1970* (Baltimore, 1970), p 93.

11. Schlesinger, *Thousand Days*, pp 380, 388–89.

12. U.S. Presidents, *Kennedy, 1961*, p 354.

13. Schlesinger, *Thousand Days*, p 391; Jean Edward Smith, *The Defense of Berlin* (Baltimore, 1963), p 250.

14. Memo, President Kennedy to the Secretary of Defense, Aug 14, 1961, National Security

File, DOD 8/61, Box 273–274, John F. Kennedy Library, Waltham, Mass.

15. Wolfe, *Soviet Power*, p 94.

16. Lt Col Clifford J. Lawrence, Jr. (ANG), *The Air National Guard in the Berlin Crisis, 1961* (Report 3629, Air War College, Maxwell AFB, Ala., 1968), p 13 [hereafter cited as Lawrence, *ANG in the Berlin Crisis*]; DOD, *SECDEF Report for FY 61*, p 14.

17. Lawrence, *ANG in the Berlin Crisis*, p 14.

18. Schlesinger, *Thousand Days*, pp 395–96; DOD, *SECDEF Report for FY 62*, p 22; NGAUS, *Official Proceedings at the NGAUS Eighty-Third General Conference* (Las Vegas, Nev., Oct 2–5, 1961), p 75; Lawrence, *ANG in the Berlin Crisis*, p 15.

19. Lawrence, *ANG in the Berlin Crisis*, pp 15–16; Maj James C. Elliott (USAF), "The Recall Story: To Maintain the Peace," *Air Force and Space Digest*, Jan 1962, pp 84, 88; Royce E. Eckwright, *Air National Guard Deployment to U.S. Air Force Europe (USAFE) Area 1961–1962* (Lindsey Air Station, Germany, 1962), p 7 [hereafter cited at Eckwright, *ANG to USAFE*]; NGB, Fact Sheet 302–76, p 3.

20. Eckwright, *ANG to USAFE*, pp 14–15.

21. "The Air National Guard in the Berlin Crisis," *National Guardsman*, Sep 1962, p 18 [hereafter cited as "ANG in the Berlin Crisis," *Guardsman*].

22. NGAUS, *1961 Proceedings*, p 80.

23. SAF Eugene M. Zuckert, "Air Reserve Forces Prove Readiness," *Air Reservist*. Jun/Jul 1962, p 7.

24. U.S. Congress, Senate, Committee on Appropriations, *Hearings on DOD Appropriations for Fiscal Year 1963*, 87th Cong, 2d sess (Washington, 1962), p 85.

25. Schlesinger, *Thousand Days*, p 388; Robert F. Futrell, *Ideas, Concepts, Doctrines: A History of Basic Thinking in the United States Air Force, 1907–1964* (Maxwell AFB, Ala., 1971), II, 614; Eckwright, *ANG to USAFE*, pp 39, 78, 89–91; "ANG in the Berlin Crisis," *Guardsman*, pp 15, 17, 35–36.

26. Elliott, "Recall Story," p 88; Lawrence, *ANG in the Berlin Crisis*, p 36; Eckwright, *ANG to USAFE*, pp 36, 95; Hoover intvw, May 30, 1978; 131st TFW, *History of the 131st TFW, 1 October 1961 to 20 August 1962* (Robertson ANG Base, Lambert Field, St. Louis, Mo., n.d.), pp iii–iv; "ANG in the Berlin Crisis," *Guardsman*, p 35; ltr, Maj Gen Winston P. Wilson, Assistant Chief NGB, Air to the Adjutants General of all States, Puerto Rico, and the District of Columbia, subj: Mobilization Problems, Mar 15, 1962. (Copy provided to author by the Office ANG History, Alcoa, Tenn.)

27. Hoover intvw, May 30, 1978; Eckwright, *ANG to USAFE*, p 35.

28. "ANG in the Berlin Crisis," *Guardsman*, p 35; 131st TFW, *Hist, Oct–Aug 62*, p iv; TAC, *History, 1 July–31 December 1962* (Langley AFB, Va., n.d.), p 48; Seventeenth Air Force, *History, Headquarters 17th Air Force, 1 July–31 December 1961* (Ramstein AB, Germany, n.d.), p 19; Eckwright, *ANG to USAFE*, p 78; news release, 102nd TFW, n.d., NGAUS Files, Washington; Wilson intvw, Dec 17–18, 1978.

29. Eckwright, *ANG to USAFE*, p 58; 7121st TFW, *History of the 7121st Tactical Wing, 1 October 1961–31 December 1961* (Etain AB, France, n.d.), p 4. (The prefix "7" was added to the elements of the Ohio ANG's 121st TFW that deployed to Europe in Operation Stair Step. The wing operated under an ad hoc split wing concept with the bulk of its units retained under the 121st TFW designation in Ohio.)

30. Twelfth Air Force, *History of the 12th Air Force (TAC), 1 July–31 December 1961* (Waco, Tex., n.d.), Pt I, p 34; Francis and Katherine Drake, "The Inside Story of Stairstep," *Readers Digest*, May 1962, p 210.

31. 17th AF, *Hist, Jul–Dec 61*, p 27.

32. Eckwright, *ANG to USAFE*, pp 14–16, 25, 28; 17th AF, *Hist, Jul–Dec 61*, pp 12–13; news release, DOD, subj: Exercise Checkmate, Sep 2, 1961, NGAUS Files, Washington; "Troop Buildup in Europe Grows," *New York Times*, Oct 15, 1961, p 44.

33. Drake, "Inside Story," p 210; Eckwright, *ANG to USAFE*, p 31; Elliott, "Recall Story," p 84; James C. Elliott, *The Modern Army and Air National Guard* (Princeton, N.J., 1965), p 26; U.S. Congress, House, Committee on Armed Services, *Hearings on Military Reserve Posture*, 87th Cong, 2d sess (Washington, 1962), p 5686; *The Air Reservist*, Sep 1961, p 10.

34. Elliott, "Recall Story," p 84; Eckwright, *ANG to USAFE*, pp 17, 31.

35. Elliott, "Recall Story," p 84; Drake, "Inside Story," p 212; Eckwright, *ANG to USAFE*, p 31.

36. Drake, "Inside Story," pp 208–10, 212, 218; Elliott, "Recall Story," p 84; statement, Maj Gen Chester McCarty, Asst Chief of Staff for Reserve Forces, HQ USAF, before the House Armed Services Committee, n.d.; MR, Maj Evelyn Watkins, Assistant Director, Information and Motivation, subj: Information on Recall, Feb 9, 1962.

37. Drake, "Inside Story," pp 208–10, 212, 218; Elliott, "Recall Story," p 84; intvw, author with Gen Curtis E. LeMay, Sep 14, 1978.

38. Hoover intvw, May 30, 1978.

39. Eckwright, *ANG to USAFE*, pp 60–63.

40. *Ibid.*, p 33; Lawrence, *ANG in the Berlin Crisis*, p 23; Elliott, "Recall Story," p 87.

41. Eckwright, *ANG to USAFE*, p 58; Lawrence, *ANG in the Berlin Crisis*, p 23; NGB, *Annual Report of the Chief, NGB for the Fiscal Year Ending 30 June 1962* (Washington, 1962), p 21.

42. Eckwright, *ANG to USAFE*, pp 20, 34, 39–40; Hoover intvw, May 30, 1978; 7121st TFW, *Hist, Oct–Dec 61*, p 4; Lawrence, *ANG in the Berlin Crisis*, p 20.

43. 17th AF, *Hist, Jul–Dec 61*, p 19.

44. Eckwright, *ANG to USAFE*, pp 64–66; 166th Tactical Fighter Squadron, in *History of the 7121st Tactical Wing, 1* January–30 June 1962 (Etain AB, France, n.d.), Sec XVI, p 9; Wilson intvw, Dec 17–18, 1978.

45. "ANG in the Berlin Crisis," *Guardsman*, p 19; Eckwright, *ANG to USAFE*, p 15; Zuckert, "Reserve Forces Prove Readiness," pp 3–4; NGB, "Compact History of the National Guard," Fact Sheet 102–76, Apr 1976, p 4.

46. 121st TFW, *History of the 121st TFW, 1 October 1961–20 August 1962* (Lockbourne AFB, Ohio, n.d.), p 9; Zuckert, "Reserve Forces Prove Readiness," pp 3–7; Eckwright, *ANG to USAFE*, pp 89–91; Lawrence, *ANG in the Berlin Crisis*, p 49.

47. Eckwright, *ANG to USAFE*, pp 91–92.

48. LeMay intvw, Sep 14, 1978.

49. NGB, *Report for FY 62, p 22;* NGAUS, *Official Proceedings at the NGAUS Eighty-Fourth General Conference* (Denver, Colo., Sep 17–20, 1962), pp 255–56.

50. Pesch intvw, Jun 25, 1978.

51. Ltr, VC to DPL, subj: Increased Readiness for TAC M–Day Air Reserve Forces Units, May 7, 1962, in TAC, *History, 1 July–31 December 1962* (Langley AFB, Va., n.d.), p 15; memo, Maj Gen Winston P. Wilson, Deputy Chief, NGB to the Adjutants General, subj: Manpower Authorization Policy and Procedures, Dec 26, 1961, NGAUS Files, Washington; ltr, TAC to HQ USAF, subj: Reorganization of ANG Tactical Wings, Jun 26, 1962, in TAC, *Hist, Jul–Dec 62* (Langley AFB, Va., n.d.), p 50 [hereafter cited at TAC ltr, Jun 1962 in TAC, *Hist, Jul–Dec 62*]; TAC, *Hist, Jul–Dec 62*, p 52; NGAUS, *1962 Proceedings*, p 255; NGB, Report for FY 62, p 22.

52. NGAUS, *1962 Proceedings*, p 255; U.S. Congress, Senate, Committee on Armed Services, *Hearings on Authorizing the President to Order Units and Members in the Ready Reserve to Active Duty for Not More Than Twelve Months and for Other Purposes*, 87th Cong, 2d sess (Washington, 1962), p 8.

53. Ltr, NGB to Demobilized ANG units, subj: Survey of Reserve Forces Being Released from Active Duty, Sep 27, 1962, cited in Lawrence, *ANG in the Berlin Crisis*, p 45; Futrell, *U.S. Air Force, 1907–1964*, p 622.

54. TAC ltr, Jun 26, 1962 in TAC, *Hist, Jul–Dec 62*, p 17.

Chapter VI

Vindication, 1963–1969

1. Abott A. Brayton, "American Reserve Policies Since World War II," *Military Affairs*, Dec 1972, p 142; NGB, *Annual Report of the Chief, NGB for the Fiscal Year Ending 30 June 1963* (Washington, 1963), p 6; NGB, *Annual Report of the Chief, NGB for the Fiscal Year Ending 30 June 1969* (Washington, 1970), p 7.

2. DOD, *Annual Report of the Secretary of Defense, July 1, 1965 to June 30, 1966* (Washington, 1967), p 30; DOD, *Annual Report of the Secretary of Defense, July 1, 1967 to June 30, 1968* (Washington, 1971), pp 34, 39.

3. DOD, *Annual Report of the Secretary of Defense, July 1, 1963 to June 30, 1964* (Washington, 1966), pp 3, 16, 22–23.

4. DOD, *SECDEF Report for FY 64*, p 24; Brayton, "Reserve Policies," p 141; "Herbert Subcommittee Blasts Realignment," *National Guardsman*, Oct 1962, p 3.

5. DOD, *Annual Report of the Secretary of Defense, July 1, 1962 to June 30, 1963* (Washington, 1964), pp 26–27; NGAUS, *1962 Proceedings*, pp 196–98; DOD, *SECDEF Report for FY 64*, p 24.

6. DOD, *Annual Report of the Secretary of Defense, July 1, 1964 to June 30, 1965* (Washington, 1967), pp 28–29; NGAUS, *Official Proceedings at the NGAUS Eighty-Seventh General Conference* (Miami Beach, Fla., Sep 27–30, 1965), pp 38–39; Brayton, "Reserve Policies," p 141; Col Robert E. Buechler (ANG), "Air National Guard-Air Force Reserve Merger" (Thesis 2681, Air War College, Maxwell AFB, Ala., 1965), p 1; memo, SAF to SECDEF, Jan 11, 1965, p 1, Records of the SAF, WNRC; memo, Special Assistant to the SAF for Manpower, Personnel, and Reserve Forces to SAF, Nov 10, 1964, p 1, Records of the SAF, WNRC.

7. Brayton, "Reserve Policies," pp 141–42.

8. Futrell, *U.S. Air Force, 1907–1964*, p 622; NGAUS, *Official Proceedings at the NGAUS Eighty-Fifth General Conference* (Philadelphia, Sep 30, 1963), p 70; DOD, *SECDEF Report for FY 63*, p 24; U.S. Congress, House, Committee on Appropriations, *Hearings on Appropriations for FY 64*, 88th Cong, 1st sess (Washington, 1963), p 352.

9. Report, Reserve Forces Ad Hoc Group, Realistic Training for Air Reserve Forces, Dec 13, 1963, in *AFCRF History, 1 Jul–31 Dec 1963* (Washington, n.d.), Atch 2, pp 1–16 [hereafter cited as Ad Hoc Group, Realistic Training].

10. Ad Hoc Group, Realistic Training, pp 7–24; Final Report of ARFPC Meeting 37, History of the ANG Pilot Training Program, 1950–1952, p 10. Document provided to author by Gerald Cantwell, Director of Historical Services, HQ Air Force Reserve.

11. AFR 45–60, Programming, Equipping, and Maintaining the Capability of the Air Force Ready Reserve Forces, Feb 13, 1963, p 1; TAC, *History, 1 Jan–30 Jun 1963* (Langley AFB, Va., n.d.), p 140.

12. U.S. Congress, Senate, Committee on Appropriations, *Hearings on DOD Appropriations for FY 65*, 88th Cong, 2d sess (Washington, 1964), pp 400–02 [hereafter cited as Senate, *FY 65 DOD Appropriations*]; U.S. Congress, House, Committee on Appropriations, *Hearings on DOD Appropriations for FY 65*, 88th Cong, 2d sess (Washington, 1964), pp 735–36; NGB, *Annual Report of the Chief, NGB for the Fiscal Year Ending 30 June 1964* (Washington, 1964); p 63; NGAUS, *Official Proceedings at the NGAUS Eighty-Sixth General Conference* (Detroit, Mich., Sep 28–Oct 1, 1964), pp 74–75; DOD, *SECDEF Report for FY 65*, pp 31, 79.

13. DOD, *SECDEF Report for FY 65*, pp 78–79; NGB, *Annual Report of the Chief, NGB for the Fiscal Year Ending 30 June 1965* (Washington, 1965), p 41.

14. Senate, *FY 65 DOD Appropriations*, p 400.

15. DOD, *SECDEF Report for FY 65*, pp 79–80.

16. *Ibid.*

17. NGB, *Report for FY 60* pp 8–9; NGB, *Report for FY 65*, p 46.

18. Wilson intvw, Dec 17–18, 1978.

19. DOD, *Annual Report of the Secretary of Defense, July 1, 1965 to June 30, 1966* (Washington, 1967), p 31; ltr, Gen J. B. Lampert, Deputy to the Assistant SECDEF to Congressman William T. Cahill, Re: President Johnson's decision not to mobilize the reserve for Vietnam, Aug 2, 1967, Box 182, ND 13/FG 13, Papers of Lyndon B. Johnson, Lyndon Baines Johnson Library, Austin, Tex.

20. NGB, *Annual Report of the Chief, NGB for the Fiscal Year Ending 30 June 1966* (Washington, 1966), p 40; untitled news item, *Air Reservist*, Feb 1967, p 4; NGAUS, *Official Proceedings at the Eighty-Eighth General Conference* (Phoenix, Ariz., Oct 17–20, 1966), pp 41–43; Gen John P. McConnell, "Our Air Force Reserve Components," Convention, New York, Jun 29, 1966, reprinted in *The Air Force Policy Letter for Commanders*, Aug 1966, pp 19–23; Wilson intvw, Dec 17–18, 1978.

21. NGB, *An NGB Activity Input to Project Corona Harvest on ANG Support of U.S. Air Force Operations in SEA, 1954 to March 31, 1968* (Washington, 1970), IV, 3–4, 10–11, I, 1, 9, III, 45, Doc K160–80, CVAH(S); Talking Paper, DAF/HQ USAF, Palace Alert, Nov 28, 1969, p 3, Doc K160.801245–1, AFSHRC, Maxwell AFB, Ala.; Carl Berger, ed, *The United States Air Force in Southeast Asia, 1961–1973* (Washington, 1977), p 187; Wilson intvw, Dec 17–18, 1978; NGB, *Annual Review, FY 1976, Chief, NGB* (Washington, n.d.), p 55.

22. NGAUS, *1966 Proceedings*, pp 98, 100–101; Statement of SECDEF Robert S. McNamara before a joint session of the Senate Armed Services Committee and the Senate Subcommittee on DOD Appropriations on the FY 1967–71 Defense Program and the FY 1967 Defense Budget, n.d., released by the Senate Armed Services Committee and the Senate Subcommittee on DOD Appropriations; Wilson intvw, Dec 17–18, 1978; Gen Nathan F. Twining, *Neither Liberty nor Safety: A Hard Look at U.S. Military Policy and Strategy* (New York, 1966), p 248.

23. NGAUS, *Official Proceedings at the NGAUS Eighty-Ninth General Conference* (Washington, Sep 18–21, 1967), p 38; Wilson intvw, Dec 17–18, 1978.

24. NGAUG, *1967 Proceedings*, pp 51–52.

25. *Ibid.*, pp 36–37.

26. "What's in Store for the ANG?" *The National Guardsman*, Jul 1967, pp 10–12, 38.

27. Maj Robert Hunter (USAF), "The Reserve Forces and the Total Force Concept," *Air Force*, Jan 1973, pp 54–59; Wilson intvw, Dec 17–18, 1978; Brayton, "Reserve Policies," p 142.

28. NGAUS, *1967 Proceedings* p 121; T. E. Greene and A. Lavish, *The Air Reserve Forces Study, Volume III: Tactical Fighter Forces* (Santa Monica, 1967), pp 3, 10–11, 13, 15.

29. Director of Management Analysis, HQ USAF, Tactical Fighter and Reconnaissance Forces (Active/ANG) Dec 15, 1965, in Greene and Lavish, *Air Reserve Study*, p 31.

30. Greene and Lavish, *Air Reserve Study*, pp 32–33.

31. *Ibid.*, p v.

32. *Ibid.*, p vi.

33. *Ibid.*, pp vii–viii.

34. Greene and Lavish, *Air Reserve Study*, in NGAUS, *1967 Proceedings*, p 123.

35. *Ibid.*, pp 125–26; Brayton, "Reserve Policies," p 142.

36. "Washington Report," *The Air Reservist*, Dec 1967/Jan 1968, p 3; ltr, SECDEF to Gov John Connally (Tex.), Re: Future of Texas ANG FIS Units, Dec 19, 1968, Box 183, ND 13/FG 13, Lyndon Baines Johnson Library; memo, AFCC to SAF, subj: Roles and Missions for Air Reserve Forces, Feb 17, 1968, Doc K168.03–3, AFSHRC, Maxwell AFB, Ala.; Wilson intvw, Dec 17–18, 1978.

37. Lyndon Baines Johnson, *The Vantage Point: Perspectives of the Presidency, 1963–1969* (New York, 1971), pp 385–87; Townsend Hoopes, *The Limits of Intervention* (New York, 1969), pp 136–37; memo, NGB to AFCHO, subj: Chronology of ANG Activities Affecting Mobilization (Jan 1968), Mar 13, 1968, Doc K160.80103–5, AFCHO, Washington; DOD, *Annual Report of the SECDEF July 1, 1967 to June 30, 1968* (Washington, 1971), p 39.

38. NGB, *Annual Report of the Chief, NGB for the Fiscal Year Ending 30 June 1968* (Washington, 1968), p 7; "The Call Up," *Air Reservist*, Mar 1968, p 2; "The Air Guard in the Korean Crisis," *National Guardsman*, Mar 1968, p 2.

39. Wilson intvw, Dec 17–18, 1978; 140th TFW, *History of the 140th TFW, 26 Jan 1968–30 Apr 1969* (Buckley ANGB, Colo., 1969), p 1; memo, Assistant SAF (Manpower and Reserve) to Assistant SECDEF (Manpower and Reserve), subj: Lessons Learned from Limited Mobilizations, Jan 10, 1969, (provided to author by HQ USAF, Directorate of Plans, DCS/OP&R).

40. Johnson, *Vantage Point*, pp 385–422; Hoopes, Limits, pp 159–181; Wilson intvw, Dec 17–18, 1978.

41. NGAUS, *Official Proceedings at the NGAUS Ninetieth General Conference* (Hot Springs, Ark., Oct 7–10, 1968), p 70; Pesch intvw, Jun 25, 1978; Wilson intvw, Dec 17–18, 1978; DOD, *Report for FY 68*, p 39.

42. "New Mobilization Directive Reflects Pueblo Lessons," *National Guardsman*, Dec 1970, p 27; Maj William W. Basnett, "A Com-

parison of TAC and Reserve Forces Organizational Structures and Associated Problems," (Research Study, Air University, Maxwell AFB, Ala., 1971), pp 13–16, 30–31 [hereafter cited as Basnett, "Comparison of TAC and Reserve Structures"].

43. Ohio Adjutant General, *1969 Annual Report, The Adjutant General's Department* (Columbus, Ohio, Nov 1969), p 35; Basnett, "Comparison of TAC and Reserve Structures," pp 10–11; 140th TFW, *Hist, Jan–Apr 69*, p 4.

44. DOD, *Report for FY 68*, p 39.

45. NGB, *Report for FY 68*, pp 7–8; NGB, *Report for FY 69*, pp 11–12.

46. NGB, "Facts and Figures on ANG Mobilizations of 26 Jan and 13 May 1968," Fact Sheet 18, Sep 18, 1968, p 1, Doc K160.801951–1, CVAH(S), Washington.

47. 140th TFW, *Hist, Jan 68–Apr 69*, pp 1, 5. (The 120th TFS was part of the 140th TFW and its history for this period is contained in the 140th's.) NGB, *Report for FY 68*, p 7; AFCHO, *Department of the Air Force Historical Summary, July 1 1968 to June 30, 1969* (Washington, 1973), p 7; NGB, *Report for FY 69*, p 11.

48. NGB, *Report for FY 69*, p 11.

49. AFCHO, *DAF Summary, Jul 68–Jun 69*, p 42; 140th TFW, *Hist, Jan 68–Apr 69*, p 6; NGB, *Report for FY 69*, p 11.

50. Untitled News Item, *Air Reservist*, Aug/Sep 1968, p 5.

51. 35th TFW, *History of the 35th TFW, April–June 1968* (Phan Rang AB, Republic of Vietnam, n.d.), p 5.

52. U.S. Congress, Senate, Committee on Armed Services, *Hearings on Nominations of John L. McLucas to be Secretary of the Air Force and Gen George S. Brown to be Chief of Staff, U.S. Air Force*, 93rd Cong, 1st sess (Washington, 1973), p 18.

53. Wilson intvw, Dec 17–18, 1978.

54. Fifth Air Force, *History of 5th Air Force, 1 July 1968–30 June 1969* (Kunsan AB, Republic of Korea, 1971), Narrative, I, 112–14; Lt Col W. D. McGleason (ANG), "Guardsmen on the Hot Spot," *National Guardsman*, Jan 1969, p 2; "Service to the Nation," *National Guardsman*, Jan 1970, pp 4–5; 354th TFW, *History of the 354th TFW, 1 July 1968–30 September 1968*, (Kunsan AB, Republic of Korea, n.d.), pp 2–3.

55. 354th TFW, *Hist, Jul–Sep 68*, pp 5–7; "Service to the Nation," *National Guardsman*, Jan 1970, pp 4–5.

56. 354th TFW, *History of the 354th TFW, 1 Oct–31 Dec 1968* (Kunsan AB, Republic of

Korea, n.d.), p 4; 354th TFW, *Hist, Jul–Sep 68,* p 12.

57.   354th TFW, *History of the 354th TFW, 1 Jan–31 Mar 1969* (Kunsan AB, Republic of Korea, n.d.), pp i, 5–9.

58.   5th AF, *Hist, Jul 68–Jun 69,* p 117; NGB, *Report for FY 69,* p 12; 354th TFW, *History of the 354th TFW, 1 April–June 1969* (Kunsan AB, Republic of Korea, n.d.), p i.

59.   123rd TRW, *History of the 123rd TRW, 1 Jul–31 Dec 1968* (Richards-Gebaur AFB, Mo., n.d.), pp 6–9, 21; 123rd TRW, *History of the 123rd TRW, 1 Jan–9 June 1969* (Richards-Gebaur AFB, Mo., n.d.), pp 10–12.

60.   123rd TRW, *Hist, Jul–Dec 68,* pp 24–26; 5th AF, *Hist, Jul 68–Jun 69,* pp 119–23; NGB, *Report for FY 69,* pp 11–12.

61.   123rd TRW, *Hist, Jul–Dec 68,* p 25; NGB, *Report for FY 68,* pp 7–8; NGB, *Report for FY 69,* pp 11–12.

62.   123rd TRW, *Hist, Jul–Dec 68,* p 9; 123rd TRW, *Hist, Jan–Jun 69,* p 1. (In addition to the active duty assignments discussed in the narrative, two ANG F–100 units activated in January 1968—Washington, D.C.'s 113th TFG and Atlantic City's 117th TFG—were transferred to Myrtle Beach AFB, S.C. They formed a training unit to prepare Air Force pilots to fly F–100s in SEA. Furthermore, numerous ANG technical organizations including communications, weather, and Ground Electronics Engineering and Installation Agency (GEEIA) units were mobilized along with their parent tactical organizations. Air Guardsmen in these technical units were reassigned on an individual basis throughout the Air Force. See NGB, *Report for FY 68, pp* 7–10; NGB, *Report for FY 69,* p 12; Benton, *Air Weather Flights,* pp 61–62, 72.)

63.   LeMay intvw, Sep 14, 1978; Wilson intvw, Dec 17–18, 1978; Lt Col Edward Y. Hill (ANG), "How U.S. Air Force Tactical Fighter Forces Can Retain Combat Effectiveness Under Budget Restraints During the 1970–1980 Time Frame" (Professional Study 3980, Air War College, Maxwell AFB, Ala., 1970), p 9.

Chapter VII

Epilogue: The Air National Guard and the Total Force

1.   AFR 45–1, "Purpose, Policy and Responsibilities for Air Reserve Force (ARF)," Mar 3, 1975, p 1; Patricia R. Muncy, "Seminar Spotlight: New Posture for Reserve Forces," *Air Force,* Nov 1970, p 104; Weigley, *Way of War,* pp 468–69.

2.   Weigley, *Way of War,* pp 468–69; W. W. Rostow, *The Diffusion of Power: An Essay in Recent History* (New York, 1972), pp 547–49.

3.   "Dr. Marrs Cites Advances in Total Force Plan," *Officer,* Nov 1971, p 20; Rostow, *Diffusion of Power,* p 549; AFR 45–1, p 1; NGAUS, *1969 Proceedings,* p 76.

4.   Wilson intvw, Dec 17–18, 1978; Maj Robert Hunter (USAF), "The Reserve Forces and the Total Force Concept," *Air Force,* Jan 1973, pp 54–59.

5.   NGAUS, *1963 Proceedings,* p 116.

6.   Roy A. Werner, "The Readiness of U.S. Reserve Components," in *Supplementary Military Forces: Reserves, Militias, Auxiliaries,* edited by Louis A. Zurcher and Gwyn Harries-Jenkins (Beverly Hills, Calif., 1978), p 77.

7.   *Ibid.,* p 84.

8.   Wilson intvw, Dec 17–18, 1978; intvw, author with Maj Gen Francis S. Greenlief (Nat Guard, Ret), Washington, D.C., Jun 23, 1978.

9.   Capt John P. Silliman, Jr. (ANG), "Air National Guard Technicians: Status Quo vs Active Duty Guardsmen" (Air Command and Staff College Research Study 2315–77, Maxwell AFB, Ala., 1977), pp 5–12.

Glossary

AAF	Army Air Forces
AAG	Air Adjutant General
AB	Air Base
ACAS–1	Assistant Chief of Air Staff, Personnel
ACAS–3	Assistant Chief of Air Staff, Operations, Commitments, and Requirements
ACW	aircraft control and warning
ADC	Air Defense Command
AF	Air Force
AFA	Air Force Association
AFB	Air Force Base
AFCAG	Air Adjutant General, United States Air Force
AFCC	Air Force Chief of Staff
AFCHO	Office of Air Force History
AFCRF	Air Force Assistant Chief of Staff, Reserve Forces
AFCVC	Air Force Vice Chief of Staff
AFCVS	Air Force Vice Chief of Staff
AFR	Air Force Regulation
AFR	Air Force Reserve
AFSHRC	Albert F. Simpson Historical Research Center
AG	Adjutant General
AGAUS	Adjutants General Association of the United States
ANG	Air National Guard
ANGB	Air National Guard Base
ANGUS	Air National Guard of the United States
ARF	Air Reserve Force
ARFPC	Air Reserve Forces Policy Committee
asst	assistant
CG	commanding general
CNG	Chief, National Guard Division
CONAC	Continental Air Command
Cong	Congress
CVAH(S)	Office of Air Force History
DAF	Department of the Air Force
DC/AS	Deputy Chief, Air Staff
DCS	Deputy Chief of Staff
D–Day	The unnamed day on which hostilities, anoperation, or an exercise commences, or is to commence.
div	division

DO	Director of Operations
doc	document
DOD	Department of Defense
DPL	Director of Plans
ed	editor
EO	executive order
FBW	fighter bomber wing
FIS	fighter interceptor squadron
FY	fiscal year
GEEIA	Ground Electronics Engineering and Installation Agency
hist	history
HQ	headquarters
H.R.	House Resolution
intvw	interview
JCS	Joint Chiefs of Staff
JCSM	Joint Chiefs of Staff Memorandum
LC	Library of Congress
ltr	letter
MAC	Military Airlift Command
MAJCOM	major command
MATS	Military Air Transport Service
MD	Manuscript Division
M–Day	mobilization day
mgt	management
MR	memorandum for record
NARS	National Archives and Records Service
NATO	North Atlantic Treaty Organization
n.d.	no date
NGAUS	National Guard Association of the United States
NGB	National Guard Bureau
NGD	National Guard Division
NRP	National Reserve Plan
NSC	National Security Council
p(p)	page(s)
PL	Public Law
P&O	Plans and Operations

pres	president
re	refer, reference
rep	representative
RG	record group
ROA	Reserve Officers' Association
ROTC	Reserve Officers' Training Corps
RPRB	Reserve Program Review Board
R&R	routing and record
S.	Senate
SAC	Strategic Air Command
SAF	Secretary of the Air Force
SARF	Special Assistant to the Chief of Stafff or Reserve Forces
SEA	Southeast Asia
SECDEF	Secretary of Defense
secy	secretary
sess	session
subj	subject
TAC	Tactical Air Command
TACAN	tactical air navigation
TFG	tactical fighter group
TFS	tactical fighter squadron
TFW	tactical fighter wing
T/O&E	Table of Organization and Equipment
TRS	tactical reconnaissance squadron
TRW	tactical reconnaissance wing
UMT	universal military training
USAF	United States Air Force
USAFE	United States Air Forces in Europe
USSR	Union of Soviet Socialist Republics
VC	Vice Chief
VCOS	Vice Chief of Staff
vol	volume
WNRC	Washington National Records Center

Bibliography

I. MANUSCRIPT COLLECTIONS

Abilene, Kansas. Dwight D. Eisenhower Library.
    Dwight D. Eisenhower Papers.
    Bryce Harlow Papers.
Austin, Texas. Lyndon B. Johnson Library.
    Lyndon B. Johnson Papers.
Maxwell Air Force Base, Alabama. USAF Historical Research Center.
    Ennis C. Whitehead Papers.
Waltham, Massachusetts. John F. Kennedy Library.
    John F. Kennedy Papers.
Washington, D.C. Library of Congress, Manuscript Division.
    General Henry H. Arnold Papers.
    General Muir S. Fairchild Papers.
    General Curtis E. LeMay Papers.
    General Carl Spaatz Papers.
    General Nathan F. Twining Papers.
    General Hoyt S. Vandenberg Papers
    General Thomas D. White Papers.

II. PUBLIC RECORDS AND DOCUMENTS, UNPUBLISHED

Alcoa, Tennessee. Office of Air National Guard (ANG) History. Wilson, Maj Gen Winston P. Letter to Adjutant Generals of all States, Puerto Rico, and the District of Columbia. Subject: Mobilization Problems. March 15, 1962. Copy provided to author by Office of ANG History.

Independence, Missouri. Harry S. Truman Library. "Selected Documents from the Records of the President's Advisory Commission on UMT." Washington, D.C., n.d.

Maxwell Air Force Base, Alabama. Albert F. Simpson Historical Research Center (AFSHRC). Air Force Chief of Staff to Secretary of the Air Force. Roles and Missions for Air Reserve Forces. Memo, February 17, 1968. Document K168.03–3.

Department of the Air Force/HQ USAF. "Palace Alert Talking Paper." November 28, 1969. Document K160.801245–1.

Douglas, James H., Jr., Secretary of the Air Force. "Special Report on the Reserve Forces of the U.S. Air Force 25 December 1957." Document K168.041–8.

Partridge, Maj Gen Earle E. "Address to the National Convention of the Air National Guard Association." Columbus, Ohio, September 17, 1947. Document 410.16l–10.

National Guard Bureau (NGB). "The Air National Guard Summary." Report, NGB, Washington, D.C., March 31, 1949. Document 160.801197.

Suitland, Maryland. Washington National Records Center. Record Group 168. Records of the National Guard Bureau, 1945–1954.

Record Group 319. Records of the Army Staff, NGB. Decimal File 1951–1952.

Washington, D.C. HQ United States Air Force. Selected Records of the Secretary of the Air Force, 1955–1969.

Washington, D.C. National Archives. Record Group 18. Army Adjutant General Central File 381. File Postwar Vol 2.

Record Group 340. Records of the Secretary of the Air Force, 1947–1954.

Record Group 341. Records of the Air Force Chief of Staff, 1947–1955.

Washington, D.C. National Guard Association of the United States (NGAUS). Adjutants General Association of the U.S. Stenographic Transcripts of annual meetings, 1946–1954. *Guardsman* Files, 1946–1960. NGAUS Files, 1946–1960.

Washington, D.C. National Security Council (NSC). NSC 5420/2. Reserve Mobilization Requirements. Washington, D.C.: NSC, June 17, 1954. Copy of paper provided to author by NSC.

Washington, D.C.: Office of Air Force History (AFCHO). Air Defense Command Historical Documents. AFCHO.

McConnell, Brig Gen J. P. "The Air Reserve and National Guard." Lecture to the Air War College, November 29, 1948, Maxwell Air Force Base, Alabama. AFCHO. Sturm File. AFCHO.

NGB to AFCC. Mobilizations of the ANG. Memo, July 26, 1974. Document K160.801–1. AFCHO.

NGB to AFCHO. Chronology of ANG Activities Affecting Mobilization (Jan 1968). Memo, March 13, 1968. Document K160.80103–5. AFCHO.

Wright-Patterson Air Force Base, Ohio. Air Force Museum. ANG File L2.

III. PUBLIC RECORDS AND DOCUMENTS, PUBLISHED

Berger, Carl, ed. *The United States Air Force in Southeast Asia, 1961–1973*. Washington: Office of Air Force History, 1977.

Galloway, Eileen. *History of U.S. Military Policy on Reserve Forces, 1775–1957*. Washington: Government Printing Office, 1957.

Office of Air Force History. *Department of the Air Force Historical Summary, January 1968–June 1969*. Washington: Government Printing Office, 1973.

Office of Defense Mobilization. *Manpower Resources for National Security: A Report to the President by the Director of the Office of Defense Mobilization, January 6, 1954*. Washington: Government Printing Office, 1954.

Ohio Adjutant General. *1969 Annual Report: The Adjutant General's Department*. Columbus, Ohio, 1969.

U.S. Congress. House. Select Committee on Post War Military Policy. *Hearings before the Select Committee on Post War Military Policy to Establish a Single Department of the Armed Forces.* 78th Cong, 2d sess, 1944.

————————. Select Committee on Postwar Military Policy. *Hearings on Universal Military Training*. 79th Cong, 1st sess, 1945.

————————. Committee on Military Affairs. *Hearings on Universal Military Training*. 79th Cong, 1st sess, 1945.

————————. Subcommittee of the Committee on Appropriations. *Hearings on the Military Establishment's Appropriations Bill for (FY) 1948*. 80th Cong, 1st sess, 1947.

————————. Subcommittee of the Committee on Appropriations. *Hearings on National Military Establishment Appropriations Bill for (FY) 1949*. 80th Cong, 2d sess, 1948.

————————. Committee on Armed Services. *Hearings on the Bill to Authorize the Composition of the Army of the United States and the Air Force of the United States and for Other Purposes.* 81st Cong, 1st sess, 1949.

————————. Subcommittee of the Committee on Appropriations. *Hearings on Department of Defense Appropriations for Fiscal Year 1951. Part Three. Department of the Air Force.* 81st Cong, 2d sess, 1950.

————————. Subcommittee of the Committee on Appropriations. *Hearings on DOD Appropriations for (FY) 1952. Part Four. Department of the Air Force.* 82d Cong, 1st sess, 1951.

————————. Subcommittee of the Committee on Armed Services. *Hearings on Reserve Components.* 82d Cong, 1st sess, 1951.

————————. Subcommittee of the Committee on Armed Services. *Hearings on the Air Force Reserve Program.* 83d Cong, 2d sess, April 1954.

————————. Subcommittee No 1 of the Committee on Armed Services. *Hearings on Review of Reserve Program.* 85th Cong, 1st sess, 1957.

————————. Subcommittee No 3 of the Committee on Armed Services. *Hearings on Review of the Reserve Program.* 86th Cong, 2d sess, 1960.

————————. Committee on Armed Services. *Hearings on Military Reserve Posture.* 87th Cong, 2d sess, 1962.

————————. Subcommittee of the Committee on Appropriations. *Hearings on DOD Appropriations for (FY) 1964.* 88th Cong, 1st sess, 1963.

————————. Subcommittee of the Committee on Appropriations. *Hearings on DOD Appropriations for (FY) 1965.* 88th Cong, 2d sess, 1964.

U.S. Congress. Senate. Committee on Armed Services. *Hearings on the National Defense Establishment (Unification of the Armed Services).* 80th Cong, 1st sess, 1947.

————————. Subcommittee of the Committee on Armed Services. *Hearings on Armed Forces Reserve Act (of 1952).* 82d Cong, 2d ess, 1952.

————————. Subcommittee of the Committee on Appropriations. *Hearings on Department of Defense (DOD) Appropriations for (FY) 1954.* 83d Cong, 1st sess, 1953.

————————. Committee on Armed Services. Status of Reserve and National Guard Forces. Report of the Interim Subcommittee on Preparedness. 83d Cong, 2d sess, 1954.

————————. Committee on Armed Services. *Hearings on a National Reserve Plan.* 84th Cong, 1st sess, 1955.

————————. Committee on Appropriations. *Hearings on DOD Appropriations for (FY) 1963.* 87th Cong, 2d sess, 1962.

————————. Committee on Armed Services. *Hearings Authorizing the President to Order Units and Members in the Ready Reserve to Active Duty for Not More than Twelve Months and for Other Purposes.* 87th Cong, 2d sess, 1962.

————————. Subcommittee of the Committee on Appropriations. *Hearings on DOD Appropriations for (FY) 1965.* 88th Cong, 2d sess, 1964.

————————. Committee on Armed Services. *Hearings on Nominations of John L. McLucas to be Secretary of the Air Force and General George S. Brown to be Chief of Staff, U.S. Air Force.* 93d Cong, 1st sess, 1973.

————————. Committee on Armed Services and Subcommittee on DOD Appropriations. Statement of Secretary of Defense Robert S. McNamara before a Joint Session of the Senate Armed Services Committee and the Senate Subcommittee on DOD Appropriations on the FY 1967–71 Defense Program and the FY 1967 Defense Budget. Released by the Senate Armed Services Committee and the Subcommittee on DOD Appropriations, n.d.

U.S. Department of Defense. *First Annual Report of the Secretary of Defense to the President. Appendix E.* Washington: Government Printing Office, 1948.

————————. *Report of the Committee on Civilian Components.* Washington: Government Printing Office, 1948.

————————. *Semi-Annual Report of the Secretary of Defense,* Washington: Government Printing Office: *January 1 to June 30, 1953* (1953), *January 1 to June 30, 1954* (1955), *January–June 1957* (1958),

————————. *Annual Report of the Secretary of Defense,* Washington: Government Printing Office: *July 1, 1958 to June 30, 1959* (1960), *July 1, 1959 to June 30, 1960* (1960), *July 1, 1961 to June 30, 1962* (1962), *July 1, 1962 to June 30, 1963* (1964), *July 1, 1963 to June 30, 1964* (1966), *July 1, 1964 to June 30, 1965* (1967), *July 1, 1965 to June 30, 1966* (1967), *July 1, 1967 to June 30, 1968* (1971).

National Guard Bureau. *Annual Report of the Chief, National Guard Bureau for the Fiscal Year,* Washington: Government Printing Office: *Ending 30 June 1946* (1946), *Ending 30 June 1947* (1947), *Ending 30 June 1948* (1948), *Ending 30 June 1949* (1949), *Ending 30 June 1950* (1950), *Ending 30 June 1951* (1951), *Ending 30 June 1952* (1952), *Ending 30 June 1953* (1953), *Ending 30 June 1957* (1957), *Ending 30 June 1958* (1958), *Ending 30 June 1959* (1960), *Ending 30 June 1960* (1960), *Ending 30 June 1969* (1969).

————————. *Annual Report of the Chief, NGB for the Fiscal Year,* Washington: Departments of the Army and Air Force: *Ending 30 June 1961* (1961), *Ending 30 June 1962* (1962), *Ending 30 June 1963* (1963), *Ending 30 June 1964* (1964), *Ending 30 June 1965* (1965), *Ending 30 June 1966* (1966), *Ending 30 June 1968* (1968).

————————. *Annual Review, FY 1976, Chief, NGB.* Washington: Government Printing Office, n.d.

——————— . "Brief History of Air National Guard Mobilizations." Fact Sheet 302–76, November 1976.

——————— . "Compact History of the National Guard." Fact Sheet 102–76, April 1976.

——————— . "Congressional Budget Appropriations, FY 1948 1976." Fact Sheet 114–77, May 1977.

——————— . "Facts and Figures on ANG Mobilizations of 26 January and 13 May 1968." Fact Sheet 18, September 1968. Document K160.801951–1, AFCHO, Washington, D.C.

USAF Historical Division, Research Studies Institute, "Air Reserve Unit Participation in the Korean War," Maxwell Air Force Base, Ala., 1954.

U.S. National Security Training Commission. *Twentieth Century Minuteman: A Report to the President on the Reserve Forces Training Program, December 1, 1953.*

Public Papers of the Presidents of the United States: John F. Kennedy, 1961. Washington: Office of the Federal Register, National Archives and Records Service, 1962.

IV. OFFICIAL STUDIES

Air Defense Command (ADC). *Air Defense Command History, March 1946 to June 1947.* Mitchel Air Force Base, New York: ADC, 1948.

——————— . *The Air Defense of the U.S.: A Study of the Work of ADC and its Predecessors through June 1951.* Mitchel Air Force Base, New York: ADC, 1952.

——————— . *History of ADC, July 1957–December 1957.* Ent Air Force Base, Colo.: ADC, n.d.

——————— . *Semi-Annual Historical Report, 1 January–30 June 1953.* Ent Air Force Base, Colo.: ADC, 1954.

——————— . *Supporting Documents: History of Air Defense Command, March 1946 to June 1947.* Mitchel Air Force Base, New York: ADC, 1947.

——————— . *Supporting Documents: History of Air Defense Command, July 1947–November 1948.* Mitchel Air Force Base, New York: ADC, 1947.

Air Reserve Forces Policy Committee (ARFPC). History of ANG Pilot Training Program, 1950–1962. Copy of document provided to author by Gerald Cantwell, Director of Historical Services, HQ Air Force Reserve, Robins Air Force Base, Ga.

Continental Air Command (CONAC). *History of the CONAC, 1 December 1948–30 December 1949.* Mitchel Air Force Base, New York: CONAC, 1950.

——————— . *Continental Air Command History for July-December 1950.* Mitchel Air Force Base, New York: CONAC, 1951.

——————— . *Supporting Documents: History of CONAC, July 1950 to 31 December 1950, Vol II.* Mitchel Air Force Base, New York: CONAC, 1951.

——————— . *History of CONAC,* Mitchel Air Force Base, New York: CONAC: *for 1 January to 30 June 1951* (1951), *for 1 July–31 December 1953* (1954), *for January–June* (1954), *for January–June 1955* (1956), *for January–June 1957* (1958), *for July–December 1957* (n.d.), *for January–June 1958* (1959), *for July–December 1959* (1960), *January–June 1960* (n.d.), *for 1 July 1960 through 30 June 1961* (n.d.).

——————— . *Supporting Documents: History of the CONAC,* Mitchel Air Force Base, New York: CONAC: *for January–June 1955, Vol V* (1956), *July-December 1959, Vol II* (n.d.).

Eckwright, Royce E. *Air National Guard Deployment to U.S. Air Force in Europe (USAFE) Area 1961–1962.* Lindsey Air Station, Germany: USAFE, 1962.

Futrell, Robert F. *Ideas, Concepts, Doctrine: A History of Basic Thinking in the United States Air Force, 1907–1964, Vol II.* Maxwell Air Force Base, Ala., 1971.

USAF Historical Study No 72: U.S. Air Force Operations in Korea, 1 November 1950–30 June 1952. Maxwell Air Force Base, Ala.: USAF Historical Division, Air University, 1953.

Goldberg, Alfred. *History, Headquarters U.S. Air Force, 1 July 1950 to 30 June 1951.* Maxwell Air Force Base, Ala.: Air University Historical Office, 1955.

Greene, T. E. and Lavish, A. *The Air Reserve Forces Study, Vol III: Tactical Fighter Forces.* Santa Monica, Calif.: RAND Corporation, 1967.

Hennessy, Juliette A. *The United States Army Air Arm, April 1861 to April 1917.* USAF Historical Studies: No 98. Maxwell Air Force Base, Ala.: USAF Historical Division, Research Studies Institute, Air University, 1958.

McMullen, Richard F. *Air Defense Command Historical Study No. 38: The Air National Guard in Air Defense, 1946–1971.* Ent Air Force Base, Colo.: Air Defense Command, n.d.

Office of the Assistant Chief of Staff for Reserve Forces (AFCRF). *History of the AFCRF, 1 July–31 December 1963.* Washington: HQ USAF, n.d.

Office of the Secretary of the Air Force. *History of the Office of the Secretary of the Air Force, 1 January 1952–30 June 1952, Vol I.* Washington: Department of the Air Force, 1952.

Office of the Secretary of the Air Force/Assistant for Manpower, Personnel and Reserve Forces. *History of the Office of the Special Assistant for Manpower, Personnel and Reserve Forces.* Washington: Department of the Air Force, n.d.

Ray, Thomas W. *Air Defense Command Study No 23: The Air National Guard Manned Interceptor Force, 1946–1964.* Ent Air Force Base, Colo.: Air Defense Command, 1964.

Special Assistant to the Chief of Staff for Reserve Forces (SARF). *Historical Summary of SARF, 1 July to 31 December 1950.* Washington: SARF, 1951.

———————. *Historical Summary, Office of the SARF,* Washington: HQ USAF: *1 January–30 June 1951* (n.d.), *1 July–31 December 1951* (1952).

Tactical Air Command (TAC). *History of the TAC,* Langley Air Force Base, Va.: TAC: *1 July–30 November 1950* (1951), *1 July–31 December 1960* (n.d.), *1 January–30 June 1961* (n.d.), *1 July–31 December 1962* (n.d.), *1 January–30 June 1963* (n.d.).

National Guard Bureau. *An Activity Input to Project Corona Harvest on ANG Support of U.S. Air Force Operations in SEA, 1954 to March 31, 1968.* Washington: NGB, 1970. Document K160.80. AFCHO, Washington, D.C.

First Air Force. *History, 1st Air Force,* Mitchel Air Force Base, New York: First Air Force: *March 31 to December 31, 1946* (1947), *1 July to 31 December 1950* (1951).

Fifth Air Force. *History of the 5th Air Force, 1 July 1968–30 June 1969, Narrative, Vol One.* Republic of Korea: HQ Fifth Air Force, 1971.

Tenth Air Force. *Historical Data, 10th Air Force, 1 July 1949 to 31 December 1949, Vol IV, No 2.* Selfridge Air Force Base, Mich.: Tenth Air Force, 1950. AFSHRC Document 830.01.

Twelfth Air Force. *History of the 12th Air Force (TAC),* Waco, Texas: Twelfth Air Force: *1 July–31 December 1960, Part I* (n.d.), *1 July–31 December 1961, Narrative, Part I* (n.d.).

Fifteenth Air Force. *History of the 15th Air Force (SAC),* March Air Force Base, Calif.: Fifteenth Air Force: *July–December 1951* (1952), *January–June 1952* (1952), *July–December 1952* (1953).

Seventeenth Air Force. *History, Headquarters 17th Air Force, July–31 December 1961.* Ramstein Air Base, Germany: HQ Seventeenth Air Force, n.d.

35th Tactical Fighter Wing. *History of the 35th TFW, April–June 1968.* Phan Rang Air Base, Republic of Vietnam: 35th TFW, n.d.

116th Fighter Bomber Wing (FBW). *History of the 116th FBW,* George Air Force Base, Calif.: 116th FBW: *1 November–31 December 1950* (n.d.), *1 January–31 March 1951* (n.d.)

121st Tactical Fighter Wing (TFW). *History of the 121st TFW, 1 October–20 August 1962.* Lockbourne Air Force Base, Ohio: 121st TFW, n.d.

131st Tactical Fighter Wing. *History of the 131st TFW, 1 October 1961 to 20 August 1962.* Robertson Air National Guard Base, Lambert Field, St. Louis, Mo.: 131st TFW, n.d.

123rd Tactical Reconnaissance Wing (TRW). *History of the 123rd TRW,* Richards-Gebaur Air Force Base, Mo.: 123rd TRW: *1 July–31 December 1968* (n.d.), *1 January–9 June 1969* (n.d.).

136th Fighter Bomber Wing (FBW). *History of the 136th FBW,* Langley Air Force Base, Va.: 136th FBW: *26 October–31 December 1950* (n.d.), *1 January–31 March 1951* (n.d.).

———————. *History of the 136th FBW, 1 April–30 June 1951.* Langley Air Force Base, Va. and Itazuke Air Base, Japan: 136th FBW, n.d.

140th Tactical Fighter Wing. *History of the 140th TFW, 26 January 1968–30 April 1969.* Buckley Air National Guard Base, Colo.: 140th TFW, 1969.

354th Tactical Fighter Wing. *History of the 354th TFW,* Kunsan Air Base, Republic of Korea: 354th TFW: *1 July 1968–30 September 1968* (n.d.), *1 October–31 December 1968* (n.d.), *1 January–31 March 1969* (n.d.), *1 April–June 1969* (n.d.).

7121st Tactical Fighter Wing. *History of the 7121st Tactical Fighter Wing,* Etain Air Base, France: 7121st TFW: *1 October–31 December 1961* (n.d.), *1 January–31 June 1962* (n.d.).

V. INTERVIEWS

Greenlief, Maj Gen Francis S., NGAUS, Ret, Executive Vice President, NGAUS, Washington, D.C., June 23, 1978.

Hoover, Brig Gen Paul E., Ohio National Guard, Worthington, Ohio, May 30, 1978.

Johnson, Gen Leon W., USAF, Ret, McLean, Virginia, June 25, 1978.

LeMay, Gen Curtis E., USAF, Ret, Pentagon, Washington, D.C., September 14, 1978.

Metcalf, Curtis E., Deputy Chief, Plans and Operations, Air Force Division/NGB, Pentagon, Washington, D.C., October 18, 1977.

Pesch, Maj Gen John J., ANGUS, Ret, Arlington, Virginia, June 25, 1978.

Stuart, Harold, Tulsa, Oklahoma, August 28, 1978.

Wilson, Maj Gen Winston P., ANGUS, Ret, Forrest City, Arkansas, December 17–18, 1978.

VI. BOOKS

Davis, Vincent. *Postwar Defense Policy and the U.S. Navy, 1943–1946.* Chapel Hill: University of North Carolina Press, 1962.

Derthick, Martha. *The National Guard in Politics.* Cambridge: Harvard University Press, 1965.

Eisenhower, Dwight David. *Mandate for Change: The White House Years, 1953–1956.* Garden City, N.Y.: Doubleday, 1963.

Elliott, James C. *The Modern Army and Air National Guard.* Princeton, N.J.: D. Van Nostrand, 1965.

Futrell, Robert F. *The United States Air Force in Korea, 1950–1953.* New York: Duell, Sloan and Pearce, 1961.

Clines, Carroll V. *The Compact History of the United States Air Force.* New York: Hawthorn Books, 1973.

Goldberg, Alfred, ed. *A History of the United States Air Force, 1907–1957.* Princeton, N.J.: D. Van Nostrand, 1957.

Hill, Jim Dan. *The Minute Man in Peace and War: A History of the National Guard.* Harrisburg, Pa.: Stackpole, 1964.

Hoopes, Townsend. *The Limits of Intervention.* New York: David McKay, 1969.

Johnson, Lyndon Baines. *The Vantage Point: Perspectives of the Presidency, 1963–1969.* New York: Holt, Rinehart and Winston, 1971.

Kinnard, Douglas. *President Eisenhower and Strategy Management: A Study in Defense Politics.* Lexington, Ky.: University Press of Kentucky, 1977.

Kissinger, Henry A. *The Necessity for Choice: Prospects of American Foreign Policy.* New York: Harper, 1961.

Levantrosser, William F. *Congress and the Citizen Soldier: Legislative Policy-Making for the Federal Armed Forces Reserve.* Columbus, Ohio: Ohio State University Press, 1967.

Pearson, Henry G. *A Businessman in Uniform, Raynal Cawthorne Bolling.* New York: Duffield and Co, 1923.

Riker, William H. *Soldiers of the States—The Role of the National Guard in American Democracy.* Washington: Public Affairs Press, 1967.

Rostow, W. W. *The Diffusion of Power: An Essay in Recent History.* McMillan, 1972.

Schlesinger, Arthur M., Jr. *A Thousand Days: John F. Kennedy in the White House.* Boston: Houghton Mifflin, 1965.

Sharff, Lee E. *1977 National Guard Almanac.* Washington: Uniformed Services Almanac, Inc, 1977.

Sherry, Michael S. *Preparing for the Next War: American Plans for Postwar Defense, 1941–1945.* New Haven: Yale University Press, 1977.

Smith, Jean Edward. *The Defense of Berlin.* Baltimore: Johns Hopkins University Press, 1963.

Smith, Perry, McCoy. *The Air Force Plans for Peace, 1943–1945.* Baltimore: Johns Hopkins University Press, 1970.

Taylor, Maxwell P. *The Uncertain Trumpet.* New York: Harper, 1960.

Twining, Gen Nathan P. *Neither Liberty Nor Safety: A Hard Look at U.S. Military Policy and Strategy.* New York: Holt, Rinehart and Winston, 1966.

Weigley, Russell F. *American Way of War: A History of United States Military Strategy and Policy.* New York: McMillan, 1973.

——————— . *History of the United States Army.* New York: McMillan, 1967.

——————— . *Towards an American Army: Military Thought from Washington to Marshall.* New York: Columbia University Press, 1962.

Wolfe, Thomas W. *Soviet Power and Europe, 1945–1970.* Baltimore: Johns Hopkins University Press, 1970.

VII.   ARTICLES

"Air Force Rapped for Policy on Air Guard Planes." *Air Force Times,* May 2, 1959, p 1.

"Air Guard Gets Transports, Starfighters." *Air Force Times,* January 23, 1960, p 1.

"The Air Guard in the Korean Crisis." *National Guardsman,* March 1968, pp 2–4.

"The Air National Guard." *Air Reservist,* February 1966, pp 4–5.

"The Air National Guard in the Berlin Crisis." *National Guardsman,* September 1962, pp 14–19, 35–36.

"Another ANG Wing Flying F–84 Jets Joins NATO Forces." *Air Reserve Forces Review,* June 1952, p 13.

Baldwin, Hanson W. "The Military Reserve Bill: An Analysis of Objections to Defense Measure Before the House." *New York Times,* June 9, 1955, p 1.

Brayton, Abott A. "American Reserve Policies Since World War II." *Military Affairs XXXVI* (December 1972), 139–144.

Drake, Francis and Katherine. "The Inside Story of Stairstep." *Readers Digest,* May 1962, pp 207–218.

Elliott, Maj James C. "The Recall Story: To Maintain the Peace." *Air Force and Space Digest,* January 1962, pp 84–88.

Evans, C. William. "War Roles Written for the ANG." *National Guardsman,* November 1952, pp 10–11.

"Finletter Approves Long Range Plan for Air Reserve Forces." *Air Force,* October 1951, pp 3–6.

"Forrestal Has Plan to Invigorate Reserve Force." *Air Force,* January 1949, pp 32–33.

"Guard Association Demands Reevaluation of General LeMay's Qualifications, Usefulness." *Army, Navy, Air Force Journal,* October 10, 1959, p 1.

"Hal Stuart Proffers Friendly Hand to Air Guard." *Air Force,* April 1951, p 40.

"Herbert Subcommittee Blasts Realignment." *National Guardsman,* October 1962, p 3.

Hunter, Maj Robert. "The Reserve Forces and the Total Force Concept." *Air Force,* January 1973, pp 54–59.

Hogan, Edmund F. "Reserve and Guard Wings Axed to 39." *Air Force,* November 1957, pp 67–69.

Information Division, Office of the Special Assistant for Reserve Forces. "Air Force's Baby: The CONAC." *Air Reserve Forces Review,* June 1949, pp 4–5.

Lanphier, Lt Col Thomas G. (Idaho Air National Guard). "Forty-Eight Air Forces Too Many." *Air Force,* January 1949, pp 11–12.

"A Look Into the Future: Long Range Policies for Reserve Forces Announced." *Air Reserve Forces Review,* January 1951, pp 2–5.

"LeMay Asks Full Merger of Reserves." *Air Force Times,* October 30, 1959, pp 1, 39.

"Dr. Marrs Cites Advances in Total Force Plan." *Officer,* November 1971, pp 20–21, 23.

"Marshall Names Eight on Reserve Policy." *New York Times,* October 28, 1950, p 6.

"Reservists Freed from Forced Duty." *New York Times,* October 24, 1950, p 20.

McConnell, Gen John P. "Our Air Force Reserve Components." Speech to the Reserve Officers Association, June 29, 1966, New York. Reprinted in *The Air Force Policy Letter for Commanders,* August 1966, pp 19–23.

McGleason, Lt Col W. D., ANG. "Guardsmen on the Hot Spot." *National Guardsman,* January 1969, pp 2–7.

Muncy, Patricia R. "Seminar Spotlight: New Posture for Reserve Forces." *Air Force,* November 1970, pp 104–109.

"New Mobilization Directive Reflects Pueblo Lessons." *National Guardsman,* December 1970, p 27.

"New Type Bombing Mission Given to Eleven F–84F Equipped Guard Units." *Air Force Times,* June 21, 1958, p 5.

National Guard Association of the United States. "A Situation Report: The Battle of Washington." *National Guardsman,* March 1949, pp 18–21.

——————— . Untitled News Item. *National Guardsman,* November 1945, p 5.

——————— . Untitled News Item. *National Guardsman,* November 1948, p 5.

"Official Text Concerning General LeMay's Reserve Forces Statement Released." *Army, Navy, Air Force* Journal, October 10, 1959, p 8.

Rhea, John. "A Vital Link." *National Guardsman,* September 1977, pp 2–6.

Ricks, Maj Gen Earl J., USAF. "The Post Korea Air National Guard." *National Guardsman,* December 1951, pp 12–13, 39.

"Service to the Nation." *National Guardsman,* January 1970, pp 4–5.

"Sixty Day Consent Tours Begin for Nine ANG Units." *Air Force Times,* August 14, 1954, p 1.

"Sound the Rally Call." *Air Reserve Forces Review,* March 1951, pp 4–5.

"Troop Buildup in Europe Grows." *New York Times,* October 15, 1961, p 44.

Untitled News Item. *Air Reserve Forces Review,* January 1962, p 12.

Untitled News Item. *The Air Reservist,* February 1967, p 4.

"Washington Report." *The Air Reservist,* December 1967–January 1968, p 3.

"What's in Store for the ANG?" *National Guardsman,* July 1967, pp 10–12, 38.

Zuckert, Eugene M., Secretary of the Air Force. "Air Reserve Forces Prove Readiness." *The Air Reservist,* June–July 1962, p 7.

VIII.   PROCEEDINGS

National Guard Association of the United States (NGAUS). *Official Proceedings at the NGAUS Sixty-Sixth General Conference.* Baltimore, Md., May 3–6, 1944.

——————— . *Official Proceedings at the NGAUS Seventieth General Conference.* St. Louis, Mo., September 27–30, 1948.

Official Proceedings at the NGAUS Seventy-Second General Conference. Washington, D.C., Octotber 23–25, 1950.

——————— . *Official Proceedings at the NGAUS Seventy-Third General Conference.* Washington, D.C., October 22–24, 1951.

——————— . *Official Proceedings at the NGAUS Seventy-Fourth General Conference.* Denver, Colo., October 6–9, 1952.

——————— . *Official Proceedings at the NGAUS Seventy-Eighth General Conference.* Spokane, Wash., October 8–11, 1956.

——————— . *Official Proceedings at the NGAUS Seventy-Ninth General Conference.* Louisville, Ky., October 7–10, 1957.

——————— . *Official Proceedings at the NGAUS Eightieth General Conference.* Atlantic City, N.J., September 29–30, and October 1–2, 1958.

——————— . *Official Proceedings at the NGAUS Eighty-First General Conference.* San Antonio, Texas, October 5–8, 1959.

——————— . *Official Proceedings at the NGAUS Eighty-Second General Conference.* Honolulu, Hawaii, October 10–14, 1960.

——————— . *Official Proceedings at the NGAUS Eighty-Third General Conference.* Las Vegas, Nev., October 2–5, 1961.

——————— . *Official Proceedings at the NGAUS Eighty-Fourth General Conference.* Denver, Colo., September 17–20, 1962.

——————— . *Official Proceedings at the NGAUS Eighty-Fifth General Conference.* Philadelphia, Pa., September 30, and October 3, 1963.

——————— . *Official Proceedings at the NGAUS Eighty-Sixth General Conference.* Detroit, Mich., September 28, and October 1, 1964.

——————— . *Official Proceedings at the NGAUS Eighty-Seventh General Conference.* Miami Beach, Fla., September 27–30, 1965.

——————— . *Official Proceedings at the NGAUS Eighty-Eighth General Conference.* Phoenix, Ariz., October 17–20, 1966.

——————— . *Official Proceedings at the NGAUS Eighty-Ninth General Conference.* Washington, D.C., September 18–21, 1967.

——————— . *Official Proceedings at the NGAUS Ninetieth General Conference.* Hot Springs, Ark., October 7–10, 1968.

IX.   UNPUBLISHED MATERIALS

Basnett, Maj William W., USAFR. "A Comparison of TAC and Reserve Forces Organizational Structures and Associated Problems." Research Study, Air University, Maxwell Air Force Base, Ala., May 1971.

Benton, Maj Duane M., ANG. "ANG Weather Flights in the Total Force Concept." Air War College Professional Study 4849, Maxwell Air Force Base, Ala., April 1973.

Buechler, Col Robert E., ANG. "Air National Guard-Air Force Reserve Merger." Air War College Thesis 2681, Maxwell Air Force Base, Ala., 1965.

Fredette, Lt Col Robert R., USAF. "Training and Operational Control of ANG Organizations." Air War College Thesis 1749, Maxwell Air Force Base, Ala., April 1960.

Gross, Charles J. "Universal Military Training: A Study in American Ideology." M.A. Thesis, Utah State University, 1973.

Hill, Lt Col Edward Y., ANG. "How U.S. Air Force Tactical Fighter Forces Can Retain Combat Effectiveness Under Budget Restraints During the 1970–1980 Time Frame." Professional Study 3980, Air War College, Maxwell Air Force Base, Ala., April 1970.

Howe, Frank L. "A Bombsight for a Freight Train: The Air National Guard, Air Defense and Federalization, 1946–1950." M.A. Thesis, Ohio State University, 1972.

Hughes, Col Clayton E., USAF. "The Air National Guard." Air War College Thesis, Maxwell Air Force Base, Ala., March 15, 1949.

Hughes, Col Clayton E., USAF, Ret. Letter to author, March 20, 1978.

Lawrence, Lt Col Clifford J., Jr., ANG. "The Air National Guard in the Berlin Crisis, 1961." Air War College Report 3629, Maxwell Air Force Base, Ala., 1968.

Reid, Col William F., USAF. "The Air National Guard." Air War College Research Paper, Maxwell Air Force Base, Ala., March 1949.

Silliman, Capt John P., Jr., ANG. "Air National Guard Technicians: Status Quo vs. Active Duty Guardsmen." Air Command and Staff College Research Study 2315–77, Maxwell Air Force Base, Ala., May 1977.

Stuart, Harold. Letter to Maj Gen John W. Huston, AFCHO, May 15, 1978.

Ward, Col Gerald C., USAF. Letter to author, March 17, 1978.

Index

INDEX